"Reading Dr. Sharon Melnick's book *In Your Power* feels like having a conversation with one of your most trusted mentors and committed advocates, and at the end you feel full of clarity and self-trust to handle any challenging situation. She offers valuable, practical, loving guidance to become the best, most powerful versions of ourselves."

—**Anne Davis Gotte, Global Vice President of Talent at Bumble, Inc.**

"Sharon Melnick has done the world a huge favor by demystifying power and making it accessible to anyone who wants to use power to create good in the world. If you feel disconnected or beaten down or know someone who is, get this book and begin accessing the power that is already within each of us. Her ability to reflect back to you your own power is unmatched."

—**Charlene Li,** *New York Times* **bestselling author of** *The Disruption Mindset,* **Chief Research Officer at PA Consulting.**

"If you have always been successful, but feel your efforts are not being recognized or valued within your organization, this book is for you. Sharon's warmth and wisdom showed me all the things I could control to be in my "power"—to start seeing myself in the way I wanted others to see me, which enabled me to achieve the promotion I had been working for my entire career but had seemed out of reach. I now feel rock-solid as a confident leader, and use the tools she taught me to navigate my new role leading the team responsible for growth of a large, multibillion-dollar, publicly traded company. She's truly changed my life."

—**Melanie Lewis, Chief Business Development Officer, Encompass Health**

"In Your Power hits between the eyes, it's so beautifully, powerfully, and honestly written. It completely impacted me, supported me, made me feel 'seen' as a Mom and head of a busines that I didn't even want to let go of the feeling at the end. I have a bazillion pink underlines, notes in the margins, and this morning I was absolutely compelled to make a video for my team reading a passage from the book as a way to start our charge for the week. Right on Dr. Menick, I love this book!"

—**Amber Vilhauer, CEO of NGNG Enterprises**

"As a girl I was taught to believe that I had power, but I wasn't shown how to access, own, or grow it. Sharon Melnick hits all of those out of the park by giving you an all-access pass to understanding how to tap into your power in the midst of chaos, with a bonus key to understanding how others operate. I'm now producing masterpieces that matter most from the boardroom to the dinner table. Now that I know how to handle situations that put me out of my power, my energy and self-happiness are at the highest ever."

—**LaTasha Stewart, Finance Executive**

"Every one of us has moments where we're not our best. We freeze up when we should talk. We snap when we should reflect. We hide when we should be bold. And in those inopportune moments, we lose ourselves. We forfeit our power to be good and do good. But thank goodness Dr. Sharon Melnick is now here to accompany us through the messy intricacies of those moments. In *In Your Power,* Sharon sits right beside us, accompanying us, whispering in our ear about how to reflect on those moments, and prepare for the next many moments with fresh eyes, new responses, and a whole heart. She asks us to face hard questions and embrace rescripted truths about ourselves. She invites us (back) to our power. You'll want to read this book v.e.r.y. slowly. Twice. You can't possibly come away unchanged for the better."

—**Ron Carucci, Managing Partner, Navalent; award-winning author of *Rising to Power* and *To Be Honest***

"Sharon is an absolute titan and valuable resource to women everywhere. She helped me create meaningful change in my career while being true to my authentic self. Your career will thank you after reading this book."

—**Neela Bushnell Hummel, Co-CEO, Abacus Wealth Partners**

"There is no topic more relevant than power right now; not just who has it and who doesn't, but how to find and unleash it, in ourselves. Dr. Melnick is to me the leading authority on the nuts and bolts of this transformation. She has equipped thousands of leaders to access more of what we're fully capable of, so that we can own where we are and move forward with certainty and confidence, to have the impact we need to have through our careers and on the world around us. This book is absolutely full of applicable frameworks, mindset shifts, and language for us to unabashedly inhabit our power. This is world-changing stuff to build a more inclusive workplace!"

—Jennifer Brown, bestselling author of
How to Be an Inclusive Leader

"In our careers and in our lives it can often feel like we have ceded control to external forces. Sharing stories and strategies learned from her experience coaching and training over 40,000 leaders, Dr. Sharon Melnick provides us with a road map to take back control of our effectiveness, increase our impact, and ultimately our happiness."

—Laine J. Cohen, Global Head of Learning, Citi

This is an illuminated book and allows us to bring the best of Dr. Sharon Melnick home. Through her genius, she provides tools and leads by example how to stand in our infinite power and how to know when we are out of alignment with our power. Each of us is born with the infinite potential to live a life of wonder and consequence on this planet. Sharon's gifts help unlock this potential in each of us, and as a result our impact is far greater than we could have ever imagined. This is a book for our times where so much sovereignty has been lost. It's one read that will change your life. I attribute so much of the ways I've elevated in my life to what she taught me about how to stand in my power."

—Teri Cochrane, CEO, The Global Sustainable
Health Institute

"Sharon has a unique approach to helping individuals identify their blind spots to success. She is one of the most thoughtful and intentional thought leaders in this arena today and is a joy to work with and know. Anyone with a desire to take their professional lives to the next level or to just live their best life should read this book."

—**Emily Pitts, Chief Diversity Officer, Lindenwood University, Retired General Partner of Edward Jones**

"WOW! The first time I heard Sharon speak about this topic I knew she was talking directly to me! What if I could be "in my power" when working with my team, my clients, even my family!? I have always been successful in my career as a Mortgage Loan Originator working on my own, avoiding managing or leading a team. I took the challenge on one year ago and with Sharon's help increased my business by 350%! I also saw changes in how I responded and behaved in other areas of my life. Being "in your power" is no joke. Take the journey in this book with Sharon. . .you will be unstoppable!"

—**Jacqueline Frank, SVP of Mortgage Lending**

"I am so thankful to Dr. Sharon Melnick's advisement for me to think differently and be "in my power." Her ideas and techniques have turned me into an enterprise-wide leader with emotional intelligence. I strongly believe this book will help many to regain control, be intentional, and act with high emotional intelligence."

—**Tushar Nuwal, Vice President of Business Development and Alliance Management, Pharmaceutical Company**

"Dr. Sharon Melnick's book is a game changer. It's profoundly impacted my life by giving me the tools to stand fully in my own power; to cut through the noise in my mind and to be a powerful and effective global leader raising millions of dollars, and running a multi-million dollar business. Get ready to dog ear its pages!"

—**Sara Vetter, CEO, The Soul of Money Institute; Major Gifts Officer, The Pachamama Alliance**

"*In Your Power* is what every female leader needs now. It specifically goes into the root of issues that interfere with mental well-being and success. Her tools and insights are incredibly practical to own my power in new ways. I learned things I haven't found anywhere else and highly recommend it for anyone wanting a new toolkit for leading."

—Kristen Clark, serial entrepreneur, CEO, Prajna Strategy and Granate

"Over the course of my 24-year career, despite continuous promotions and rising through the ranks, I found that I was losing both my power and my voice. I was overwhelmed, burned out, and emotionally hijacked by my leader and certain team members. Disappointed, discouraged, and disheartened, I felt like I had peaked and there were no signs of hope or improvement. Then I started working with Dr. Sharon Melnick to learn the tools, tips, and techniques developed through her years of research and experience, that are covered in this book. And **WOW**, things began to change dramatically! They have helped me beyond measure to react less, focus on what I can control, stop the mental and emotional "swirl," and regain my power. Through her approach, I'm now clearer, calmer, and focused on what I want to accomplish both personally and professionally. This book is a must-read for anyone looking to regain or stay in their power!"

—Jennifer Lokenvitz Schwitzer, Associate General Counsel, U.S. Venture, Inc

"Dr. Melnick has, once again, gifted us with another body of research-based work and a logical plan to advance goals, both professionally and personally. Our women leader participants rave about the successes they have in using the tools in the "power portals" that she's taught in her trainings and this new book *In Your Power: React Less, Regain Control, and Raise Others* We can channel that resilience into the power to make the changes we wish to see in the world and in our own lives. We definitely plan to incorporate Dr. Melnick's new research into our executive leadership development program."

—April Benetello, CEO, Momentum Leaders

IN

YOUR

POWER

IN

YOUR

POWER

Sharon Melnick, PhD

IN YOUR POWER

React Less, Regain Control, Raise Others

WILEY

Published by John Wiley & Sons, Inc., Hoboken, New Jersey.
Published simultaneously in Canada.

For general information on our other products and services or for technical support, please contact our Customer Care Department within the United States at (800) 762-2974, outside the United States at (317) 572-3993 or fax (317) 572-4002.

Wiley also publishes its books in a variety of electronic formats. Some content that appears in print may not be available in electronic formats. For more information about Wiley products, visit our web site at www.wiley.com.

Library of Congress Cataloging-in-Publication Data

Names: Melnick, Sharon, author.
Title: In your power : react less, regain control, raise others / Sharon
  Melnick.
Description: Hoboken, New Jersey : Wiley, [2023] | Includes index.
Identifiers: LCCN 2022029470 (print) | LCCN 2022029471 (ebook) | ISBN
  9781119898863 (cloth) | ISBN 9781119899105 (adobe pdf) | ISBN
  9781119899099 (epub)
Subjects: LCSH: Resilience (Personality trait) | Self-control.
Classification: LCC BF698.35.R47 M47 2023 (print) | LCC BF698.35.R47
  (ebook) | DDC 155.2/4—dc23/eng/20220729
LC record available at https://lccn.loc.gov/2022029470
LC ebook record available at https://lccn.loc.gov/2022029471

Cover Design: Wiley
Cover Image: © AlexZ/Adobe Stock
Author Photo: Courtesy of Alyssa Peek
SKY10039401_120122

To my clients, who are in their power and raising everyone around them. You inspire me.

Contents

Contents

Introduction

"**I** can't sleep. I can't focus. It's like I'm under siege," Mary shared.

"He's squeezing me out and trying to lower my ownership stake." In her partnership group in a financial firm, Mary told me the senior partner started spreading rumors that she's a bully and the team is afraid of her. The young analysts joined in. She tried to speak to the offending partner, but he reacted with hostility, making the situation worse. She didn't feel she could get a fair response from the HR director or from their regional head because they were longtime buddies of his. She feared her only way out was to leave the firm. But that would be a big blow to her reputation, and why should *she* have to sacrifice all of the clientele she had worked for 20 years to establish?

The senior partner also criticized her for her "quality over quantity" client service approach. "He's making me feel like a failure. I've lost my confidence, and now I'm even questioning— maybe I *should* change, and maybe I really am a bully."

Mary felt powerless.

So did Steve. He was the head of a fast-growing technology start-up, and his team members' repeated mistakes were like nails on a chalkboard to him. "I can't *get them* to be more careful and to follow through on their work plans," he explained. He was getting impatient and would react, thinking, "They're lazy," and also questioning, "Am I a bad leader?" He brought his irritation home to his wife, which he knew was unfair.[1]

Mary and Steve were in situations that are similar to those many of us face: You feel that *other people* determine what happens to *you*. Their behavior 'gets to you', and puts you into a mental swirl. You rehash the scenario, convincing yourself they're wrong or that there's something wrong with you. You get hijacked and react emotionally instead of responding with thoughtful intention. You see limited options to resolve the problem because whatever you've tried hasn't worked. You feel trapped. You want to be a role model for others or be the bigger person in the scenario, but you can see you are showing up as a diminished version of yourself.

This is what it's like when you are "out of your power."

You want *relief*. You want the other person to do what you think they should do, believing that is the only way to achieve a good or fair outcome. What you really want is to get back to your calm confident self and refocus on living your life and making a difference for others in your company, community, or family. You want to be back "in your power."

If this describes how you are feeling anywhere in your life, this book is for you.

I share the psychological insights and strategies you can use to immediately stop the mental swirl and quickly recover to be "good in you." With fresh ways of overcoming your automatic reactions, you'll be free from the effects of other people on you. You'll achieve bigger business results, get promoted, improve the culture, and connect with difficult loved ones.

You'll shift your experience from that of the thermometer to the thermostat. When you are the **thermometer** your mental and emotional state goes up and down according to other people's behavior. You fixate on others' actions and see yourself at their mercy, as if "others act, all I can do is react." The climate outside of you determines the weather inside of you. You experience yourself as the casualty, not the creator of the outcome.

As the thermostat, instead *you* set the tone of your interactions with others, no matter what their behavior is, and you set the temperature of your internal state as well. You are able to bring people along in your vision. The thermostat harmonizes all the conditions in a room—the humidity, air flow, movement of people—to reach the decided-upon temperature. As the thermostat, you can steward the whole situation to make it better.

When you're in your power, you make an impact not by reacting to the behavior of people who are limited, but rather by raising yourself and others to be limitless.

By the end of my first discussion with Mary, she regained this sense of control and confidence. She stopped taking the situation personally, her emotional upset evaporated, and she slept well that night. She no longer looked to others to know her worth. Within days, the discussions she initiated with her partners led them to cease badmouthing her. She earned so much respect from them and for her client service approach that within 60 days they voted *her* Partner in Charge of the group. Within 90 days, she brought in the biggest deal of her career, producing a windfall they all benefitted from now that she'd begun enforcing their contractual agreement to do an equal draw on profits. Then she led an approach to diversify the talent in their group, and together they've grown the pie.

Mary got back in her power!

I have coached and trained over 40,000 senior leaders, entrepreneurs, and professionals in all levels of organizations around the world, and what I've found is that in the challenging situations where you find yourself off your game, *the underlying issue* is always that you're pulled out of your power.

We are made to feel powerless in many ways. We feel unseen, unheard, or can't make an impact on people who are important to us in our professional and personal lives. We may be dismissed, overlooked, or uncredited by a manager, or sabotaged by a colleague. We can't convince executive peers to move past corporate scorecards toward true transformation in the culture. We might feel disrespected by a bully boss, a difficult family member, or be overloaded with more than our fair share of work. We can't get our team members to live up to our expectations or respect our leadership. We don't get our needs met by a partner or friend. We're made to second guess ourselves.

Business as usual can put us out of our power by piling on excessive demands and constant change. In the workplace and culture at large, we don't feel psychologically safe, and these places are rife with harms in the form of inequitable pay and advancement, microaggressions, and violence. On social media, we have reason to fear we'll be cancelled or trolled. Political systems make us feel our values are not protected, or are violated.

Being out of your power is not a sign of some inherent weakness within you. Usually it means you care—about getting a good result, about fairness and respect, and about the greater good. Everyone can get out of their power regardless of how emotionally intelligent or highly accomplished they are. An acquaintance of mine is a former army general. His son verbally attacks him regularly and every day he has the sinking feeling he's a bad father. As we'll explore in the next chapter, we are even biologically hardwired to get kicked out of our power.

When we get out of our power we do what we can to help us regain control. We blame the offending person for what they've done, or haven't done, and plan what we'll say to them if we have the chance. We seek sympathy in venting to others. We spin about whether to stay or go and then get to the point we start to disengage. We try to not think about the situation by drinking, numbing ourselves with social media, or other unhealthy habits.

Well-meaning advice from friends, family, or blog writers tells us to "let it go; just leave! give it time; be persistent!" This advice offers encouragement rather than true empowerment.

It suggests we grit our way through the problem or continue to do things that aren't working. It doesn't address that something fundamental to you is being crossed—your sense of self, your truth, your boundaries, your vision, your sense of fairness about the way the world should work, or all of these.

Wrestling with these situations can interfere with our mental well-being and contribute to burnout over and above our culture of "too much to do." We can even develop mental health symptoms, such as anxiety, which comes from thoughts about lacking a sense of control. Or depression, which can come from anger that is turned against oneself when no recourse is available. Emotions and behavior from past traumas can be reactivated, and post-traumatic symptoms can develop when you experience the situation as inescapable.

Not having an effective way to navigate these scenarios derails careers. I've seen it be a major reason people leave an organization (or relationship) or decide to stay but just go through the motions, which is not who you are. The temptation is to avoid collaborating with the other person, eroding connection and trust among coworkers, friends, and family members. Leaders can react with overwhelm or pursue their own agenda rather than serve the team.

Being out of your power destroys dreams and kills joy.

More than ever we are determined to overturn these situations when we face them, personally or collectively. We are fed up with situations where someone else's actions make you feel bad about your value or constrain your success. With the ongoing stress of pandemic-related circumstances, economic uncertainty, and an overdue reckoning on social injustices, our resilience is worn down.

We are factoring in our mental well-being and prioritizing environments where we can do meaningful work drama-free. We're ready to be the change we want to see in the world, making things better for all involved. We want to go beyond the temporary effects of a massage, a manicure, or a good workout. We seek a practical response repertoire we can use in the heat of the moment to further our goals and experience lasting well-being.

Being in your power is the ultimate form of self care. It is the root cause solution for the successful life you want.

***

As a business psychologist and executive coach, I began to make the connection between being out of our power as adults and insights I learned from 10 years of research at Harvard Medical School in my early career. My initial focus was on studying what we bring with us from childhood into our parenting in the next generation. For people who had difficult experiences, I came up with methods to heal the wounds, become their own person, transcend their patterns, and act toward their children in a way they would have wanted for their own life.

Without realizing it, in my research I had been putting together the psychological processes of getting back in your power. Over 20 years of coaching clients, I heard about the issues they were struggling with in their workplace, and I started to see how the approaches I had developed for helping people overcome early trauma-related patterns in their parenting applied to a broad range of work and social environments in which people don't feel seen, heard, or can't have the impact they're here for.

And I needed this myself! I was a person who reacted all day long to other people and got tossed about by matters large and small that didn't go my way. If a friend said something ambiguous to me, I'd spend the rest of my day rehashing it. I sought others' approval and tried to prevent their disapproval. Books told me to "look within," but all I found was a cacophony of self-criticism. Life happened *to* me. When I used my voice, I didn't see it have an impact. As is true for so many, being out of my power had become my way of being in the world. I plunged myself into learning how I could coach people to apply these approaches in work challenges, starting with how I could use them to build ownership over myself as well.

From coaching thousands to be confident influential leaders, I've observed that the biggest unlock to business outcomes rarely comes from one or another specific tactic but rather from knowing how to get in and stay in their power. It comes from their new way of understanding what the problem is, the energy they emit, and the command with which they bring others along into win-win solutions.

***

The word "power" is loaded. We associate it with being predatory, selfish, or manipulative and with people abusing their power. Being in your power is *not* about wielding your power *over* others or achieving your ends through force. This happens with people who are *in* power but not in *their* power. They may behave in these ways because of insecurity, fearing that if they don't show they are powerful, they will be subject in the same ways to others' power.

Research suggests that, as the saying goes, power can go to your head. Studies show that high-power individuals *are* more likely to direct their energies in pursuit of their own goals and that their empathy can be reduced.[2]

Being in your power has a different character. The word "power" comes from the Latin root "posse," which means "to be able." In your power is your ability to stay "good in you," no matter what's going on around you. Being in your power is the *ability* to alchemize the challenging aspects of what goes on outside of you in order to get "into a good place" inside of you *so that* you can then take actions to achieve your aims and make the situation as you envision it should be outside of you.

Being "in your power" actually encompasses two abilities: To be in your power and to use your power as a force for good. The "for good" piece is key. I want to redefine "power" so we embrace it as a force for good.

When I refer to using your power, I mean the *power to use yourself as an instrument to make a situation better*. The power to get a better result, to resolve friction at root cause, to implement innovative ideas, or to create a culture in which you and others thrive. It's the potential of this positive use of power that led Ron Carucci, expert on executive success and author of *Rising to Power*, to say what he found in his 10-year study among those who assume leadership positions is that the biggest abuse of power is not using it![3]

When you are in your power, you have a sense of control over your own mental and emotional state, thoughts, and actions—you respond rather than react. You decide who you are and what you will and won't accept—you own your choices. The course of your life isn't happening *to* you, it's happening from you, through you, and for you.

You achieve your desired impact to make the situation better, not only for you but for *everyone* involved.

In your power, you stop taking things personally or holding onto them. Your well-being is preserved regardless of others' behavior because other people are not the supply line to your emotional oxygen, you are. You don't have to worry about their judgments of you, because you decide who you are. That gives you freedom!

In your power, you're Teflon to the negative effects of situations—you can see them as they unfold in real time, understand everyone's motivations and needs, and respond strategically. You model new standards and hold space for new conversations. You also know how to quickly step back into your power if you do get kicked out of it.

What you say is heard, you get the outcome you want, the situation gets resolved at root cause. You are proud of how you handled it; it doesn't fester or continue to drain you. Your energy is freed up to devote to the people and activities you love and the contribution you are here to make. You are able to inspire and lift others, empowering them with your power. You leave the situation better than it was when you came into it.

When you are in your power, you raise everyone around you.

You'll see the effects everywhere in your life. Being in your power:

Fuels resilience and mental well-being. It gives you a calm, clear mind so you can hold onto your important thoughts. And have renewable energy.

Allows you to resolve problems rather than deciding to leave. Being able to handle unyielding situations allows you, if it's the right fit, to stay and rise in the organization, transform a poisonous relationship into a fruitful collaboration, and bring a huge win to the team—or grow your own company.

Enables you to make a difference for others. You can grow power in other people once you've grown it in yourself.[4] Being able to make a bigger impact makes my clients giddy and brings the delight back into work.

Helps you cope with societal injustice and change it. Systemic inequities must be resolved by dismantling the structures that hold them in place, that is the only and ultimate fix. Until that is complete, being in your power can help you personally deal with injustices—helping you not be triggered and overcome their personal effects on you. Being in your power will set you up to sustain yourself and respond effectively and emphatically so you can be an agent of change.

In the following chapters, I'm going to show you how much power you have, right now, within you, that you can use immediately to start feeling good in you and achieve the change you desire. I take you on a tour of what I call Power Portals. They are like doorways that lead to new ways of understanding the situation you are struggling with and how you can transform it. There are 12 of them.

The first six Portals will show you how to get in your power and stay there when challenged. The next six Portals show you how to use your power for the good of all, both in interpersonal scenarios and in positions of power, regardless of what role you are in. You'll learn from a wealth of stories of others who were challenged and out of their power and then turned their situations around to get buy-in for their ideas, get promoted, get the team performance they wanted, or resolve personal friction to strengthen a relationship.

As you learn to access the power the Portals open your eyes to, you will find that being *in your power becomes a lifestyle.* You'll walk in the world as an infinite creative force to make any situation serve your good intentions and steward outcomes where everyone wins. In your power you are a Change Agent, simply by the way you show up.

Around the time this book was starting to become a possibility, I had a call with a colleague of mine, Jo, who's a senior HR leader. A few days prior she had left her role as the HR lead in a start-up after one year, saying about the experience, "It was like quicksand, but I persevered." She was confused: "I was hired to bring in a new vision, and then the founders blocked the vision." She started to question herself: "Am I smart enough to do this? I became afraid of saying the wrong thing when these jackasses say the first thing that comes to mind. I felt like I was losing my mind." She confessed: "I know that whole idea of putting your oxygen mask on first before you can do it for others, but I lost that ability even though this wasn't my first rodeo. I'm usually the one telling *other* people how to handle this."

What does one do in this situation? "I went to people I follow on Instagram searching for a quote or a meme that could help me. I saw a video by a guru telling me how I should look in the mirror and tell myself I believe in me. That helped for 30 seconds." Then she said to me, "I know I have that within me, but I'm unable to find it and tap into it now. I wish there was a place I could go and fill up how to be in my power, how I could find this within rather than have to seek it elsewhere or through other people. Can you recommend a book I could read over and over again to regain it?"

I shared with her my framework for understanding her situation to ensure it doesn't happen again. At the end of our conversation she said, "This is the first time I've felt calm in months."

Oh, and about that book recommendation she asked about, "I got you, Jo. Here it is."

PART I

Be the Thermostat (Not the Thermometer)

CHAPTER 1

From Out of Your Power to In Your Power

"It is never too late to be who you might have been."

—George Eliot, pen name of English author Mary Ann Evans

E arly in my career, I had tickets to a rock concert in Washington, DC, one of those blockbuster lineups with all your favorite musicians. As the stands were starting to fill, I noticed a cluster of people in the row ahead of mine, and to my surprise I recognized one of them. It was Tipper Gore, wife of then Vice President Al Gore. She was a strong advocate for policies to improve the lives of women and children, and I thought we might have synergy in our missions. Without a moment's hesitation, I marched over to her, reached out to shake her hand, and said, "Hi! I'm Dr. Sharon Melnick. I do psychology research at Harvard Medical School on how parents who grew up in difficult circumstances can have resilience and confidence to break intergenerational cycles . . ."

Tipper's interest was piqued, and we chatted about our work and about her daughters. Suddenly, she turned to her Chief of Staff and said, "Melissa, could you get Dr. Melnick's contact information? We want to invite her to the White House to share the policy implications of her research."

On the flight home, I thought about how fortunate I am that from early in my life, starting at about age five, I have known what work I wanted to do in the world. I wanted to help people turn their private suffering into powerful service and make the contribution they're here to make.

This is what I was *here for*, what I had studied for so long and worked so hard for. Now maybe I had made a connection that would make that dream a reality. I wrote a short description of the research and emailed it to Melissa.

A few weeks later, as I was lacing up my sneakers to go for a run, my phone rings. It was Melissa! She filled me in about Tipper's initiatives helping millions of families around the country, and at a certain point she popped the question, "Will you come down to the White House to share the policy implications of your research?"

My heart raced with nervous excitement imagining how I could make such an impact. So what do you think I said?

Well, of course, I said . . .

"No."

I didn't exactly say no; I said, "I'm not sure I know enough yet from the research. Let me get back to you when we know more." (It's okay, go ahead and gasp.)

Why? I pictured myself sitting around that table at the White House presenting our findings to Tipper and a group of important policy makers. Even though I had won an award for my work, I was convinced that those people would think I wasn't smart enough. So I prioritized what I thought *they might think about me* over the once-in-a-lifetime contribution I could have made to the lives of millions of families.[1] I gave them all the power to determine what impact I could or couldn't make.

Even if I was in my power during other parts of my day, in that moment I was pulled out of my power. Whether its someone else's behavior or something that gets activated in ourselves, we shift into a state in which our thoughts, emotions, and actions align to disempower us.

If you can think of being in your power as a state you can get out of, then by definition it's a state you can come back into. When you *name* it, you *contain* it. You can know when you're in and when you're out.

Returning to this state is inherently within your control even though the catalyzing event may not have been. You want to devote your energies to making this your default state. It crystallizes your intention—there aren't 10 things you have to "work on" in yourself, *just one* to cultivate.

The phrase "out of your power" also reminds you that you've disconnected from a *source* of this power within you and outside of you. It's state you get into, it's not *you*. This will help you have less self-judgment if your prior approaches haven't worked or if you still react despite your best intentions not to. In this chapter you will learn what puts you into an out-of-your-power state and keeps you there, and what it takes to get back in your power. (As it turns out, I was invited again to present at the White House about 15 years later and said "yes". As you start to act "in your power", you magnetize opportunities to you.)

To become more conscious and in command of being in your power, let's first understand its three essential attributes:

1. A Sense of Agency

You see yourself as the creator of your life. You think, "I *can*."

Life is not happening *to* you. You maximize what you can control. You always see options, and you are intentional in your choice of responses. You see yourself as responsible for your thoughts, feelings, and actions. You make choices about whether your current situation is right for you—appreciating that you *always have a choice*. You operate in your stride, without limits or interference.

2. A Sense of Sovereignty

You own who you are. You think, "I *am*."

You have an inviolable sense of yourself. You write the narrative about yourself and rewrite narratives that have been put on you. You consciously decide what you believe about yourself, *you* determine whether you are worthy and enough. You are sure of your values, what you stand for, and what you are here for. Though you learn from others, you trust your own counsel rather than outsourcing your opinion of yourself to others, or second-guess.

What you think, feel, and say all align and inform how you act. You are able to say yes when you genuinely mean it, and say no when you don't. You are able to ask for what you want and speak your truth without fear of reprisal. You're driven by your values, not what other people impose on you or how you're trying to get other people to think of you.

You know how to create the mental and emotional "weather" inside of you and surrounding you. You recover quickly back into your center if you react emotionally. You know inner peace.

You know what you want and enjoy the choices you make for yourself. You know how to fill your own needs, so you don't have to pressure anyone else or make them wrong for not giving you what you need. When others do support and love you, you can take it in and be filled up by it.

3. A Sense of Efficacy

Your efforts effect change. You think, "I *make an impact*."

Your actions have the desired results. You can act to make your situation better—not only for yourself but for everyone involved. The way you communicate "lands." You turn a *no* into a *yes*. You move others to action.

You can look beyond the finite problem to see infinite possible solutions. You understand all angles in the context, taking into consideration yours *and* others' needs, and pursue win-win solutions. You resolve the underlying problem at root cause. You attach your own goals to the betterment of all.

You know how to get out of bad situations and find or create good new ones. Your approach transcends the current paradigm.

In sum, these three attributes of being in your power characterize being in—and staying in—your flow. These descriptions hint at the vast array of possible things you can control, ways you can manage yourself, and find resolution, no matter the challenges you are facing.

What Happens When You Are Kicked Out of Your Power?

Getting kicked out of your power starts when something happens to emotionally hijack you. Each person experiences this in their own way, ranging from an intense internal alarm to a subtle sensation. Maybe you get a pit in your stomach or constriction in your chest or throat. It might be like a streak of electricity coursing through your veins or conversely, energy draining out of you like rain down the side of a window. Perhaps you want to do a silent scream or maybe you simply notice a blip on your emotional EKG.

After our initial emotional response, our thoughts put us into a mental swirl. Your reaction beelines to your worst insecurities, immediately thinking that others' actions mean you are not enough or you don't matter. Our minds become noisy as we blame the offending person for what they did wrong and think what they should have done instead. We carry the experience with us into our next meeting, into our family life, and into restless nights. We feel as if the other person or people have all the power to determine how the situation unfolds. And we feel made small.

Then we act. In the heat of the moment, we might react in a defensive tone. We might avoid, such as not sending an email we know we should send. We numb ourselves with food, drink, drugs, or online entertainment binges. We go on the offensive, strategizing how to get one up on the offender by putting them one down. We might vent endlessly to anyone who will listen. Or we might appear as the swan on a lake, displaying calm above the water while full of commotion below the surface.

This describes an acute reaction to an interaction you may have on any given day, but when you have to interact with that person or system over time your response becomes an automatic patterned approach to that important relationship or your life in general (and a natural adaptation can be to dull our emotions to spare ourselves the pain).

You might even hold *yourself* hostage with self-doubt when alone with your thoughts (even despite objective evidence you are crushing it). Once this spiraling occurs, you start to develop the sense that the frustrating situation is just the way things are or turn the accusatory lens on yourself: "This is just the way I am."

You might be quite in your power in some but not other areas of your life. You may *know in your mind* you are really good at what you do but *in your bones* you still question yourself. You may have a group of supportive friends and a family who loves you but can't get your manager to see you. You may be a successful entrepreneur, but your children or your partner make you feel disrespected. It confounds you.

We all have the resources within us to make agency, sovereignty, and efficacy our default state so that even when we are pulled out of our power for a time, we can quickly get back in our power. But we also all have response patterns built into our human nature that will put us out of our power and keep us there if we are not intentional.

Three Power Derailers: Overcome Your Hardwiring to Be in Your Power

Human nature sets us up to be kicked out of our power—and stay there—when a situation:

1. Seems out of your control;
2. Activates an unresolved pattern in you; and
3. Is not improved by your attempts to make it better.

We are even hardwired through evolution to have these derailers determine our responses. But once we are aware of them, we can override them. First let's start with an understanding of how these three derailers operate.

We Focus on What We *Can't* Control

We only get out of our power when the problem seems out of our control. When you focus on what you can't control, you *leak your power*. Your nervous system's resources are redirected toward monitoring incoming information about any potential threats to physical survival or emotional well-being.

These threat detection parts of your brain are like a Marine sentry on the lookout 24/7/365. When a threat is perceived, the Marine sentry sounds an alarm to begin problem-solving to cope with it. Our minds are programmed to focus much more on what we *can't control* in a threatening situation than what we *can.* Your attention will naturally be pulled to the ways you feel "done to," assessing the list of factors out of your control.

We have a built-in follow-up response, which allows us to get back into a place of safety within, once we learn that the stimuli in the environment are no longer a threat. But when we focus too intently on what we can't control, our attention loops only on the threat. Then the Marine sentry can't signal it's okay to let our guard down.

Our acute sensitivity to such threats was demonstrated by a study done with college students. They were asked to write about interpersonal situations in which they had power over others, then ones in which others had power over them, and then complete a cognitive task. Even a brief experience of being out of one's power—simply by writing about a situation in which they felt powerless for a few minutes—reduced their sense of agency and what they thought they could control.[2]

When threatened, the brain also filters all incoming information through one question: "How will this affect *me*?" *The survival mechanism of your brain literally sets you up to take things personally.* While in early human evolution the threats we had to be alert to were primarily about our physical safety, David Rock, author of *Your Brain at Work*, highlights that today threats to our status, certainty, autonomy, related-ness, and fairness (SCARF) are primary.[3] We are wired to be social, and we are constantly looking to other people in order to assess how safe we are and how well we are doing. We micro-track and then interpret other people's behavior. This is espe-cially true if you're in a lower power position; you'll pay greater systematic attention to behavior of the person in the higher power position.[4]

Over time your brain associates this "How will this affect me?" question with the more general question "*What does this mean about me?*" This leads us to the second factor that derails us from being in our power: a personal subconscious reaction you have to the perceived threat.

We Act Out of an Unresolved Pattern

When you become stuck out of power, it's because there is a personal "hook" that gives the situation a disproportionate effect on you. Your brain associates the current situation with a prior experience that registered strongly with you emotionally, and you perceive the theme is related or being reenacted in the current situation.

Every human has had some—or far too many—experiences that have caused us to feel powerless. In order to try to control and make sense of it, we tried to explain and assign a meaning to it, which will remain as an unresolved source of fear, pain, or self-doubt unless actively processed. This is like "kindling" inside of our psyches. Other people's actions, or the circumstances we're in, can act like a match that lights it afire. These are triggers, a painful reminder of similarly themed past experiences. They teleport us into a reexperience of powerlessness.

Our kindling leads us to personalize the situation, making it about issues from our past rather than seeing it objectively in the present. This subconscious process elevates the perceived gravity of the current situation as implying something about *who you are, beyond the current specifics*. We're often unaware of our kindling because it is embedded deeply in our psyche.

For example, let's say a colleague left you off an email chain for a meeting. If you are in your power, you might approach the colleague to discuss the value you could bring to the meeting or why it would be helpful for you to hear what the attendees discuss, and then ask to be included. But if an unresolved pattern gets triggered, you might instead ruminate about how you've been left out, telling yourself, "I'm not respected," "I'm not smart enough to be invited to the table," or "They're trying to margin-alize me," fully convinced that's what objectively transpired.

Even though the specifics of the current scenario might differ markedly from the situations you faced earlier in your life, your mind has connected the current and the past events through a chain of associations. Suddenly, a situation has become a refer-endum on your worth instead of an everyday interaction among flawed humans.

Then *here's the clincher*: When our kindling has been alighted and we're stuck out of our power, we often look to involve other people in shoring ourselves up. We'll seek their validation and acknowledgment, try to prove ourselves even more, or vent to seek sympathy. We'll hold back to prevent them from criticizing or rejecting us and wait for their permission to boldly do what we know we should. We'll try to please and be perfect in order to not disappoint them. You *give away your power* trying to change peo-ple and circumstances outside of you in order to fix something that is insecure inside of you.

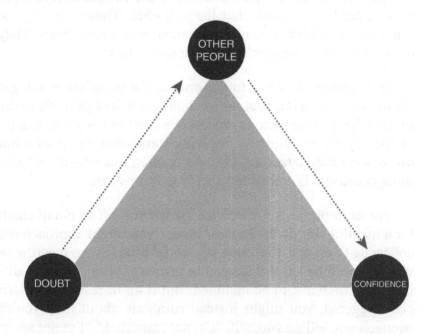

As I introduced in my first book, *Success Under Stress*, this diagram shows you the visual of how we commonly *give our power away*. You'll act toward other people (depicted as the arrow up the left-hand side of the triangle) in order to get other people to act toward you (depicted as the arrow down the right-hand side of the triangle) *so that* you can feel secure in yourself. Your time, energy, and attention go toward managing other people's perceptions of you. You outsource your evaluation of yourself to others and overweight their opinions. In short, you involve other people in your own efforts to feel worthy inside. I call these approaches "Indirect."

With an Indirect approach, *it matters* how others think and act toward you because you *need* their input in order to be in your power inside yourself. By setting up a formula where you have to go through others in order to get the thing you need most inside of you, this *gives away* your power. It sets you up to be the thermometer.

I was the thermometer when I held myself back from an opportunity to make an impact on millions of people's lives because I was worried about what the people around the White House table would think of me.

Indirect behaviors are completely normal. As infants, we are biologically hardwired to seek caring responsiveness from important people in our life. It's the way human babies learn to calm their own nervous system and internalize whether we are worthy of being cared for. Just as we need to breathe in oxygen to grow physically, we must take in "emotional oxygen" from caregivers in order to grow our self-esteem. As a child grows up, we come to *see and know ourselves through the eyes of important others*. Our parents' love and attention, teachers' evaluation and praise, and peers' approval and appreciation are the mechanisms by which we come to know ourselves—favorably or not. Similarly, we are hardwired to avoid physical or emotional harm and be afraid of getting "kicked out the tribe."

In short, important people in our early lives serve as a "secure base,"[5] and when we have a responsive caregiver, we go to them in order to be safe, soothed, and assured we matter. From this home base we get the fill-up we need to go conquer the world.

Indirect behaviors start off as adaptive. Because we have learned to know ourselves through others' eyes and regulate ourselves through others' input, many of us continue this approach to feeling secure in ourselves in adulthood. What I discovered in my research at Harvard Medical School is:

What you have been doing right to try to build your sense of power within (i.e., through other people) is the very approach keeping you out of your power now.

If you haven't built the ability to be in your power from your own means, you may keep going to other people to try to get into that state in yourself. And if you don't get the response you *need* from them, then you're going to try harder to get it from them. It becomes a vicious cycle—you put yourself out of your power and then blame the other person for not being a good source of helping you be in your power.

You can learn to stop yourself from making any specific disempowering situation into a general conclusion that you are not enough or unworthy.

The fix is to Go Direct, which means you source your worthiness from within, independent of others' evaluations of you. You feel filled by a sense of reward and satisfaction from your contributions. You source your sense of purpose from *your Source*, however you define it. You become a secure base for yourself to always come home to. Then you have the fill-up you need, as Jo said, to go out and be the one who raises others.

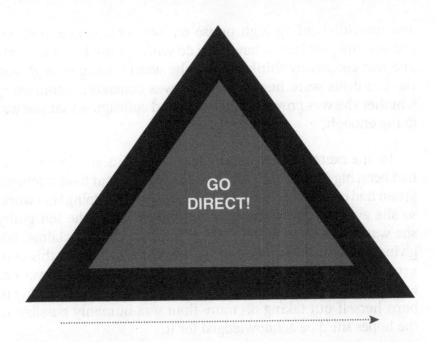

If you were thinking of this concept in terms of love, Indirect behaviors are like trying to "get love". Go Direct is "be love." Go Direct is "feel loveable"—because *that* you *can* control. Then it doesn't matter how limited anyone in your personal life or work family is. (To do this, you need to discover what your kindling is and learn to Go Direct, as I will guide you to do in subsequent chapters. Note: There are four specific types of Indirect behaviors, and generic advice can be counterproductive for certain types. Go to **www.inyourpowerbook.com** to take the full Power Profile assessment for personalized learning.)

My client Susan was able to quickly get back in her power this way after years of being stuck in an out-of-power quagmire. A leader in the long-term disability division of an insurance company, she always had more claims to process than she could get through. Despite backlog being due to the company's bureaucratic processes and challenges in hiring adequate staff, and notwithstanding high praise on her performance reviews, she saw the problem as having to do with *her* not being enough. She was constantly thinking that she wasn't doing enough and the fire drills were hers to fix. She was constantly monitoring whether she was proving to her boss and colleagues that she was doing enough.

In one exercise together, she had an aha insight. Her mother had been big into volunteering and helping out at food kitchens. Susan had resented all the time her mother spent doing that work, so she avoided doing any such volunteer work. She felt guilty she was not doing enough—not processing enough claims, not giving enough in her community life. Once she made this connection she was able to break the hold that kindling had over her and *have a new experience of herself as enough* without having to burn herself out taking on more than was humanly possible in the hopes she'd be acknowledged for it.

Often the situation throwing us out of our power does, in itself, present real threats to our goals for ourselves and to our well-being. Getting back in our power, then, requires strategic problem-solving that addresses the true issues with effectiveness. This third derailer explains how our brains can work against us taking those approaches.

We Take Flawed Approaches to Trying to Fix the Problem

Our natural emotional stress response can derail our effective problem-solving, so we *overlook the unused power we already have*. When out of our power in an emotional state, you can only see a narrow range of options (which may be the same lack of options already thought of, and usually pertain only to how the other person should change). The increased levels of stress hormones in the brain constrict our ability for pattern recognition by shrinking the database searched by the brain.[6]

Our brains interpret new information in a way that is consistent with the way you recently interpreted this or another situation, so an out-of-your-power cycle can keep you looping on the same understanding of limited options.[7] Research on the brains of people in high power and low power positions revealed that the while the goal-oriented centers of a high-power persons' brain are active, there is little active goal seeking among the low-power subjects.[8]

I often hear from clients, "Well, I said something but . . ." with the net that they didn't get a cooperative response or even one at all. This was the case for one of my clients, Tara, who was able to turn her situation around after our first session. She was in sales at a Fortune 100 company. She told me she was ready to leave because her manager of six years had systematically denied every request for more resources and better assignments, reserving those for the younger men in the group. It was affecting her income, and she was to the point she had what she termed a "victim mentality." We agreed that she would give her best shot at influencing her manager, and if that didn't work, we'd pivot to plan B and seek a new job for her to move into.

She had described the manager as being narcissistic and only managing up, which to her meant never being supported because it was all about him. But knowing this about him gave me a great clue about how she might be able to influence him. We carefully scripted her ask, which instead of being about what *she* wanted would allow him to see how her requests would help *him* to look good for having granted them.

The next week she emailed to say she met with him and got everything she asked for (and more!) Not only did she stay with the company, but in the subsequent four months she brought in the biggest deal of her career, was promoted, and pocketed an extra $100k in commission. In the position she was promoted to, she was able to improve the process by which deals got assigned and resources were accessed by the sales team, and in that way she was able to raise the rest of the whole sales team up as well.

This is just one small example of the blind spots we have. Though it's never okay for a manager or anyone else to deflect requests for support, you also want to appreciate that you have available to you a vast repertoire of influencing approaches that you might be overlooking.

This "blind spot" approach starts to form an out-of-your-power vicious cycle. We set ourselves up to stay stuck by having limited or ineffective approaches, then we blame the other person for not being cooperative and deepen our hurt that we are not supported, further curtailing our effective approaches.

The more power we hold inside of us and use (not leak, give away, or overlook), the more we have what we want for our life and the bigger our impact with less effort.

Turning a Vicious Cycle into a Virtuous One

These three biologically hardwired processes *are the factory settings of your human condition*, designed to help you cope with threatening situations. They are instinctive and start out being adaptive.

But these tendencies keep you living your life to satisfy basic biological needs when what you want is to live your life on your terms and to make the contribution you are here for. In your power, you *choose* how to respond in the face of challenges that could otherwise keep you in survival. You take situations where you and others were stuck in patterns, and you make a new way. You create a virtuous cycle.

On the virtuous cycle of being in your power:

1. **You maximize what you *can* control.** You have a sense of agency. You stop leaking your power.

2. **You decide who you want to be and don't personalize or get triggered.** You are sovereign over yourself. You stop giving away your power. You source confidence from within and you don't need the other person to change, or to validate you, in order to be in your flow.

3. **Your approaches are strategic and therefore effective**. You have efficacy. You no longer overlook the power you already have. Your problem-solving helps you get the outcome you want and the collaboration is better than you originally imagined.

On the virtuous cycle, life gets better and better. You trust things will work out for you because you know how to make it so. Your energy is unleashed toward your goals. Ownership of your value is strengthened because the environment actually reflects your talents. Confidence begets boldness and willingness to take risks and share your powerful truths. You get buy-in for your ideas, attract opportunities, sponsors, and partners, and grow your platform. You attract opportunities like new and next-level roles, speaking opportunities to help you bring your vision to life. The more you are in your power, the more power you have, so you can share it with others, which is a win-win and grows your impact.

Expect that across a typical day or week you will be kicked out of your power and have the immediate opportunity to get back in. With proactive practice of the approaches in this book, your bouts of being out of your power will be less frequent and less intense—you will build the muscle memory to come back into your power faster and stay longer. Make it the purpose of your life to stay in—and get back into—your power.

***

Now it's time for you to tap the sense of where you are at your starting point. You can do two exercises. First, take the next full minute and think of a time in your life or an ongoing interaction in which you haven't felt or don't feel in your power. Notice where you feel it in your body, the thoughts you have, and the actions you were tempted to take. This is a good set of cues for you to know you've been kicked out.

Now take a full minute to think of a time where you felt in your power or handled an ongoing situation in that way. Notice where you feel it in your body, the thoughts associated with it, and the responses you are tempted to make/have made. You want this to become your new "home" state of being.

Going forward you can notice when you are out of your power and how you know you are still in your power. Being out of your power is a known experience and will start to become old hat—you can be aware of its early warning signs and welcome it saying, "OOPs" (out of power signal) and have it be the cue to use approaches in this book to get back in.

How well are you already doing at being in your power? You can answer the questions in the quick self-assessment below the chapter summary to get a high-level temperature check.

For the full assessment about where you are in your power (or not), and to get recommendations that are personal for your situation, go to **www.inyourpowerbook.com**.

In Your Power Practices: In and Out of Your Power

1. In your power is a state of being you can get kicked out of and get back into. In your power has three attributes: agency, sovereignty, and efficacy. What do these words mean to you?
2. There are three "factory settings" we have as humans that keep us out of our power:
   2.1. We focus on what we can't control. This *leaks our power*.

2.2. We act out of personalized unresolved patterns—we have kindling of a doubt or negative conviction about ourselves deep in our psyche that can get reactivated causing us to react personally. This doubt or criticism of ourselves causes us to involve other people in order to feel worthy inside ourselves. This sets us up to *give our power away* by trying to change people and circumstances outside of us in order to fix something that is experienced inside of us.

2.3 Our stress response sets us up to get myopic and take flawed approaches to solving our out-of-power problems. We *overlook* the power we already have.

3. Staying out of your power creates a vicious cycle, but practicing being in your power creates a virtuous cycle. What situations do you find where you are in a vicious cycle? Where are you/can you create a virtuous cycle?

4. Learn the signals of when you are in your power and out of your power. For each, where do you feel it in your body, what thoughts do you have, and what actions are you tempted to take?

5. Go to **www.inyourpowerbook.com** for a more in-depth assessment of where you are in your power, or not, along with recommendations that are personal to your situation.

"Are you In Your Power?" Assessment

I. **Do you feel more like the "thermometer" or the "thermostat" on a typical day?**

   1. *Mostly the thermometer; I react to and play off others' moods and actions.*

   2. *I feel like both.*

   3. *I'm usually the thermostat; I create the "weather" around me.*

II. **How often do you react emotionally, not respond with thoughtful intention?**

   1. *Very often.*

   2. *Sometimes.*

   3. *Rarely.*

III. **When you get emotionally hijacked by a situation, how quickly do you recover and stop obsessing about it?**

   1. *I rehash it all day and for several days or weeks.*

   2. *I might carry it with me throughout the day, but then I start to feel better.*

   3. *I get back to my center quickly.*

IV. **When you're in a situation that's not going your way, how often do you blame the other person(s)?**

   1. *I often blame the other person and stay mad at them for not changing.*

   2. *I blame the other person, but over time I also can see how I could learn from it.*

   3. *I know how to see the ways any situation can serve my growth and my life goals.*

V. **How often do you worry about other's judgments?**

   1. *I often worry about what other people will think about me.*

2. *Sometimes I worry about what others think, but other times I know who I am and don't worry.*

3. *I am confident; I focus on the work or supporting others, not on judgments.*

VI. How often do you get deflated because you don't feel heard?

1. *Often—regularly I feel that I've said something multiple times but people don't listen or do what I ask.*

2. *Sometimes.*

3. *Not much—I know how to communicate with others effectively so they understand me and take action on my ideas.*

VII. How well do you set boundaries and share your truth?

1. *Not well at all—I say "yes" when I mean "no". I get angry at others for crossing my boundaries, but I don't say anything. I don't feel comfortable sharing my truth.*

2. *Sometimes but only with people I feel really comfortable with.*

3. *I set boundaries, I minimize my interactions with toxic people, and I share my truth. I feel great about it!*

VIII. How often do you feel stuck and frustrated you can't get others to cooperate with what you need in important relationships?

1. *Often.*

2. *Sometimes.*

3. *Rarely.*

You can find out how much you are in your power by adding up the number that corresponds to your answer for each question.

(continued)

If you got a score of 20 and above, congratulations; you spend a good deal of your life in your power and probably are a great role model, leader, and mentor for others!

If you got a score of 16–20, you have some experience being in and staying in your power, but might feel there are still too many times you can get kicked out of your power. You're starting at a great place, and there's many strategies that will help you stay in your power.

If you got a score of 15 or below, you're spending a good deal of your time out of your power. I'm excited for you to learn many strategies to get into and stay in your power!

CHAPTER 2

From Chaos to Control

"You always had the power, my dear. You just needed to learn it for yourself."

—Glinda the Good Witch, from *The Wizard of Oz*

I want to open your eyes to just how much power you truly have.

A surprising feature of the human mind is that when we focus intently on something, we become blind to many other things that are within our field of vision. A famous study conducted by Harvard researchers demonstrated this by testing two teams of students. One team in black shirts and one in white were asked to pass a basketball to the other players on their team. Other students were then asked to view the short videotape and to count how many times the basketball was passed among the white t-shirt players. Keeping count was tricky because the players from the two teams were circulating all around one another. So the viewers had to really pay close attention to the white t-shirt players.

What many didn't pay any attention to—didn't even see at all!—was that a student dressed up in a hairy black gorilla suit strolled right into the middle of the two teams, paused for a moment to beat her chest, and then leisurely strolled on. The researchers have shown this video to hundreds of thousands of viewers and about 50% of them did not notice the gorilla *at all*. What's more, most people who didn't spot it adamantly refused to believe it, even complaining that they must have been shown a different video. The researchers explain that "we experience far less of our visual world than we think we do . . . we are completely unaware of those aspects of our world that fall outside of our attention."[1,2]

When out of your power, you get *myopic*. You are so focused on the things going wrong that you don't see the many possibilities for making things better.

I want to take you on a 360-degree tour of the lush landscape of these opportunities you might not be seeing now. Think of a frustrating situation you feel stuck in and imagine that in any direction you look, there are doorways that when you open them give you a new vista. There you discover new ways of understanding the situation and new set of tools to make it better. These doorways are what I call a Power Portal.

A portal is "a way to get or do something." Think of web portals; they provide us with access to a wealth of learning and community. Power Portals provide us with new ways of seeing, feeling, and acting so that we can be in our power. Accessing a portal transports you from a situation that makes you feel small and defensive into a whole new world in which you are strong and full of purpose.

In this chapter, I will briefly introduce you to each of the 12 Power Portals. You will have a repertoire for dealing with challenges that allows you to be "good in you" *no matter* how others are behaving.

In any situation when you notice you are starting to get out of your power, ask your go-to question: **"Where's my power?"**

The master key to accessing your power is shifting your focus from what is being done to you—on what *others* are doing—and instead focusing on what *you* can do. Turn your attention to what you can control and away from what you can't.

The 50% Rule

In my first book, *Success under Stress,* I introduced a concept that many clients and readers have reported helped them feel dramatically more in charge of their lives. In every challenging situation you find yourself in, distinguish the factors you can control, which is *your* 50%, from those you can't, which is the *other* 50%. Identify the 50% that you can control, allowing yourself to not be preoccupied by the other 50% where you leak your power.

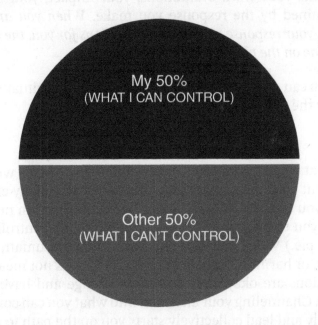

You might be thinking, "Sounds good in theory, Doc, but 50% is way too optimistic; I can only control about 10% to 20% of what's going on at best!" Or you might be thinking, "But the 50% I can't control *is* the problem; how can I not focus on that?" And it might seem like you would be letting the bully on the playground get away with their bad behavior, giving them a free pass. You may be thinking, "They *should* change, they should admit they've been wrong; they should stop treating me that way."

Yes, they probably should. And they may or may not be capable to. Getting them to change *is not* your responsibility or within your ability. Being in your power *is*. I want to show you that fixing them is not the only way to get the outcome you want; there's *so* much more you can control than you think you can.

Taking your focus off what you can't control and shifting it to what you can is not letting the bully get the better of you. On the school playground the teacher doesn't usually see the bully's behavior when it starts; they usually only turn their head to notice as you are making your response. In the playground of your life, your work evaluations, your impact, your sanity are determined by the response you make. *When you are in your power, your response creates new conditions for you, the bully, and everyone on the playground.*

You can always control what *you* bring to any situation, which is why the 50% Rule is:

Be Impeccable for your 50%.

That means, take 100% responsibility for what is within your 50%. Put your time and energy into being maximally effective at what you can control. (My fellow perfectionists: I'm not encouraging you to be a control freak; that would be controlling 100% of the pie.) When you face conditions that are unfair, discriminatory, or harmful, focusing on your 50% does not mean outside conditions are okay, they still must change and have accountability. Channeling your attention into what you can control individually and lead collectively starts you on the path to do that.

Think of a challenging situation that is putting you out of your power and what you can and can't control. Take a piece of paper now, draw a big circle with a horizontal line through the middle, and start writing down things you can control in your 50% above the line and those you can't control (the other 50%) below the line. This exercise orients your attention toward what you can control. I've heard from so many training participants how this idea has been immediately liberating. This is a warm-up, to get the creative juices flowing with what you already see in your control. The full effect of the creative power you have can be found in the 12 power portals.

The first six portals are meant to help you "get your own affairs in order" inside so that you can be in your power. The second six portals will leverage all the clarity and confidence that you built in the first six. They will help you use your power with other people in order to change the dynamic and make the world more as you think it should be. Altogether, the portals help you be *in your power*, give you *interpersonal* power, and know how to channel the power you have once *in power*. In each portal, you'll read stories of professionals like you who were in a crunch and used the strategies within to create notable wins across their organization or industry and to experience freedom from patterns they struggled with for a long time.

Portal One: Precision

In order to move beyond an out-of-your power situation, you have to have a clear picture of the future you want *and* the role you play in it. Declaring what you want in the fog of your disempowerment starts a new momentum. In this portal, you will quantify the outcomes you want and then articulate what I call your Horizon Point—*who you need to show up as* in order to achieve the desired outcome (because *that* you can control). Specifying this idea of who you want to be as a leader/contributor/collaborator sets you up to be intentional, not reactive. Being able to show up in this way immediately puts you in your power because you choose this persona, and when embodying it you are already participating in the interaction *on your own terms*. You'll also define how to lead others toward win-win outcomes *they want*, which helps you be in your power.

Portal Two: Perspective

Your brain operates in a way that's surprisingly similar to the algorithms on LinkedIn, Facebook, or TikTok: whatever thoughts you have, your world gives you more experiences like these. Unlike those algorithms, you have control over how you train your brain.

You'll learn about the psychological mechanisms that filter and determine your understanding of any situation. You'll start by learning the one question that flips your script from victim to victor on demand. You'll identify research-backed beliefs and mindsets to put you in your power, along with built-in cognitive biases that keep you in tunnel vision. You'll stop seeing the situation as a finite problem and start to see infinite solutions.

You'll view your challenges through multiple new lenses, each progressively zooming out from your current one, starting with a three-dimensional understanding of what's going on between you and the other person and ending with macro views such as the relevance of human history and planetary trends. These perspectives are like pouring a chemical solution on invisible magic ink, the underlying problem and bigger-picture solution reveal themselves.

Portal Three: Physiology

Out-of-your-power situations cause emotional hijack. Whether you get riled up or sunken, without tools to work out your emotional reaction, you will carry that off-kilter state into the next meeting (or next day or decade). You'll learn to move emotions through and recover quickly so that you don't stay as full of electricity or lethargy. You will learn a suite of practical exercises to immediately refind calm and your ability to think clearly instead of keeping on replaying the aggravating or hurtful situation in your mind.

You'll learn to use your agency to choose pleasure and joy over anger and disappointment. When you proactively fill your own needs in this way, you inspire others to want to give to you (and give to themselves as well)—raising everyone around you.

Portal Four: Purpose

Out of your power, you give your power away. Connection to your purpose is blocked. Your purpose is what makes you feel alive, it's a motivation and energy source that is always available for you to tap, and connecting to it can instantly eject you out of the mental swirl. You will learn to identify and act in the service of your purpose lifting yourself from your small game. No longer thinking, "Who am I to . . ." or looking to others' expectations of you, you'll learn to play your big game—this is the life and work you're *here for*. It will give you a sense of satisfaction and impact that feeds your power, and freedom from the judgments of others.

Portal Five: Psyche

What puts you out of your power? We all have kindling inside of us that is derived from prior similarly themed experiences and might be phrased as a doubting question, "Am I good enough?" or as a conviction, "I'm not worthy." The current situation is a match that ignites this kindling, setting you up to react defensively, take situations personally, and have a hard time letting them go. This is the personal *hook* that is the core of what makes you susceptible to getting kicked out of your power.

As long as you have this place of powerless that you go to within you, other people's actions and external circumstances can send you there without your permission or forewarning.

You will learn the *real reasons* you developed this narrative for your life—it's not what pop psychology says and it's not because of what's happened to you in your life. You will reclaim the narrative and be able to tell a whole new empowering story about your life.

If you are at the point where you are aware of your triggers but can't seem to move past them, you'll learn ways of transcending these past experiences and live a legendary post-story life.

Portal Six: Proficiency

There are times you can change the result you're getting in an out-of-your-power scenario through means that are entirely under your control because it has to do with your own skills and know-how. You'll use your knowledge strategically to influence the perception of you by decision makers who overlook or sabotage your talents. Leveraging your own proficiency can give you a sense of security that no matter what thwarting challenges you're facing, *you* can control the achievement of your goals and life plan. As you showcase you are a valuable, if not indispensable, contributor to others' success, you'll be sought-after and untouchable. And if you have doubts about your competence, you'll defang them.

Portal Seven: Persuasion

One of the most common reasons we feel out of our power is that we haven't been able to get someone to buy into our ideas or take action on our requests. We blame the other person for being obstinate, but it may be the case you could be more effective in your approach to influencing. You will learn to have x-ray vision into the minds of decision makers and interaction partners so you can unlock other people's energy to support your ideas and help you leverage your power. You'll learn five hidden ways of strategically messaging your requests and bring others along in your vision so you can turn any "no" into a "yes."

Portal Eight: Partnership

We stay spinning out of our power when we have not found a way to engage others in helping solve the difficulty we're having. We are reluctant to or intimidated by raising the issue because we don't know what to say or how to say it. Or we've tried ways that weren't effective and now everyone is more entrenched yet sees fewer options to broach it.

I share my POWERS framework for raising issues in a way that helps the other person see that they have a stake in helping you solve the problem and motivates them to partner with you in finding win-win solutions. You will feel powerful as you approach these stuck scenarios with the mindset of a steward who leads a process in which everyone benefits, and you'll know how to handle situations with grace.

Portal Nine: Protection

Even if the continued problem really does lie on the other person's side of the street and you've tried to use your power with little effect, you can *always* protect yourself. They might be dishing it out, but you don't have to *take it*.

You will learn an extensive repertoire of strategies to ensure that other people's unaware, thoughtless, or mean behavior does not affect you or cause overwhelm. Forms of protection include setting boundaries and barriers, bringing the interaction onto your own terms, and continuing to engage without absorbing the situation's negative effect.

There's a special section with an array of strategies for dealing with a narcissist, or anyone who criticizes and lies. (If you are already skipping ahead to those pages saying, "I need that now!" just make sure to come back right after you've gone through that portal because the strategies in the book build on one another.)

Portal 10: Powerful Truth

A powerful truth introduces a new level of your authenticity and humanity, which requires the people around you to pay attention to you with a new level of engagement and urgency. Speaking your truth introduces what you want and need, and it aligns what you think and feel with what you say and do. It uses your voice and brings into form what has been unspoken. When you don't share your powerful truth, you are filled with regret that you missed an opportunity.

You will learn when and how to share your powerful truth so you engage others in taking action to move beyond the status quo. You'll learn to channel your anger into the strategic display of emotion and how to respond to and neutralize micro-aggressions. You'll be inspired by numerous examples to use your voice to hold others accountable and represent yourself in the world.

Portal 11: People

Once you have reliable strategies to access your power on your own then other people can play an important supplemental role in bringing you back there and helping you stay there. Some moments we are so disconnected from our inner resources that we *need* scaffolding from outside of us to bring us back to ourselves, and trusted and caring others can help us calm our physical bodies and heal from shame. People mirror back to you aspects of your own magnificence that you have forgotten, the effect of which is even more amplified with the right posse of people. People play a practical role as an extension of your network, mentoring and sponsoring you to further your vision and expand your impact.

Portal 12: Position

We tend to think that the power we have in our position is defined by the responsibilities outlined in the job description but generally we have more power in any given position than we realize and are harnessing. You'll learn best practices to use the power you have and to leverage that which you are overlooking to create a better outcome for your team or organization. You learn to use who you are as an in-your-power person to amplify others, including as a sponsor and ally. Also part of the power of your position is to grow and use your platform to expand your voice and create movement toward the world as you think it should be.

***

How to Begin Accessing the Portals

You are a creative force and you now see you have an abundance of options for regaining control and making disempowering situations better for you and everyone. Once you are familiar with all the portals, you can look around to the portal you need most and walk through it in real time. But that's overwhelming when you are first starting out, so my recommendation is that you go through the book learning and practicing them in the intended order. The portals to be 'in your power' set a strong foundation for you to have interpersonal power, and the portals, while modular, refer back to and build on one another to keep you on the virtuous cycle. That said, if there are a few portals that are screaming your name with the promise of an immediate solution to a current challenge, then have at it and go read them now (but do come back to the rest of them in order)!

I hope your head is now alight with a sense of possibility about how *you* will be able to step into your power. Let's walk through the first door.

In Your Power Practices: From Chaos to Control

1. Open your mind to the possibility that you have more power in any situation than you are currently seeing for yourself. You might start by doing a Power Inventory—make a list of all the ways you see yourself having power now. (And then let's compare it to the list you will make after reading the book.)

2. In any challenging interaction, start by asking, Where's my power? Focus on what you can control in your 50% of any interaction. Apply the 50% diagram to a challenging situation: What is in your 50% and you could start to control right away, and what factors are in the other 50%?

3. Make the 50% Rule your mantra: Be Impeccable for your 50%!

4. There are 12 Power Portals that reveal new ways of seeing, feeling, and acting—in any moment you are kicked out of your power, know that you can walk through the door of the one or more of these portals to stay in your center and lead a new resolution.

5. It's best to learn and practice the portals in the intended order, but if there's a few that are screaming your name to be accessed right now, then go for it (and when you're done applying what you learned there, go back to read the other ones).

PART II

Portals to Be In Your Power

CHAPTER 3

Precision: From Instinctive to Intentional

"The only person you are destined to become is the person you decide to be."

—Ralph Waldo Emerson, American Essayist

Our whole lives are dedicated to getting what we want, yet we often don't know what we want. This is especially true in circumstances when you are out of your power. In the crunch the first thing we want is just relief. The plea in your mind is, "Just make them stop it!"

Gaining clarity about the outcome you want in any situation in which you feel out of your power is the first step to getting off your heels and starting to move the situation in a forward direction. Refocusing your vision on the positive outcome you seek breaks the hold of the stress response on your brain, which has been fixing your attention on a running list of all the things that are wrong about the situation. You might have even lost any vision of a better future, captured by thoughts like "It's never going to feel different than it feels now." You make imagined futures based on the way you feel now and forecast unwanted outcomes: "I don't think I can take this anymore. I might have to leave."

In order to eject yourself from the vortex of being out of your power, you have to have a clear picture of the future you want *and* the role you play in it. In the portal of Precision, you will develop this clarity and know how to start participating in situations on your own terms.

The Three Questions for Creating New Outcomes When Out of Your Power

The first question I ask clients who feel stuck is, "If you could wave a magic wand, what is the outcome you want in this situation?" They'll often respond, "That's a good question!" indicating that's not where their attention has been. A sign that you are still in the stress loop is that it's hard to see above all the problems in the situation.

I received a call from Bo, who shared a detailed description of discriminatory behavior she had been experiencing at her fintech company. When she raised the issue and offered specific cases in point, she was naysaid. Understandably, she felt powerless to solve the problem, and she hired me to help her navigate it. When I asked her the magic wand question, she gave me a long list of her boss's bad behavior, while at the same time enumerating a long list of her successes. It was baffling how her quantifiable value could not be recognized.

She seemed to be leaning in the direction of wanting to fight for recognition or to get accountability for her manager's behavior, but I stayed listening actively to know what *she really* wanted. So I asked her again.

She thought about it and confirmed that she didn't want to fight. Rather, she wanted to leave and do so with a sense of grace. Having to zero in on what she *really wanted* helped her choose her health and peace of mind. Her sense of relief was palpable, her shoulders dropped and the muscles in her face relaxed. This clarity immediately broke the grip of her months-long spiral, and we pivoted our discussion to how she could set up her team for continued success and make sure they knew she cared about them. We also talked about how she could protect her reputation and showcase her contributions as she sought a new position. Precision opened the way for her to figure out what to do next.

When you answer the magic wand question you immediately override the emotional hijacking of your brain, replacing it with the problem-solving capacity of your frontal lobe. This clearing of the fog is the first step to having a sense of agency. It gives you a destination you can adjust your GPS in the service of. You'll notice that ideas for possible steps you can take will start to appear.

As you practice, you can take this question "from good to great." The second question for activating the power of precision is, "What outcome could I work toward that would be in the best interest of all?" This question helps you see all the people who might be affected by the challenging scenario, and from this expanded view, you may see further ways of improving the situation. The more you are working in the service of an outcome that aligns with what others want, the more you unlock their energy too. This is where you start to bring to life the idea of using your power as a force for good.

One of the best examples of this is from Nobel Peace Prize winner Nelson Mandela. He was imprisoned in 1962 on Robben Island, in squalid conditions and with meager rations, for his efforts to secure equal freedoms for Black South Africans. In 1985, Mandela refused an offer of release from then South African President Botha because it came with no significant commitments to reform the political system.

Mandela was eager for release, but he knew what he stood for. He issued a statement from his prison cell explaining "I cherish my own freedom dearly. But I care even more for your freedom," speaking of his fellow Black South Africans. "If Botha truly wants a political solution to South Africa's continued turmoil, the government should legalize the African National Congress, permit free political activity and commit itself to end apartheid."[1]

I visited Robben Island Prison on a trip to South Africa and witnessed the brutal conditions Mandela had lived in. If he had focused on his own personal outcome, he would have likely chosen the comforts of release. He had a clear vision about what's in it for everyone, which was powerful leverage in furthering negotiations that ultimately achieved all of those objectives, leading to a new constitution, his later release from prison—and to his election as the first Black President of the country.

You may not be accustomed to training yourself to ask the question "What's in the best interest of all?" but you can see how this clarity provides a go-forward vision that marshals others' energy and partnership.

Consider a situation you are facing now that has you spinning on what should you do, and identify (1) If you could wave a magic wand, what is the outcome you want in this situation? and (2) What outcome could you work toward that would be in the best interest of all?

_____

_____

_____

Once you have clarity on the way forward, the third question starts to give you a sense of control over moving toward those outcomes. What's the best thing and ultimately the *only* thing you can control in your 50%? That's right, you and who *you* show up as. The third question is:

Who Do You Need to Show Up as in Order to Move the Situation in That Direction?

With this question you add in the element of the role that *you* can play in moving yourself and everyone toward that outcome. You said you want to be the thermostat, here's your chance! It's helpful to have an intention that you can articulate even before you get into the disempowering situation; then you can anchor yourself to it if you get pulled off your center.

I call this concept your Horizon Point. This is a brief but precise description of how you want to show up that helps you stay focused on the outcome you've identified. Just like its literal meaning, your Horizon Point is a visual focal point, an anchor. It declares who you want to show up as, thus imposing an intention on the situation. In the skies, like in your daily life with people and internally triggering thoughts, there will be turbulence, storms, and air traffic to steer clear of. You are the pilot, able to use the controls available to course-correct toward the outcome you define.

Experts in air navigation have a rule of thumb known as the 1 in 60 rule. For every 1 degree a plane veers off its course, it misses its target destination by 1 mile for every 60 miles you fly. A plane that starts 1 degree off course flying from one coast of the United States to the other would arrive 50 miles away from the airport. Without intention, you might show up a "few degrees" off who you need to show up as, then miss the mark of the perception you intend to create or the contribution you're here to make.[2]

To craft your Horizon Point, you make two lists, so get out your notepad or electronic device. On the left, list the qualities and attributes *you want to show up with*. Consider adding in your superpowers and any strengths you want to make sure to imbue. That might look like:

Calm

Confident

Collaborative

Positive

On the right you list the qualities that are needed of you in your role. Ask yourself, what does the organization or the group (or your family) need for you to show up as? You might even want to pull out your job description to see how the company has described the requirements. If you are a service provider, think of what your clients are looking for in a provider even beyond the job description so you can distinguish yourself. If you're looking to improve an issue in your personal life, what does your spouse or your family or community need from you? This list might look like:

Problem-solver

Leader

Communicates well

Knowledgeable

Strategic; Visionary

It will be hard to remember all you just wrote down in the middle of a meeting where you are getting kicked of your power. You don't want to have to say, "Hold on a minute everyone, I have to find that scrap of paper I wrote down from this book I was reading." Instead you want to capture the essence of this intention so you can easily remember it.

You want to identify a Horizon Point that is at the sweet spot intersection of these two, both bringing forth your natural strengths *and* reflecting intelligence on how you need to show up for your role in the situation. In order to make yours user-friendly, what you can do is boil down these two lists to a concise phrase that captures the essence of the combination of these two intentions. This encapsulating phrase may not capture every word you wrote down but should reflect what's really the heart of the matter. It could also refer to an image or a tangible feeling in your body.

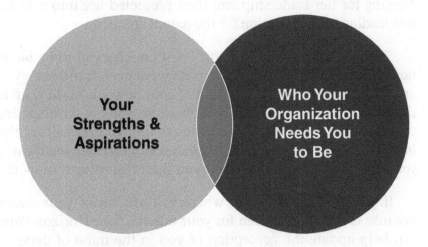

Jeannine was executive for supply chain at an international fashion company, which was in the midst of an overhaul of its operations. There was a lot of friction in the competing interests of creative designers and supply chain folks about the materials to work with. Jeannine felt unsupported and personally attacked in management team meetings without air cover from her CEO and was frustrated at the lack of uptake for the change process. She developed a short fuse at work and brought the stress into her nightly dinners with her husband. She was ready to leave her job. Here are highlights of her lists. She wanted to show up as:

Rational, not reactive;

Be a positive collaborator who is above the fray;

Be a calm, steady role model and the person who guides others to embrace change.

Her encapsulating phrase was "Poised Change Agent." As she encountered irritating situations, she would ask herself, "What would a Poised Change Agent do?" She told me that this actually made it fun to navigate all of the hassles of the supply chain changes. With precision of who she wanted to show up as, she was able to stay calm and keep the big picture in mind. She became the go-to person helping team leaders to adopt the change. Within two months, the CEO gave her a shout out at a senior management meeting for her leadership and then promoted her into a global role leading transformation for the parent company.

Showing up at your Horizon Point enables you to be *intentional, not reactive.* One of the fastest ways to shift the energy in any situation in which you are out of your power is to show up in the service of your Horizon Point because you are participating on your own terms. Those you're interacting will notice *immediately.* Because *you see you that way, others see you the way you want them to*, and that earns you their respect and support.

If you are in a situation where you are out of your power because of not feeling seen for your talents, your Horizon Point can help update the perception of you in the mind of decision makers. You can adapt your question, "What's in the best interest of all?" to "What is the perception needed of me in the minds of decision makers?" The answer becomes your intention.

Liza was in one of my coaching programs for mid-career talent. She was a talented manager at a biotech firm but had been passed over twice for promotion, and she felt unsupported and disrespected, at a loss what she could do to get her manager to give her more stimulating work and a promotion. She was ready to leave the organization but instead put herself through this process of identifying her Horizon Point. Qualities she wanted to show up with were:

Be confident, make a more meaningful contribution to their patients, be someone who's heard, have more stimulating work.

The list for those the organization wanted of her was:

Strategic. Impactful. Influential. Brings new ideas.

The phrase she chose was "*Strategic Influencer.*" That's who she wanted to be! I suggested that before every meeting she ask herself, "How can I be a Strategic Influencer?" and that she use language to support her Horizon Point such as "My strategic recommendation is . . ." She delegated work and crafted a plan to expand an existing product. In short order, she became more influential.

Liza had been trying for more than 18 months to get her boss to see her as ready for the next level, and she would regularly feel deflated when she wasn't. Instead, start seeing *yourself* in the way you want others to see you. In your power, *you* control the perception of you from the inside out. You own the narrative about you. Three months later her manager called a meeting with her to say how much more strategic Liza had been, and the buzz she had created with her ideas. And to tell Liza she put in for her promotion, even though it would be six months before the next cycle.

The brief phrasing of your Horizon Point helps you to remember it in the heat of the moment. It creates a picture for the subconscious mind, overriding out of your power reactions. When you successfully act in alignment with your Horizon Point, you experience a brief surge of the chemical dopamine in your brain, which reinforces how good it feels to be in that grounded and centered place that *you* have chosen for yourself. As James Clear says in his popular book *Atomic Habits*, every time you [show up as your Horizon Point], "it's like casting a vote for the kind of person you want to become." You will start to absorb this intention into your self-image, making it easier and more automatic to show up this way with each new situation.[3]

You can use your Horizon Point intention to remind you how you can shift focus from your personal woes and be a creative force for good. Tushar Nuwal was the head of business development for a pharmaceutical company. His responsibility, as part of the leadership team, was to grow the company and its product portfolio through strategic partnerships and collaborations. Tushar was faced with a challenge when exploratory discussions started to potentially establish the company's own commercial sales and marketing infrastructure, leading Tushar to believe that his role could then be minimized or eliminated. As anyone might in that situation, he felt anxiety, and initially interpreted the situation as: "I am not being valued." He was tempted to respond aggressively. But he set his sights back on his Horizon Point, which was "Enterprise-wide leader with high emotional intelligence."

This allowed him to refocus from worrying about his functional leadership role and consider how he could make himself indispensable by serving the needs of the business as a whole. When he reached out to the relevant teams with "his listening ears on," he heard a need that he could help them fulfill. He requested his team put together the scenarios for commercializing the new product, which would realize best value in both the short and long term. He pulled a group of leaders from across the business to propose a plan, demonstrating his enterprise-wide leadership.

Tushar went on to present the business case for combining the commercialization options including his alternative approach. The management team aligned with the proposal. Not only had Tushar secured his leadership enhanced his standing but he also brought value to the whole company. And at the end of the year, the CEO shared with him how much he appreciated his initiative and way of working across the business.

Leaders can use the idea of a Horizon Point to help create team culture. It's not uncommon that I coach a leader of a team who asks me, "How can I *get* my team members to be more engaged and motivated?" I have a long list of approaches to accomplish this end, but the first question I would always ask is, "And who do *you need to be* in order for your team members to be engaged and motivated?" We're so focused on getting others to change we overlook the role we play. Start by being precise about who you need to be.

For example, Jackie was the SVP of a mortgage originator team. She had recently hired her team after years of success as a solo flier, and she was frustrated by mistakes that her new hires were making and her perception that they weren't putting in enough effort. She became narrowly focused on their inadequacies, constantly thinking "Why can't they?" and "Why don't they?" She realized that she played an important role in setting the tone and structure and organizing how to train them in a new business. She set her Horizon Point as "Calm, Clear Thinker." That allowed her to take a patient and organized new approach to teaching her staff the ins and outs of bringing in clients and getting mortgages approved quickly. Together they grew the business 350% that year.

Now it's your turn; are you ready? Create your two columns:

Qualities and attributes I want to show up with	What my team/role/clients/ family need from me

Once you've got your two lists, go through them and pick out the words you think are the most important, capturing who you want to show up as. When it comes to what the company wants from you, or your partner or children, extract the thing that is most important to them. Some of the words and phrases on your list are going to be redundant, such as "confident" and "self-assured", so choose which one of them resonates most with you emotionally.

Now, boil the list down to a few words. Play around with combinations. You want to come up with a phrase that feels right. You want it to light you up. Sometimes that involves just some wordsmithing! Don't obsess over it, start the exercise today and let it marinate. Your Horizon Point can evolve over time, you can have a placeholder until you land on the phrase that's right for you. Yes, you can steal from the client stories I shared royalty free. And yes, you can have a Horizon Point for work and one for your home life.

"Who are you at your Horizon Point"

_____

You can be creative about your encapsulating phrase. If you have a different style in which you'd like to state your intention, go for it! For instance, my client who was a personal development coach had a dream to appear on the *Oprah* show but felt marginalized in her field. Her phrase was "That Oprah girl!" and by consciously tapping into that positive experience of herself each day, she saw enormous growth in her platform and is in demand as a media presenter.

Are you wondering about *my* Horizon Point? One word captures it all for me: "Uplift." It's actually more kinesthetic than a word. I experience a streaming ray of white light surrounding me, guiding me how to bring more humanity to any scenario and support each person—myself and the other(s)—to be in their power. When I feel powerless, it ejects me out of my impatience or blame and nudges me to act from my "better angels." My Horizon Point suffuses me with an energy that tells me I can be a force for good, creating the world as I think it should be right there in that interaction.

Bring Your Horizon Point into Your Every Day

You've come up with your Horizon Point statement; now the question is how can you make it second nature and be able to show up that way, even in the heat of the moment when you can feel yourself starting to leak your power. First order of business, you can't keep your Horizon Point statement written on a scrap of paper and hope it will infuse into your life. You have to embody it.

So right now, think about who you want to be at your Horizon Point. Then "upload" the energy of that person, in other words, "become" that person now. Be that version of you through any and all of your senses. As you do this, notice what you naturally do to become your Horizon Point. Did you change your breathing? Did you say something to yourself? Did you change your posture? Did you call up a memory from the past when you were that way? Take notes on what the sensory access points are. You can consciously use these cues for getting into your Horizon Point state *on demand*. If it makes it easier for you to do this, you can imagine you are telling an actor how to show up at your Horizon Point; how would you direct them to do so?

Now let's take it a step further so you know exactly how to act. Use a journal to get to know this version of who you want to be, try writing or meditating on just one question a day, such as: How do you dress? How do you walk? What do you talk with your colleagues and friends about? What car do you drive/transportation do you take, or where do you dwell? What thoughts predominate in your mind? What will you tolerate and what won't you tolerate? What's a small desire you want you can keep front of mind today, and what's your biggest desire you can hold the energy of every day? How do you respond when kicked out of your power? Get to know this persona, and practice walking around as that person—even if you have to start doing so in your own bedroom before you do so at work!

You can also script how you would respond in situations where you are kicked out of your power. Think of the people who press your buttons and anticipate how you'd respond to them when in your Horizon Point state. Pre-rehearse this response and you're more likely to carry it out when it happens.

Your Horizon Point gives you ownership. Give yourself permission to want what you want. Enjoy being at your Horizon Point and the outcomes you create by being that person.

Make showing up at your Horizon Point the new purpose of your life. You just have to remind yourself to do so during busy days. Easy! Post a sticky note with your Horizon Point statement on your computer. Take a photo representing how you want to show up and make it your screen saver or stow it in your wallet. Think of an object that can act like a totem that reminds you of your Horizon Point whenever you catch a glimpse of it and put it on your desk or on your kitchen counter.

I upload my Horizon Point before I give a speech or enter with a client or prospect or any time I'm directly addressing someone about a situation in which I'm out of my power. This intention connects me to the energy of uplift so others can feel it from me, too. And when I'm in the rays of light of my Horizon Point, if I ever feel wobbly about being able to stay there, one of the most likely things I'll reach for is to shift my perspective, which you will learn in the next portal.

In Your Power Practices: Precision

1. Answer the three questions that help you know what outcome you want for any situation that puts you out of your power. "If you could wave a magic wand, what outcome do you want?" Unlock others' energy by broadening the question "What outcome is in the best interest of all?"

2. Ask yourself, "Who do I need to be in order to move the situation toward the desired outcome?" This is your Horizon Point. Focus on it to help you be intentional, not reactive, in who you show up as.

3. Go through the exercise to determine your Horizon Point—that sweet spot intersection between who you want to be and what the organization/role/your family needs from you. Capture the essence of your Horizon Point with an easily recallable encapsulating phrase.

4. Upload your Horizon Point into your body. Notice what you do to become that person. You can step into your Horizon Point on demand in any situation where you're kicked out of your power.

5. Who are you at your Horizon Point? (You can find a database of Horizon Point statements to inspire you—and upload yours—at **www.inyourpowerbook.com**.)

CHAPTER 4

Perspective: From Casualty to Creator

"No problem can be solved from the same level of consciousness that created it."

—Albert Einstein

"I just met with my leader, and she's promoting two of my colleagues, but not me. One of them has even been with the company for less than a year!"

Nikki had good reason to feel she'd earned a promotion. She'd been in charge of creating a new dashboard for tracking progress with the company's diversity, equity, and inclusion efforts, which was so well regarded that the chief human resources officer had given her a big shout-out. And the retention initiative she spearheaded was praised by senior leaders. But her boss told her she wasn't ready for the next step up, senior director position. That triggered her to start doubting herself. "I started questioning my value and my trajectory, and I started thinking maybe I just wasn't worthy."

You can probably relate to how Nikki felt. When your contributions are clearly valuable, and even more than your peers', and yet you're not advanced appropriately for them, you feel undervalued. This was the second time she was passed over; she was beleaguered and angry.

> "Why is my boss promoting people with less experience than me? Why is this happening to me?"

When it seems like bad things are happening, I have a go-to question that puts me back in power. I encouraged her to consider this question:

How might this be happening *for* me instead of *to* me?

This question immediately shifts your focus onto what you *can* control and how the situation may offer you opportunities.

> "All my negative thoughts started to dissipate. To think this is happening *for* me helps me see I could be learning something from it. I could be growing from it, and I should use this moment to pivot versus staying stuck."

She was starting to be open that this unfolding of events might be what I saw as "a prompt from the universe," signaling that it was no longer a good match between her talents and available roles. I prompted her to go further with her review of how this could be happening *for* her: She'd given her boss all the leverage to decide when she was ready for promotion, she decided to take that power back. The job she regretted not being promoted into wasn't even one she really wanted; she wanted *more*. She believed she was ready for a vice president–level job that would allow her to use her talents and thought leadership for transformative impact on the company's whole culture. She's now in the advanced stage of interviewing for Vice President and Chief People Officer roles.

> "I know that if I go somewhere else there will be similar personalities, and politics is even more difficult to manage the higher you go. So actually, it was good for me to go through this."

Here she sums up the change in her point of view: *"If it's happening **to you**, you're the victim. If it's happening **for you**, you're the victor."*

In the portal of Perspective, you will learn that we all have the power to consciously look at challenging situations from different angles and to be open to a deeper truth that might be revealed. Like Nikki, you can have a single thought that shifts your perspective and poof, like magic, all of a sudden a landscape that was humiliating and obstructive is expansive and brimming with possibilities.

When you try on a new perspective, it's like when you go to the eye doctor and look through a series of lenses. One finally snaps into place, and voila! You can see clearly. Ah, that feels right! Seeing through your new lens brings relief with its clarity, and you can feel deep within you how right your new way of thinking is. That helps you to keep reminding yourself to look through your new lens until it becomes second nature for you. Your life will always move in the direction of your strongest and most frequent thoughts.

Henry Ford famously said, "If you think you can and if you think you can't, you're right." Beliefs are like the CEO of your mind—they set the direction of our life and often override rational evidence. They determine what you think is permissible and possible for you, or not. Your beliefs are the default lens through which you interpret everything you experience. They influence all of your thoughts, emotions, and behavior, whether you're aware of that or not.

And the hold they have over you tends to be reinforced over time by the confirmation bias, that gripping default wired into all of our brains that leads us to see what we're expecting to see (and not see what you don't expect to see). If you think your manager is not supportive, you'll play gotcha anytime they act that way and fail to take into account when they are supportive.

We're all subject to this bias, including me:

I'm a runner, and some years ago, I started feeling a searing pain in my left foot. I had to stop running, and I felt the pain even when I was just sitting at my desk coaching. I went to a chiropractor and a podiatrist, begging them, "Please fix my foot!" Nothing worked. Then, on a weekend getaway, I told a friend about the pain. She asked, "Have you tried wearing one size larger sneaker?" I thanked her for her suggestion, but lovingly mocked her. "I've always worn the same size shoe. How could that be the problem!" She also suggested, "Maybe your toe rings are causing the pain." Similarly: "But I've worn my toe rings for 20 years. I love them, and they've never caused me a problem yet!" After a few weeks, now more desperate, I decided to indulge these ideas I believed to be overly pragmatic. I removed the toe rings and tried on my first pair of half size bigger sneakers. From day 1, the pain vanished! I had continued to suffer and problem-solve ineffectively simply because I was stuck in my belief about what the solution needed to be.

You Can't Grow Past Your Beliefs, But You Can Change Them

We have many types and layers of beliefs; some of them are so foundational we are not even aware they play a role in our day-to-day life, but they determine your go-to understanding in situations that put you out of your power. For example, do you believe people are flawed but basically have positive intent, or do you believe people are selfish and out to get you? Do you believe things happen randomly and by luck, or do you believe everything happens for a reason, even if you're not aware of what the reason is yet? Are difficult people obstacles in your way, or have they been brought into your life to be teachers?

When it comes to being in your power, there are a few key beliefs that we all seem to have as a baseline. You want to become aware of your beliefs so that you can choose either to embrace them or change them, intentionally. One is that we tend to believe either in a world of scarcity or of abundance.

A belief in scarcity leads you to see a "finite pie." In the corporate workplace, you'll focus on there being fewer and fewer positions as people rise through the ranks. If you run your own business, you'll worry about the limited number of clients and customers out there to serve. In your personal life, you might be pessimistic about the limited number of possible romantic partners you could be happy with or friends you can make. But you can change your perspective.

Albert Einstein said, "Imagination is more important than knowledge. For knowledge is limited to all we now know and understand, while imagination embraces the entire world, and all there ever will be to know and understand."

The choice to embrace an abundance mindset puts you immediately back in your power. A belief in abundance allows you to see that the world is full of opportunities. The pie isn't finite. You can *make* it bigger, for yourself and others.[1] Nikki started to think, "There are companies out there who will find value in my talents" (or for your situation it might be, "Or I'll find a different department, or start my own company," or in your personal life, "If this dating situation doesn't work out, I'll be sad, but I'm a 'catch' and I'll find someone who is *even more right* for me"). This perspective keeps you from leaking your power by attaching all your control onto a certain outcome just because its the only one you can see. It's a big world. And there's plenty of ways this could play out to serve your life.

In your power you can look beyond the finite problem and see infinite solutions.

Here's a great exercise to help you nurture this perspective. Imagine walking into a networking event with 100 people with the intention to meet at least one head of a medium-sized company because they are the target clients for your service. After talking with a small group of new acquaintances, you head to the bar to refill your glass, and on the way, you catch the eye of an old colleague and walk over to say hi. He introduces you to the pod of people he's talking to, and in that group is the leader of a medium-sized company. Bingo! Now rewind. Maybe if you hadn't headed to the bar, you wouldn't have spotted your old colleague. It might have happened differently: In this possible scenario, the host of the event greeted you when you walked in and you had a brief conversation about what you do and that you were hoping to connect with leaders of mid-sized companies. She is friends with an attendee who's a company leader having relevant challenges and walks you over to introduce you. Or alternatively, maybe you arrive late to the event and that company leader has already left. But among a group of the remaining people that you chat with is that leader's mentee. You make a good connection with the mentee, and he introduces you to the company leader the next day.

Keep playing the scenario out, and you will see that there are infinite ways to meet the leaders who need your services, but you can't know or control all the ways it could happen. What you *can* control is continuing to show up at your Horizon Point with a clear intention.

An abundance mindset and seeing infinite options is key to being in your power because it will help you not overstay in situations trying to make it work when there are other opportunities you are missing out on simply because you don't trust they are there. An abundance mindset takes the pressure off any given person to give you what you need, because you have infinite ways of getting what you need and what you want.

A great way to keep tapping the power of the abundance perspective is to note every occasion that supports this viewpoint. Stack up the evidence to reinforce this mindset until it's become so engrained in you that you expect abundance in your world.

Your Ability Is Infinite if You Keep Cultivating It

The next change in perspective is choosing to believe in your ability to grow. Psychologist Carol Dweck discovered that some of us believe we have a basically fixed set of abilities, while others believe we can always grow our talents.

If you have a fixed mindset with respect to a challenging situation, you will see the situation as it is *now*—and finite. You'll come to the conclusion: "This is the way this person is," and be resentful of them. Your mind will be closed to trying new approaches, concluding, "This is the best level of collaboration we can get to." You'll see yourself as limited, too. "This is just who I am."

With a growth mindset, you see failures or impasses as opportunities to learn. You embrace that you can get where you want to go but just haven't gotten there yet. "Not yet" fosters hope and perseverance, as well as agility. You're open to, even excited about, trying new things. (Aren't we all a work in progress?)

My client Grace is a gold star example of growth mindset for staying in your power. She was serving our country overseas, leading and protecting people under her mandate during dangerous operations. But when she returned to the US, the government institution she worked for accused her of violating protocol by sharing some information in a press conference before release of it had been approved (even though she had in fact not done so). She was temporarily removed from her post and subjected to a yearlong bloody slog of an investigation. She found herself questioning her leadership and grappling with a sense of betrayal. "Imagine how much trust and belief you have to have in your country to pick up sticks and go live in authoritarian regimes and drag your children around the world. It's something you do with your heart," she told me. She received no trust in return.

The situation was devastating, but at the same time she didn't let it keep her out of her power. Instead, she kept coming back to focus on how the challenge would strengthen her, how she would get to the other side of the bridge. She kept being open to figuring out why it's happening *for* her, trusting everyday some reason would unfold in order to help her move forward with courage. Soon, requests started coming in from the highest levels in her institution for her to tell her story, and she saw the opportunity to help reform the institution. Also, she had reason to believe gender bias was involved in the decision to investigate her, and she imagined once resolved, she would educate women's audiences and advocate for reforms in her institution.

And that's exactly what she did when, a year later, she was fully vindicated and reinstated! She is now leading a high priority global collaboration initiative. As we reflected on her experience, she shared, "Having gone through this I feel in every part of me there's this comfort I can give myself, like I no longer rule my life looking for approval or needing everyone to like me. I now see I am going to need this level of self-trust and power I've built in order to lead at this level."

The growth perspective zooms you out from your current viewpoint and can take the edge off or coexist with the anger at being acted upon because you see the situation has meaning for you; there is a purpose for having to go through it. You're being readied for a bigger mission.

***

Get a 3D Perspective on the Situation

So often when we're experiencing difficulty with someone, we see their behavior through a narrow lens. We focus on their character. They're acting the way they are because they're selfish, power hungry, pathetically insecure, or have no emotional intelligence.

We aren't seeing all sorts of other possible explanations, having to do with the features of the broader context. You want to keep zooming out until you can see clearly from a 3D perspective.

I once coached a leadership team where one leader thought her peer was aggressive, always talking over her in meetings. Meanwhile he thought she marginalized him and was too insecure to make important decisions. They each had a one-dimensional perspective, only pointing fingers at the other.

Instead, take a 3D perspective. First, understand each person's perspective. Then understand the interactions between you and them, and finally understand the contextual factors. From this view it became clear that neither person was wrong, the leadership team structure wasn't right. They talked together to get clarity on "who does what," and now they no longer put each other out of their power.

This way we tend to focus narrowly on other people's flaws to explain difficult situations is again not our fault; it's another cognitive bias built into our brains called the fundamental attribution error. This error is the innate tendency to attribute someone's bad behavior to their character or personality, while attributing our own similar bad behavior to external situational factors outside of our control. For example, if your boss is abruptly dismissive of you when you're asking her for approval of an idea, you might attribute that to her being self-involved. But if *you* are dismissive in the same way to a direct report, you might attribute your behavior to your well-intentioned effort to give a timely response while rushing off to a meeting you're late for.

We can stop ourselves from jumping to these negative conclusions by getting a wide-angle 3D perspective of the situation.

Your first step is to try to see the situation from the point of view of the person you're having difficulty with. This allows you to meet them where they are now and then effectively move them toward a solution that's in the best interest of all. This was a huge help for Elisa, an executive in finance I coached who was having trouble with the head of the IT group. He would not submit a budget to her after she'd made multiple requests, and he was blaming her, saying he hadn't received her emails about it. She heard he was badmouthing her. The situation had gotten so tense that she was waking up with a pit in her stomach, dreading going to work each day, and whenever an email popped up with his name on it, her stomach would clench.

When I explored how she might see the situation from *his* perspective, she realized: *The CIO prides himself as the IT systems savior whose role is above having to deal with budget issues.* He probably didn't think his group should be confined by a budget because they are conducting a system transformation across the whole global organization.

Next consider the wider set of circumstances that are involved. The CEO recently mandated business unit heads take ownership of their budgets but hadn't communicated that clearly to department leaders. Also, Elisa's up for a promotion, so she's worried that she would be seen as not doing her job. In any situation of impasse, there are always these confluence of factors.

You Want to See the Hologram of Any Scenario You're Struggling With

Getting that holistic view helps you identify possibilities you haven't thought of for resolving problems. In considering the 3D perspective of a situation, you also have opportunity to think beyond the perspectives of all the people involved to factor in systemic issues that might be at play. *Often we make an under-lying systems issue into an interpersonal one.* Instead, what problems might there be in the organization's procedures or structures? What might be the root cause of the issue for both of you or for everyone?

My client, Sharon, was struggling to build her business in the world of art transactions. It's quite competitive, and she was vying with others for every opportunity. One aspect of the work is authenticating an artist's work, or as the case may be, not authenticating it. Whether it was a gallery owner, the artist and/or their family, a museum, an auction house, or an art historian, she found that she was frequently coming up against the word of others who had a vested interest in authenticating an artwork. When she couldn't get her advisements to be followed, she started to feel marginalized or that there was "something wrong with her," that she wasn't compelling enough to break through in this world.

By zooming out and observing the interactions between many stakeholders in the art world—not only her own challenges—she was able to realize the real problem was that *the industry as a whole lacked standards*. This is an issue that has wide implications, from fraudulent art sales to lawsuits over whether artworks should be repatriated to their countries of origin and much more.

She stopped focusing on particular actions with competitors and instead focused on how bad behavior was endemic in the field. As she recalls, "I set out to create a corrective for everybody." It hit her there was a lack of standards in the field—who qualifies to work in our field, or what credentials determine you are an expert. She thought to herself, "Wait a minute, I have expertise I can apply to this problem!" She developed the "Hecker Standard"™ which is an objective set of criteria to authenticate an artwork. She is now sought after as a speaker, as an expert witness, and as a university lecturer, making great progress in disseminating the standards throughout the art world. She personally stepped into her power, going as I call it, from "chasing after, to getting chased!" And the whole field benefits. You too can be that powerful.

***

A new frame of reference can come from looking at the history of a problem. Taking a historical perspective can help you understand the dynamics that got us here and provide insights into the part you can play in transforming it. Milagros Phillips is the author of *Cracking the Race Healer's Code*, and on my *Power Shift* podcast she provided this perspective on racism in the United States: "Racism is a reflection that we're all out of our power. The bottom line is that we're dealing with unhealed trauma, which when gets passed down from generation to generation dehumanizes people. It disconnects people from their true nature, which is that human beings are pure love."

She offers a perspective that helps us look at the history of painful realities such as discrimination: "Racism shows up at five different levels—the institutional, systemic, internalized, personal, and interpersonal . . . . To make a difference in the world, people need to become conscious, they need to take responsibility. They don't have to take responsibility for what they have been institutionalized into, but you need to understand and take responsibility *that you've been institutionalized*. We've internalized what we've been institutionalized into and then we act, react, and interact with each other from what we know. It doesn't make any of us a good person or a bad person, it makes you a *conditioned person*."

Many years go into the making of discriminatory behavior that denies the humanity and tangible life opportunities of another person, whether that is because of their race, gender, sexual orientation or identity, religious beliefs, national origin, or physical ability. Again Milagros Phillips: "That is why I don't do guilt and shame in my seminars for Black people or White people. We have all been trained by a dysfunctional system of traumatized people, who make laws and culture out of their traumas; the truth of who we are as human being is so much greater."

As each one of us takes responsibility for being conscious of and healing of our conditioning, we set a new standard for each person we interact with to become more conscious as well. As each of us is intentional about coming from our pure nature and not from fear, we can each play a role in not passing down "out of one's power behavior" to future generations.

You can extend your perspective past human history to gain even more insight. For example, many have "climate anxiety" or feel out of our power because of species loss and extreme natural disasters. Tenzin Seldon is a climate solutions leader recognized as the social entrepreneur "most likely to impact the next century." She shared that people ask her how she can be so calm and surrendered despite being on the forefront of understanding climate realities. "I say to them it's because I understand the millennial perspective of eons, not just 1000 years. The Earth, and nature, and the universe have a way of correcting itself, with or without humans."

Here's how she uses this perspective to allow for more solutions: "If the root of your anxiety is that human action is one of the main causes of the climate crisis, then you think only humans can solve for climate change. And that is untrue. Humans are a big part of *both* the problem and solution, but indigenous wisdom teaches us that the more you get connected to Earth, the more you understand that there are also natural systems and natural orders that are bigger than human beings that can correct themselves. The best way to change climate is to understand climate and to understand nature."

She advises that "If you're feeling that anxiety, get back in your body and walk on the sand, or walk in the trees to ground yourself."

I asked her how to apply this wisdom to the idea of how to be in your power in relation to an issue that is truly out of our control and bigger than what any of us can control. She reframed my question in way that aligned beautifully with the idea of being in your power—and helped me understand the way I was thinking about it was putting me out of my power: "I don't think climate is bigger than us. We are part of climate and climate change, we are part of climate crisis, and climate crisis is part of who we are. We have to think of ourselves as one. A small tree that's dropped and is dying is not thinking, 'I'm a small tree that's dying.' It's thinking, 'I'm part of this ecosystem. So I need the other trees to be able to live on and live with.' I think this isolationist perspective is hindering us. We need to get back to harmony with nature. I think Greta Thunberg has shown that every single voice, even a 19-year-old girl from Sweden's voice, matters in this."

Zooming out even further to the layer of the cosmos is a perspective that helps many people get back in their power. Having a belief or faith in a Creator or creative energetic force in the universe can provide a sense that there is a meaningful unfolding order—reinforcing the idea that events are happening "for you." You can reframe difficult events as holding a karmic lesson requiring you to overcome a longstanding pattern and instead to grow more empowered in yourself. You can reinforce this trust by noticing that when you stay in your power with regard to that challenge you attract more of what you want in your life. Trust in the intelligence or timing of a higher power can be a comforting guide and make us feel supported and not so alone. This surrender can give you the experience of actively "doing something" even when you're not sure what to do next with the limited information you have now.

***

Your mind is an extraordinary multileveled parallel-processing machine that you can program to work for you rather than against you, as long as you know its tendencies. The portal of Perspective helps you see you might only be stuck out of your power because of overfocus on the finite problem in front of you. Rather than thinking that how you understand the problem now is the last word, you can train your mind to see context and abundance.

Bringing a greater level of consciousness to your understanding of the situation will help you move forward from it and will enable you to bring everyone involved in the scenario along with you. To see new solutions, you can understand the history of the issue, see it from a 3D perspective or resolve it at its root cause. The version of you that feels powerless is not all of who you are, and what you are seeing of the other people involved is likely not all of who they are either. And if the current situation is not a good fit for you, then there's a big world of alternatives waiting for you.

Make each of these perspectives a screensaver of your mind. As you try on each of these perspectives, give them a "like" so the algorithm of your mind will show you more of them and shape your mindset to make these your go-to perspectives. You have infinite ways of reconnecting to your power. You are a creative force who can both overcome your personally challenging situations and contribute to overall healing and make the world the way it could be.

In order to shift your perspective you must be able to clear your emotional reactions so you can think straight. You'll learn how in the next portal.

Power Practices: Perspective

1. Ask the empowering question to shift from victim to victor: "How might this be happening *for me* instead of *to me?*
2. To see beyond the finite problem to find the infinite solutions, cultivate an abundance mentality and growth mindset.
3. See the situation as a hologram. Make it a game to understand the problem in 3D—your perspective, their perspective, and contextual factors—and see if you can find and solve the underlying problem.

4. Build insight by looking beyond the "now" moment. Understand it's history, see it as a part of an overall arc of an unfolding order, or consider being open to trusting the workings of a Creator or creative energetic force that can provide guidance.

5. Give each of these perspectives a "like" in your mind so you can shape the algorithm of your mind to make these your go-to perspectives. You are a creative force who has endless capabilities to get back in your power and contribute to making the situation better for you and everyone involved.

CHAPTER 5

Physiology: From Hijack to Natural High

"Thoughts are the language of the brain, feelings are the language of the body."
—Dr. Joe Dispenza, author of *Becoming Supernatural*

How do you know you're out of your power? Your body tells you so! Think about the ways we describe being out of our power: We get a pit in our stomach or are gut-punched; we feel paralyzed, hot under the collar, or a knife through the heart. Maybe you feel like you're swallowing your emotion or have lost your footing.

Being knocked out of your power isn't just an in-the-moment thing, though. You might carry the emotion into your next meeting and the one after that or be off-kilter the rest of the day. It's hard to focus, let alone empathize or be inspiring. If you replay the emotion-inducing event in your mind at any point in the day, you whiplash yourself to experience the event again and again.

In this state, we usually put our focus on the stressor—the situation that caused this ejection from our power. But the stressor that caused the issue needs to be distinguished from the stress reaction that it activates in your body. As the Nagoski sisters write in *Burnout*, "Addressing the cause of the stress doesn't mean you've addressed the stress itself. Your body is soaked in stress juice," wreaking the havoc just described.[1]

We have to deal with our emotions first because a state of strong emotion constrains our ability to problem-solve, have perspective, or remember the strategies you're reading here. It overwhelms your attempts to understand the events that pushed you out of your power and keeps you focused on interpretations that keep you there. The way that you can separate yourself from all the reactivity and re-experience your sovereignty happens through your body.

Whereas the rest of the portals in this book will guide you to prevent, improve, or transform the stressors that put you out of your power, in the portal of Physiology you will learn to manage your emotional reactions. You'll learn to recover from them quickly and counter negative emotions with pleasure.

Feeling an emotion is not the same as being out of your power. Emotions are physiological patterns we give meaning to and which then prompt us to take action accordingly. Getting kicked out of your power happens when you don't exercise the power you do have to deal with your emotions, so you get out of your flow or kept in a state of helplessness caused by your inner turmoil as much as the event itself.

Humanity is founded on the experience of a wide range of emotions. We've evolved to experience positive emotion such as we get when we fall in love, listen to beautiful music, accomplish moonshots, and come together in prayerful community. But human cultures are built on structures that caused out-of-power emotions. Our early ancestry lived in fear and struggle for survival, and their cultures were rooted in violence. Emotions arise in us from daily interactions today, but they tap into an archeology of accumulated emotions built up over generations that may have gone unprocessed for years and are still a stored pattern embedded in our bodies. This is one reason why we can get flooded with emotion or display disproportionate or out-of-control emotion responses.

Cultural conditioning has taught us that while it's okay to show passion when it comes to winning (such as at an athletic game), we're prohibited from having or showing negative emotion or being too emotional. (Emotions that are at all acceptable tend to have gendered prohibitions. Men are only allowed to show anger, while for women, anger is seen as unacceptable, but passive emotions such as sadness and hopelessness are okay.) We keep ourselves from our emotional expression in order to keep other people comfortable.

Thus, most of us haven't learned a good repertoire of strategies to move through our feelings and get back into calm and mental clarity. Rather, when hijacked into an emotional state, we tend to isolate, where we ruminate as we tour the museum of our hurts. We hold in or avoid feelings, which keeps stress hormones festering in our bodies and maintains self-destructive thinking patterns that can be associated with anxiety. When we don't feel we can safely express anger, we often turn it back on ourselves causing depression. We also get afraid that if we allow a tiny trickle of emotion, the dam will break and the whole reservoir will flood. Or we have pushed away emotion so consistently for so long, the well is dry—and we don't know what we feel.

Your emotions connect you to your essential truth. Anger signals to you what you won't stand for. Most people who have persisted in challenging the status quo are fueled by healthy anger. When I am angry or frustrated, I can act on my behalf (or to protect others) in a way I can't when I'm less energized. Sadness and grief are an important part of an acceptance process. They help you honor your hurt that you've had to detach from something or someone.

Disconnection from ourselves makes us less insightful about how to respond, and your response might come out sarcastic or with a tone, defeating your purpose to make the situation better. Don't be afraid to follow emotions where they lead as long as you know how to keep your hands on the steering wheel.

We would all be better served by following my favorite line from visionary and feminist icon Regena Thomashauer, aka Mama Gena: "We want to 'play all 88 keys of our emotional piano.'"[2]

***

Here are three overall approaches to using your physiology as an instrument to help you get back in and stay in your power:

Return to a State of Calm

Reconnect Your Feeling and Thinking Centers

When out of your power, your body is out of alignment. Humans are meant to balance the emotional centers of our brains: the sympathetic nervous system (SNS) with its counterpart, the parasympathetic nervous system (PNS). When you are in a calm state of power, the emotional centers and rational thinking parts of your brain are in two-way communication, conspiring together to guide you with a response to improve the situation. Yet when you're emotionally hijacked, the parts of your brain that are feeling the hurt, anger, or shame *disconnect* from the rational thinking parts of your brain. You literally are not able to access the part of your brain that can help you get back in your power. Your emotions are calling a *disconnected* phone number.

This emotional mode tries to maximize efficiency so all information is routed to grooves that are already well worn in your brain and you can only reference things you've done in the past to know how to solve current problems. Lacking a distinction between past and present, your brain experiences the current moment as a rerun of the past, giving you that doubly sinking feeling that you are back here *again*. Yet you cannot see a greater context or access lessons you've accumulated in your life.

Activate Your Safe and Social Response

You can see the bigger picture of the situation and respond with intention once you reconnect to the regions of the brain where that kind of processing takes place. This is the PNS, it's the mode in which you can feel safe and be social. The PNS helps you be cool, calm, and collected. It gives you compassion for self and for others. It enables discernment, understanding of others' motivations, and the ability to carry out power-shifting interpersonal strategies.

In this state of calm and safety, you reconnect to your identity. From there you can radiate your intentions out onto your team, your family, your community, and beyond. In this way *your ability to raise others is built into your physiology*.

All you need to do to set this empowering process in motion is to activate the chief nerve of the PNS, the vagus nerve. It signals that all is well—the threat is over: You can be calm now. You're cared for. Clarity begins here. Then you can *choose* a powerful response: the one *you* want, not one you've been triggered into.

Your Mind Follows Your Breath

One of the quickest ways to tell the vagus nerve it's okay for it to calm you down is to slow down your breathing. Here are three essential breathing exercises you can use even when you're in the middle of a meeting or difficult conversation.

Reconnection breath: The vagus nerve becomes active when your breath slows down to six breaths per minute—that's 10 seconds for each breath—and when your exhalation is longer than your inhalation. Inhale through your nose and count to five, and then exhale through your nose to the count of five. Do this for one to three minutes.

Instant calm breath: Inhale through your nose with a regular inhalation duration, and then do a second shorter inhalation to capture even more oxygen. Then do a slower than normal exhalation through your mouth.[3] (This one is easier on a video call than in person.) If you're in your own space, a great variation is to take a big breath in through your nose and let out a long sigh through your mouth (remember the exhalation is what activates your vagus nerve, so emphasize it). Especially effective is to let out a sound of "haaa" as you release your sigh. Keep doing this until you are noticeably more calm or start to feel a yawn coming on, this is a telltale sign that your nervous system is entering a calm state.

Cooling breath: When you are angry/frustrated/impatient with others, it generates a heated physical state within you. We even say, "My blood is boiling." Cooling breath will get you back to a cool, calm, and collected state in order to maintain composure and respond, not react. (I bet you're going to have a lot of opportunity to practice cooling breath!)

Open your mouth slightly and slowly breathe in as if you were sipping through a straw. Then breathe out slowly through your nose.[4] In addition to cooling breath, if in a meeting, you can sip from a glass of cold water, or if in your own environment, then try holding an ice cube in your hand or putting an ice pack on your chest.

Instant Calming Hacks with Your Senses

The SNS is activated by visual stimulation, via your sight. Try closing your eyes for a few seconds, and you will access the PNS. You will start to notice auditory cues that can help you feel present, and that your breathing relaxes.

Have you ever taken a class, maybe in yoga, in which the instructor told you to hum or chant? The calming effect of this is due to the vagus nerve being connected to your throat box. If you are in private, say, in your office after a tense meeting, stretch yourself to engage in a little humming, chanting, or singing. As part of my everyday energy practices I do a chant that is specifically designed to calm down my emotional brain while lighting up my intuition centers.

The sense of touch can also be used to stimulate the vagus nerve, just by stroking something soft, like a scarf, a furry animal friend, or alternatively running your hands along something hard and smooth, like a favorite totem rock.

In sum, start to build a repertoire of these exercises to instantly access a state of calm, return to a neutral mind, and regain a sense of harmony in your body.

***

"Feeling Is Healing"

You are not at the mercy of your emotions (even though it feels like you are). As humans, we have a range of physiological arousal that we can bear. It can be helpful to think about this in terms of the concept of windows of tolerance,[5] which suggests that we have a range of emotional arousal in which we can readily process information about people and interactions and respond effectively.

But when your emotion gets to a level outside of your window of tolerance, you will feel an urge and/or automatically react with one of the 5 Fs: fight, flight, freeze, fawn, or fix. Especially if you've had difficult or traumatic experiences earlier in your life, then you would have developed strong emotional reactions that were appropriate to the situation (such as fear, anger, or embarrassment), and these 5F automatic reactions were developed as survival behaviors to protect yourself from the overwhelming emotion. Repeatedly having to deal with these situations will have trained your physiology to respond automatically with high emotional arousal even in present-day situations that may potentially be less threatening. It can be helpful for you to become aware of your own tendency so you can recognize it in real time and become more comfortable dealing with emotions that get activated.

Fight: When you are feeling unseen, disrespected, or threatened, you might tend to "come out swinging." Do you raise your voice or become defensive? Do you react aggressively by wanting to win over the other person or confront them? Do you direct verbal barbs at those offending or undermining you (or just in your own mind)?

Flight: Do you go into avoidance mode, like avoid interacting with someone or actively not dealing with the situation? You might prefer to escape the unpleasant emotions through a Netflix binge or by starting the evening with a drink, or both. Some of us turn to substances as a means of avoidance or resort to binge eating, compulsive shopping, or other addictive behaviors. Or we've developed strategies to bypass actively feeling emotion altogether, instead intellectualizing (thinking your emotions rather than feeling them) or somatizing (your body expresses the emotions through pain or illness without consciously feeling the emotion).

Freeze: If a situation raises emotion that is especially intense and/or goes on for a considerable time, your body will become overwhelmed because of the continued effort to deal with the emotion. At that point your natural coping mechanism shifts toward a freeze response, shutting down emotionally and feeling numb.[6] You might notice you've become disengaged with your work, depressed, or burned out. Like all protective mechanisms, this was a helpful mechanism for the times you couldn't escape uncontrollable and harmful experiences, but when used in everyday scenarios that don't threaten well-being to the same extent, it can significantly disconnect you from knowing your own emotions or even remembering important parts of your experience.[7]

These three responses are built into our nervous system. Fawn and fix are behavioral responses that have been added to our repertoire over time as humans have sought to devise other strategies for coping with interpersonal stress.

Fawn: You try to please or appease those causing you harm as a way of trying to maintain connection with them safely. That might be by caregiving or rescuing them, not standing for your own needs and saying no, hoping that if you care for others they will want to care for you.

Fix: The fix response is my name for behaviors that try to deal with a hurtful person by trying to control them; examples include being overly responsible or trying to make things perfect so you are not blamed.

Do you recognize your common reactions in any of these descriptions (or a combination of them)? Think of a current situation that may be putting you out of your power. What do you do as soon as you start to get emotional?

_____

_____

_____

You want to find ways of dealing with your emotions that keep you within your window of tolerance so you can act with intention to get back into your power. To move the energy of your difficult emotions through you constructively, you have to embrace and become unafraid of your own physical sensations.[8] Here are some ways to get started doing so.

1. **Allow your emotions:** Research suggests that the life span of an emotion is only about 90 seconds. In *90 Seconds to a Life You Love,* Dr. Joan Rosenberg teaches that by staying mindfully present for that short duration and breathing through

it, you can surf the wave of emotion—allowing yourself to stay present to your emotion so you can learn from it. Many mindfulness and meditation approaches take this as their premise—thoughts and emotions will come and go. Just stay in the present moment, observe them, and allow the next thought to come.

2. **Allow your Body to Express Itself:** Regena Thomashauer suggests that the most important thing is for a woman to "feel every drop of emotion that runs through her body— with gusto. Feeling is healing." One way to do this is to put on music that matches your mood. Then get out of your head, allow yourself to sink into your body, and experience the sensation of the emotion wherever you feel it in your body. Allow yourself to sway or to move your arms, your head, or your torso in whatever way expresses those sensations. Being self-conscious about this is old school;, you're here to take back your power! Do this for at least one full song in order to start to know where emotion lives within you and follow your body's sensations (2–3 songs is even better). You'll feel more connected to yourself and back into your power.

3. **Work it out with vigor:** It's not only that we don't allow our-selves to experience our emotions, but when we experience them, we don't feel them fully enough. In their book *Burnout*, the Nagoski sisters make the important point: "Emotions are tunnels. If you go all the way through them, you get to the light at the end of the tunnel."[9] You want to, as they advise, *"complete the stress cycle."* This means, continue the approach of moving your emotions through until there is some sort of indication that there's been a physiological shift, that is, you feel better, you feel done. You have a felt sense of closure, as in, "I needed that! I can move forward now."[10] If you don't complete the stress cycle, you'll stay out of your power, not knowing the clarity and energy of being on the other side of it. You will learn to leverage this clarity in later chapters, such as if it helps you know when to set a boundary or what you want to say when sharing your powerful truth.

When It Comes to Your Emotions, If It's Not through You, It's Still in You

It's helpful to think about emotion as energy in motion. We try to suppress our emotions, or ignore them, but if they are still a part of our experience, they will rise up again in a way that feels less in our control. Have you ever thought of how much energy it takes to *not* feel your feelings? It's like encaging a tiger. You *have* the negative feelings either way, but you have to work hard physiologically to repress them. This is underscored by the main premise of Chinese medicine: to keep moving energy through you so it doesn't stagnate and cause disease. Here is a guide to strategies for feeling negative emotions intensely and complete the cycle:

Intense physical exertion channels negative emotions out of your system. Try to match the intensity of your emotion with the strength of the method you use to clear it. If you have a mild emotional response, a pleasant experience like going for a walk in nature could help ground you and move the experience through. However, if you have a strong emotion, you want to counter this with a more vigorous physical action.

My client Tom was facing a serious threat to his business because of friction with business partners, and he was angry both with himself and them. He'd been feeling depressed and was drinking more and making impulsive decisions. I told him to go hit the boxing bag a few times before our next meeting or go to the driving range and hit a bucket of golf balls, not worrying about accuracy but just to smack his anger out. In our next meeting his mental fog had cleared, and we continued to execute a strategic plan to address the problem.

I used to deploy a range of flight responses—stress eating to stuff down emotion was my go-to behavior as well as procrastinating/avoiding. This tendency would keep me preoccupied in an off-kilter state but doing nothing about it. Now as soon as I feel off inside,

I lean into the emotion and instead feel it and move it through my system. This is what enables me to recover much more quickly when kicked out of my power.

When I'm angry and frustrated, I start with the exercises I've included next. If I'm still worked up after that, my go-to tactic is hit the boxing bag in the gym in my New York City building. I think of the disempowering scenario in my mind and strike the bag with as much force as I can until I feel like my arms are going to fall off! By the end, the interaction that put me out of my power feels a distant memory, and I'm ready to step back into my Horizon Point. "Moving it through" options are infinite;, they vary according to my environment: When I can get myself to a swimming pool or an exercise bike, I go as hard as I can for sprints. If I can get myself to a beach, I slap it out among the waves in the ocean. If I'm tied to my NYC apartment, I might dance like no one's watching to a rage song in between meetings.

You want to find a repertoire of strategies that works in *your* day-to-day. Go to boxing or Zumba class. Work out vigorously (but safely) with weights. Do an in-person or online yoga class with poses that squeeze the tension out of your muscles. Chop wood. Smash pillows. Go in a room, lock the door, and throw a 90-second hissy fit. Have a good cry. Go in your car to scream, close the windows and let it rip. (If you are a parent with small children, you'll need the extra layer of problem-solving to find a place where your children won't see or hear you. Or if they are mad too, then do it all together!) Do what works for you to move that "burn the house down" feeling out!

When you don't attend to your emotions, you often end up feeling exhausted. My client, a leader in a tech company, was highly aggravated at her underperforming team members but sat in front of her computer all day, rarely moving. She didn't even realize she was so frustrated, saying she was "too exhausted" to work out—but this was only because she had so distanced herself from the physical states in her body. When she started to engage in vigorous movement it helped her to channel her frustration into productive solutions. (Is this you?) Remember—if you don't do something to move your unhealthy emotions through you, then you are carrying the effect of that frustrating person inside of you. You're letting *them* win!

Other times you might not feel the riled up energy of anger but rather the tender experience of grief or low energy signs of burnout. If so, the "move it through" strategy is different. You have to start by doing something to energize yourself enough to get back to your baseline level of energy. This might look like going for a mindful walk, allowing tears, journaling, or slow dance movement with a hand on your heart. (You want to have a range of playlists for different emotion states. You can find my constantly updated playlists for angry moments, grief, and pick-me-ups at **www.inyourpowerbook.com**.)

For acute moments of anger or frustration during a busy day, when you can't make the time for a workout, here are some ways to "get it out" in one to three minutes. You'll need a private space for these or try them outdoors or at a gym.

Push Away Breath

A lot of negative emotions stagnate around the chest area. This movement clears it away and gives you an empowering sense of taking a stand for your own space. Stand with your legs greater than shoulder width apart and raise both arms in parallel to the ground straight in front of you at shoulder level. Put both hands vertical as if you are making the motion "stop." Push your arms forward and exhale as if you are forcefully blowing air out through your mouth (as if you were pushing something away). Retract your arms, and then push away again with a similar exhalation.

Now that you have the basic motion, repeat this by twisting your body to the right side, and push away there while exhaling. Then do the same toward right in front of you and then to your left. Then back to center. Keep repeating this push forward with your arms while exhaling. Try this for two or three minutes; you will experience a clearing of negative energy in your chest. (Go to **www.inyourpowerbook.com** for a demonstration of these three exercises and songs that match the beat of the movement.)

Karate Chop

This is a great exercise to dissolve negative emotions. Have you ever been to a massage where at the end the masseur/masseuse does a rapid "karate chop" motion on your back in order to stimulate the meridians there? You can leverage this same motion. Put your arms out in front of you, palms facing each other. Alternate moving your hands up and down in a chopping motion between your belly button and your throat area. The key is to do this as vigorously as possible. Start with 30 seconds to one minute, and work your way up to more time. You'll see this gives you a lot of energy in your hands and clears away the mental swirl that comes from frustration and anger. (I've had roomfuls of corporate professionals howling with fun doing the karate chop to dissolve their frustrating emotions. I was quite nervous the first time I tried it that it would be considered too "out there" and get me laughed out of the room. But countless times trainees have told me they do it on their own with their teams and request it when they recommend training for other parts of the organization. It's energizing and helps you get it out so you can get back into your power and on with your life.)

Clearing Breath

This simple breath cleanses your mind of negative thoughts. Sit up straight and keep your spine long. Breathe out through your nose making each breath an expulsion that starts from your navel area, as if your navel is pushing the breath up and out of your body. The solar plexus is the energetic seat of your power, it is the connection point for 72,000 nerves in the body. So much emotion gets concentrated there, and this breath releases it. As you do this breath, picture the disempowering situation in front of you, or represent it with a flame, and try to blow the candle out with the force of your breath.

Feel with Those You Feel Safe With

One of the ways to soothe our sense of distress is by sharing about it with our friends, family, and colleagues. This can be a useful strategy, but there are caveats. First, move your emotion through you *first*. Second, be thoughtful about whom you trust. Has this person proven that they won't dismiss you for your full range of feelings? Is this someone who is calm and can help you get back to calm? Third, don't just vent. Venting keeps you reliving the experience, depleting rather than restoring you. It can also push people away from you if you get stuck in the rut of continuously venting to them.

Vent constructively! Ask if it's a good time to do so, don't just ambush them and launch into a rant (we've all been there). Best is to give yourself a designated amount of time, for example, 10 minutes. Maybe the first round of venting you just need to dump out what happened and how you feel about it, but after you do that, aim to turn your stream of consciousness into a set of coherent thoughts. For closure, summarize your key takeaways so you start to integrate your learnings across the emotional and rational thinking centers of your brain. Always end on a note where you commit to a constructive action and thank them for holding space for you to talk to you.

***

Fill Yourself Back Up!

You want to go beyond just relief from the bad. You want to fill up with the good. The counterbalance of pleasure and joy is important to repeatedly train your body to go from out-of-your-power to in-your-power emotional states. It's an assertion of your sovereignty akin to saying, "You can act how you act, but I'm not going to let it interfere with my life!" When you connect with your joy and pleasure, it reminds you who you are without your mental judgments of yourself and others. It gives you an expansive delicious feeling within yourself. It makes you feel unstoppable, like you can handle the out-of-your-power offender. These experiences increase happiness chemicals oxytocin and dopamine.

A regular slate of activities that bring you pleasure and joy strengthens your nervous system (e.g., live music, cooking, snuggling up in front of a fire with a good book, maintaining your garden, or hiking a beautiful mountain trail). However, you don't necessarily need to plan a big or complex event. Baby-step it.

Allow yourself to experience "glimmers", micro-moments that are antidote to the intense work of reconnecting with your power and healing negative emotion triggers.[11] Often these moments engage the senses, as in appreciating the crisp fresh air when out on your morning walk or watching a sunset not just with a cursory view but really seeing the full collage of it. Or linger on a moment someone complimented you and allow it to settle and give you a smile inside you. Flirt playfully with a special someone in your life. End your day by lighting a candle with a calming aromatic scent, and don a soft robe to feel its soothing touch on your skin. Do a double-take as you look at yourself in the mirror dressed up to go to work or out on the town, and tell yourself, "You've got it going on!"

Our bodies offer infinite gifts if we would only know to unwrap them—for example, just take in a *really* long breath or two now. See how you can feel the full expanse of it starting in your belly, expanding into your chest, and the wisping of the air all the way up into respiratory channels of your head. Something you do thousands of times a day is deeply nourishing. Same thing if you allow yourself some body stretches. It's especially good to move your body in dance—just spontaneously start dancing with your partner or your kids in the kitchen (or take a class or get on a Zoom dance break with your friends)! Reconnecting with your life force you gives you a feeling of aliveness and self-love, a reminder of you when you are in your power. Counterbalancing the intensity of the negative entrains our nervous system to recognize coming back into our power. Try to get hooked on these "glimmer" moments of deliciously filling yourself up and proactively create them.

Regena Thomashauer, founder of the School of Womanly Arts and longtime visionary on empowering women, has stood for the idea that reaching for pleasure is the antidote for allowing our emotions to feel stuffed down or our light dimmed. From her I've learned that we want to engage in "pleasure research," which *is how* you find your way back to your power. You can—and must—proactively make time and space for it in your life even when you are kicked out of your power and your attention is consumed with reactions of grief and rage.

Here's an example of her game-changing guidance for a woman who's caught in an ongoing pattern of anger and disappointment toward her husband:

"The trick for you is that you have justifiable "charge" because he has not risen in the way one might have hoped. But he can't rise higher than you are willing to choose pleasure over anger. This is the hardest thing to do because we get so much agreement from other women that men are insensitive. We are all willing to join that party saying, "Yeah, he's such a jerk." But retraining ourselves to choose pleasure over anger takes a lot of discipline and responsibility."

She continues: "This is how we can be the change we wish to see. We are not going to get anywhere with raw destructive anger. We see the lack of progress that occurs when we all resort to anger as part of the overdeveloped masculine in our culture. The question is how can we co-create pleasurably and creatively? We haven't even touched the surface of that because pleasure is unlimited. And when we as women can dispense with our anger, devote ourselves to our pleasure, and guide our men to perform at a higher level, the world will shift on its axis and we will handle things—from the intricacies of interpersonal relationships to the larger issues such as climate change—in our lifetime."

Going beyond these exercises to move emotions through your body, Mama Gena teaches that women can access the transformational power of our emotional truth by choosing to add the element of "turn on" to it. You do this by plugging into your innate experience of yourself as beautiful and magnificent and deserving that is our birthright. And then weave this aliveness in with the way you work through your out-of-power emotions. Think, for example, of dancing to a rage song—you experience the physical release of anger but also it energizes your sense of "rightness" in yourself and reminds you of your "sexy." Your "turn on" is a renewable energy source you can tap into any moment, and keeps you lit up even if others' limited behavior intrudes on you. You can stay 'in your power' no matter what.

A woman I met through Mama Gena's community, Cindy, shared that she followed this idea to re-ignite the spark she had lost in her marriage by refocusing on injecting these moments of pleasure into her days. She had been stewing with silent anger toward her husband of many years, out of her power because she blamed him for not being attentive to her. She decided to stop making him wrong for everything and take matters into her own hands. She started to dress up with radiance *just because it made her* feel sexy and special. She inserted dance breaks in her day and took nightly baths, having her young children join in the fun to set up the bath but then taking the time to soak on her own. She started to explore her own body with movement classes and sensual touch, so she knew what felt good to her and could ask for it. She started to fill her own cup, and realized she could have more of the relationship she wanted with him if she started by going first. So now if she sends him a love note, he writes one back. If she sends a flirtatious text, he eventually sends one back. And over time, he's initiating these. They have honest conversations about what they each want, and it has brought them so much closer—to the point of getting their spark back!

When a woman is in her power, she raises everyone around her!

In sum, yes to massages, a mani-pedi, or drinks with friends if you have the time and money and it feels nourishing to you, *but* you now know the fix to recover from getting kicked out of your power is to reconnect your thinking and feeling centers, and to clear away your out-of-power emotions until you complete the stress cycle and fill yourself up with joy and pleasure. This is true replenishment as antidote to burnout. *Staying in your power is the ultimate form of self-care.*

Now that you know how to deal with your emotional reactions and stay "good in you," you are free to devote yourself to the purpose that fuels your power. That's what you'll learn in the next portal.

In Your Power Practices: Physiology

1. Dealing with your emotional reactions is the place to start getting back in your power so you can separate yourself from your mental swirl and reconnect to who you are when you feel alive and powerful.
2. Activate the vagus nerve to reconnect your thinking and feeling centers, especially by breathing s-l-o-w.
3. "Feeling is Healing": Develop a reliable repertoire of strategies that work for you to "complete the stress

cycle"—whether this is breathing through it, moving your body, or vigorous exercise. Identify which of the 5 Fs (fight, flight, freeze, fawn, fix) might have been your go-to strategies to deal with emotional arousal so you can recognize your reactions in the heat of the moment and apply new strategies.

4. Cultivate daily practices where you experience pleasure and joy in micro-moments and build these experiences into your day. Begin your "pleasure research" exploration to help you know what feels good and expansive in your body and what doesn't. This is the ultimate self-care!

5. Choose pleasure over anger, and take responsibility for filling yourself up so you can offer a better collaboration with people who are putting you out of your power.

(Go to **www.inyourpowerbook.com** to see demonstrations of the techniques described and download my constantly updated playlists for anger, sadness, and turn on.)

CHAPTER 6

Purpose: From Your Small Game to Your Big Game

"The only way to make your present better is by making your future bigger."

—Dan Sullivan, Entrepreneur Coach

Your purpose gives you power. We all feel the most alive and in our flow when we are aligned with our purpose. It helps you transcend the drama of the moment and take the action that is most aligned with who you want to be in the long term. It makes you feel good and right in who you are.

Your purpose is what you are *here for,* whether in the moment or for your life. You may have multiple purposes: to be a role model for your children, to grow those on your team, to bring creative solutions to problems, to leave generational wealth, and/or to have as much fun as possible. In any given meeting or project you might also have an overarching purpose above your specific functional role, such as to lead inclusively.

Too often we find ourselves losing sight of our purpose in our daily routine. The moment-to-moment demands of our insanely full to-do lists can grab all of our attention, and then simply getting through the day becomes our purpose. But emotional overload is not the only thief, we can derail *ourselves* from acting in the service of our own purpose.

Playing Your Small Game versus Your Big Game

When I said no to the White House, I *put myself out of my power.* It had nothing to do with what Tipper Gore or her Chief of Staff said. I had an internal picture in my mind of who I thought I should be and what I should know. I fell short in my own evaluation and feared they would evaluate me similarly.

Human brains track and monitor what we believe others' opinions are of us, activating fear that they will judge, criticize, or abandon us. We're wired to attend to this threat before we can put energy into fulfilling our potential or purpose. Saying *no* to the White House was my way of reducing my fear of judgment, which I prioritized over the contribution I could have made to millions of families.

On any given day we can find ourselves doing this silent interpersonal calculation. Common examples include when you second-guess, pressure yourself to be perfect, compete to prove you're worthy, or feel guilty about not doing enough anywhere in your work-life juggling act. To the extent you don't have deep trust in yourself, you look to other people in order to know what to believe about yourself.

As referenced in Chapter 1, if you feel unworthy, self-critical, or in any way concerned about what others will think about you, you will involve other people in your effort to feel worthy and valued. These behaviors are *Indirect*—your doubts motivate you to get others to think well of you, *hoping* they will act back toward you in a way that helps you feel secure. These approaches start as adaptations to interactions with early caregivers and have the survival intention to get basic needs met (such as not getting rejected, eliciting the feeling you matter, maintaining emotional/physical safety). We'll continue to outsource our feeling about ourselves into adulthood until we can source this trust from within and from connection to our purpose.

With this Indirect approach, you allow other people's response to determine how you feel about yourself. It makes you vulnerable to be *at the effect of* their behavior, which is the thing you can *least* control. You'll never feel powerful because your energies are not going toward building it. Let's say you did a bang-up job on a presentation, but your manager didn't give you positive feedback because she was preoccupied thinking about a personal matter having nothing to do with you. You might get deflated or feel unsure about next steps to take on your goals. You *give away your power.*[1]

Indirect behaviors focus on your momentary personalized concerns such as "What will they think of me?" and "What can I do to get them to think well of me?" It's a controlling energy, not one that magnetizes. To control their perception, you might talk a lot or loud to show people how smart you are, micromanage so people think you're perfect, or not speak up with a great idea, and so forth. All the behaviors we do to please, protect, and try to be perfect are less about the actual work and more to get other people to approve, not reject, you and feel safe with them. What is the net win of these strategies? Only temporary relief from potential judgment or a quick compliment you shrug off anyway. These automatic responses get you through that situation but don't build self-reliance within. They are like a *sugar high*, a fleeting temporary bump in confidence or relief from criticism. And who is the primary beneficiary of this short-sighted strategy? Only you.

This is your "small game."

When I said *no* to the White House, I had an opportunity to play big, but I opted to play small. (Though it didn't feel like a conscious choice at the time.)

To play your "big game," Go Direct! Your big game is your purpose, your legacy, your opportunity to use your power to make the ongoing situation better. When you focus on your purpose, it's not about just what's happening in the moment, it's acting to further the values that run deep in you and that follow your long-term vision. The effect is not only for you but *all* the people who will benefit from your actions.

Purpose helps connect us to something bigger than ourselves. It lifts you up from your self-judgments, and plugs you into an overall flow of progress that puts wind behind the sails of your intentions. Its focus is less on "What do they think about me?" and more on "What am I here to do?"

A leader can only be as effective as how far out into the future they focus on with their vision for all involved. Instead of trying to get worthiness from others, you can give others a sense of worthiness. Leaders Go Direct!

Heather exemplified this shift to her big game. She worked in the equipment leasing finance department of a manufacturing company. She was frustrated with her boss and ready to leave. She didn't feel seen, so she micro-tracked what he said or didn't say to value her. She was the thermometer, getting resentful when he didn't take an opportunity to recognize her or to give her the support she asked for.

Instead, she started to focus on her purpose to be a problem-solver. A company-wide breakdown in billing systems caused consternation for hers and other groups. Passionate about resolving this major technology issue, she initiated a cross-functional meeting of all parties interested in the matter, starting the first month with the business partners she knew well. They thought the meeting was so productive they asked to invite their key colleagues. By the third month, it became the go-to meeting for company influencers. Because she was leading a process that started to get results and provided a valuable forum for "get it done" types to connect, senior leaders from across divisions were jockeying to be invited.

She lost interest in her daily monitoring of her manager's validation. In place, she poured herself into the visible win of finding an alternative to the company's broken technology issue. She had the satisfaction of getting a result, and as an extra bonus she got a lot of kudos. She made relationships that allowed her to have the influence she hoped she would have *through* her manager.

Her manager should have been recognizing her and supporting her, but he wasn't. He was still the same, but she's not playing the losing game of trying to get her validation from him. She transcended her stuck situation and became a respected thought leader who could write her *own* ticket (which led to a promotion four months later). Just as important, she enjoyed her role again.

In another example, Richard is the president of a company. He wanted to instill a greater commitment to sustainability throughout the company. But he was feeling worried about whether he was being upstaged at his company by a talented employee he'd hired to work with consultants.

This younger man he'd brought in made no bones about his aspiration to become president of the company someday, and the confidence he exuded derailed Richard into doubting himself. In our discussion, he refocused on his purpose as a leader: "He can do a great job in achieving our company goals. That's why I hired him," he said to me, but really he was reminding himself. He realized that he shouldn't see his hire as competition, reflecting, "He is my wingman. His success will be a reflection of my guidance. And he will help me achieve my big-picture vision."

Richard was able to lift himself up from playing the small game of his competitive concerns, and that allowed him to redirect his energies to playing the longer big game of driving other strategic wins for the business.

Now it's your turn:

1. What are the Indirect behaviors you do that set you up to be put out of your power? Who are you giving away your power to?
2. Where do you recognize you are playing your small game?
3. Where are you playing or could play your big game?
4. Describe what your big game looks like.
5. Take a few minutes to describe what you could do to Go Direct!

_____

_____

_____

***

Bias and Exclusion Exacerbate Doubt

The Indirect approaches I'm describing are universal, we are social beings and all humans have insecurities about how they are viewed along with common intentions to be liked and valued by others. But I want to also add needed context: It's important to be able to distinguish one's personal doubts from doubts that develop in response to structural and cultural factors in the environment that layer on top of our personal history. This is because "bias and exclusion exacerbate doubt."[2,3]

As one example, there is still a tendency to give women, in comparison to men, feedback that is vague and focused on improving their personality, not business outcomes.[4] This sows confusion and doubt in women, such as lack of clarity where they stand on the path to career advancement, what skills they have or need to develop, or why they are not tapped for key promotions. And to adapt to this critical feedback about their personality, many women scrutinize their behavior and worry if they are getting right the exact delicate balance to drive business results without being told they are "too aggressive."[5]

Women of color specifically don't see many role models who look like them in senior positions. They are not seen by decision makers as fitting the narrow stereotypical Eurocentric male criteria of a leader, and they are regularly overlooked for promotion into leadership roles for which they are qualified or already doing, albeit informally and without proper recognition.[5] Research at Eli Lilly found that Black women tend to experience low psychological safety and feel never enough despite accomplishments, Asian women experience being valued for their technical ability but not for their leadership capability, and Latinas experience invisibility.[7] A memorable way of summarizing this reality can be found in the quote "When marginalized at work, they don't just *feel* like imposters, they are *made to feel* like imposters . . . regardless of how self-assured, smart, and confident they are."[8]

These realities distract attention and perpetuate a constant unanswerable open loop of whether obstacles are due to the forces of gender and intersectional bias or whether it is "something about you" that "needs fixing." The absence of others seeing your value interferes with you having the objectivity to own your value. This energy drain can also derail your focus away from your business and life purpose (though for many women this reinforces their mission to be treated with respect and be a role model for others in the workplace). You want to be aware of these collective unconscious biases and behaviors so you can distinguish that they are not about you personally.[9] This will help you transcend the noise of other people's behaviors to own your value from within and stay focused on the contribution you're here to make. Your purpose puts you back in your power. And every person in her power is a Change Agent.

(For a deeper understanding of how to bring in objectivity to understand if you are facing bias, see Endnote 9 in this chapter).

***

Finding Your Purpose

The first step to connect with your sense of purpose is to take a little time to reflect deeply on what you see as your purpose. Have you ever written down your thoughts about what you want your purpose to be or a purpose statement?

A great exercise for doing this is based on the so-called 5 Whys.[10] It's a means of digging into any problem you want to solve. It fast-tracks you to the roots of purpose by reconnecting with why it is so important to you. With each layer deeper, you refine more clearly the essence of that core reason you're devoting your efforts to. (You can also leverage assessments such as StrengthsFinder™.)

The first why is to write an initial answer to the question:

1. What is your purpose? _____
_____.

2. Next comes: And why is that important to you? _____
_____.

3. And why is that important to you? _____
_____.

4. And why is that important to you? _____
_____.

5. And why is that important to you? _____
_____.

When I went through this exercise with my client Deborah Borg, who is the Chief Human Resources and Diversity Officer of a *Fortune* 500 company, she already had this sense of purpose vaguely in her head, so it was helpful to articulate it out loud so she could remind herself of it. She got to: "To create opportunity for our 25,000 employees and the people in their families and communities."

Like many of us who want to make a meaningful contribution, she had been putting lots of pressure on herself with concerns that as the top "people officer," all eyes were on her and then focusing on what the executive team thought about how effective she was. She'd been telling herself that she had to have all the answers about how the company could foster a more intentional culture rather than how she could be the best facilitator of change.[11]

Focused on her purpose, she realized she didn't need to have all the answers and didn't need to make sure that people thought she had them all. Your Purpose is a way of freeing yourself from expectations of other people. She told me, "The real shift for me was realizing that the most important thing is less that my point of view is adopted but that we have a consistent and harmonious view across the organization." She saw that the bigger impact she could make was to hold space for conversations (even uncomfortable ones) at the management level to get to the root cause of where the organization was resistant to change. By refocusing on the end goal, she understood that "I can still have my point of view and suggest a direction, but why do *I* need to have all the answers? This is a new space for us. We are all finding our way." That freed her from her self-doubt. "I'm not second-guessing or overthinking things or racing three steps ahead to what they are going to say. It was extremely liberating to take a different approach to the same set of problems and in moments of stress anchor back into my purpose."

I saw her showing up bigger in those conversations, and her authenticity and intentionality inspired others to do the same. Borg said, "I noticed an immediate benefit to my well-being. And over time [I] see there's been a great benefit to the organization of me being more in my power." Her senior leadership team is much more connected and aligned on issues. "We've tackled important topics that will impact our full workforce and the communities we operate in. Every so often when I get a note thanking me for the work of our team, it really feels good." Note that she was now seeing that positive evaluation of her contribution as the icing on the cake of an already deep sense of satisfaction from fulfilling her purpose, not as the necessary praise that would tell her she was on track. This is what it looks like to Go Direct.

This is an excellent example of what it feels like to be able to put yourself back in your power. You want to be able to "get the feels" from the meaningful reward of your contribution and from your own felt sense that you are living your purpose.

Lisa Earle McLeod, author of *Selling with Noble Purpose*, highlights, "People tend to think that [having a purpose] is about this inner search for your gifts. The thing that people miss about purpose is, we feel the most satisfied when we're making a difference to other people."

Connected to your purpose, you see it as *your responsibility to use your power to bring people along toward that purpose.* When you show up in your power, you raise others.

When you live and breathe your purpose, you can tap into it even when not performing a specific role. Tasha Morrison, *New York Times* bestselling author of *Be the Bridge: Pursuing God's Heart for Racial Reconciliation*, exemplified this when she said being in her power "is about understanding *who I am*.[12] I'm not defined by what I do, or who other people think I am. That was freeing for me. I'm a change agent, and bridge builder, and a leader. And I can do that in any capacity and anywhere, I can do that in the middle of the grocery store." The more you connect with your purpose, the easier it is to connect to it when you are in the throes of being pulled out of your power and the more it becomes your way of walking in the world.

Shift Your Focus to Those You're Serving

If you've ever had the idea of stepping into a more powerful version of yourself but then asked yourself "Who am I to take that on?" then you've allowed your concerns about what other people will think to determine your impact. You've put yourself out of your power with their imagined judgments.

Instead, try changing your question and ask, "Who will benefit from me speaking up, asking for resources, offering ideas, taking on more responsibility, etc.?" These people are the end users and beneficiaries of you being in your power. If you are going to worry about what other people think of you, at least worry about the right things! Instead of worrying about their judgments of you, worry about their challenges. Deepen your empathy of their plight or their customer journey, and put your worries into how you can help them. Be so filled with a sense of purpose that you have no bandwidth to think about your worries, only how to bring more value to those you can uplift. Instead of trying to feel valued, be valuable. Enjoy the experience of yourself feeling valuable.

Consciously shifting to a focus on the end users of her actions was the slight tweak my client Brenda Salce-Garcia needed. She was in a leadership position at an advertising technology company. People were working to the bone, morale was dropping, and some people had resigned. She felt that the elephant in the room was the C-suite's opportunity to set the culture. Yet she was a level below the executive team and sometimes intimidated to speak up. "I was the only woman and woman of color at that level, and newly promoted. I was nervous because I felt that if I wasn't 1000% sure I was correct, I shouldn't speak up. During that time, I was very inward, living in my head, over-analyzing everything I did or didn't do. It would exhaust me. I used up energy I needed for other efforts."

"Then," she said, "I thought of my purpose: I'm not doing this for Brenda. I have to think beyond myself. I thought about who I'm sticking up for. About my colleagues who were burning out. And my customers. I thought that's not a life I want to live where my customers walk out when there was a potential solution that's not being raised. That got me to speak up."

"I started off shaking, but from our coaching I went through with it. I asked the C-suite team: What are we doing to protect customer retention? and I tied examples of employee dissatisfaction to risk of customer retention." She said, "If we don't figure this out soon, more people are going to walk out the door, and if people walk out the door, then this whole next generation advertising platform you want to do, it's going to take a heck of a lot longer to implement." The leadership team followed her lead and even *asked her to start leading their meetings* so they could keep getting her perspective. Her energies now channeled effectively toward her purpose, and she was able to end her days being present with her husband and son.

You may have been socialized with expectations on how to act, but that is not your purpose. Your purpose is *not* "to make people comfortable." At work, your purpose is to fulfill a role that contributes to an overall result and to play your part in creating a collective culture for the organization in which everyone thrives. Get above your personal concerns, and allow this purpose to guide you. Even if you don't have all the answers, you can convey that confidently in the service of your purpose, such as "This part I know, and this part I don't have all the answers on. But here's how we're trying to figure it out, and here's why I wanted to raise this issue now even before the data is in."

Like Brenda, you might start out being scared of what other people—including senior leaders—might think of you, causing you to hold back and cautiously observe other people in order to determine what you should say and when. Get courage from standing for those you are serving. When you channel energy away from your self-judgment and into your purpose, you will experience enormous unleashing of energy that was previously trapped in your mental swirl. You are likely to experience recognition and see opportunities come to you that are even better than what you were trying to accomplish, *without trying to make it happen.*

That's what happens when you Go Direct and show up in your purpose: You play a bigger game. People are attracted to this kind of power and leadership—they want to be a part of what you are doing, follow you, and see how much higher you can take them. "I'll have what (he or) *she's* having!"

Where in your life can you shift your question from, Who am I? to, Who will benefit when I'm in my power and act in my purpose?

Be the Champion and Steward of Your Beneficiaries

Here's a related way of thinking about acting in the service of your purpose. In a study of cadets at West Point (the US military leader training academy), what do you think was in the top traits of the most successful leaders during combat? The capacity to love![13] Leaders with this trait made decisions based on the needs of their charges. These leaders saw themselves as the champions and stewards of the cadets.

You can eject yourself out of your small game by accessing your love for others. This comes naturally to you, that's why I know you're going to be good at it. I too had this inflection point recently when I was invited to keynote—wait for it—the West Point women's conference!

I was honored, and out of appreciation for their service I really wanted to give an experience that would profoundly nourish and expand them. But when it came time to write my speech, I went to that doubting place: "What could I possibly say about power and resilience to women who have survived infamous bootcamp training, coordinated logistics for hundreds of thousands on the front lines of war, and held leadership positions in one of the most male-dominated institutions on Earth? Surely all I could tell them would be things they already knew."

But I'm authoring a book on being in my power, wasn't there something in these pages that could rock their world? All

I had to do was to not get ahead of my skis and simply devote myself to them. I asked for a mini-focus group with the planning committee, and I got a laundry list of challenges they face for which I absolutely had solutions.

And, in the presentation, I set up an interactive experience where they could see themselves reflected in the eyes of their West Point sisters. So they could find that place to deeply appreciate themselves, be proud of their own sense of purpose, and help other West Point women do the same (okay, yes, a few tissues were needed, because it's such a profound experience to be recognized for your purpose).

This kind of connection to your own confidence and self-love is a shift that fuels your ability to raise others. Indirect approaches are controlling, and on some level you're trying to get people to *need you* (because when you please and are perfect, you are indispensable to them). But if you want to truly uplevel your power, show up in a way where team members/followers/clients not only need you but *want* you, meaning they want to be like you and a part of what you are doing. They *want* to have your energy; they *want* to have the impact you are having.

When you walk through your life embodying that persona and that purpose, people attach to a version of who they'd like to be themselves. And they associate this desired persona with you. This becomes an effortless way of influencing others and doesn't require a heavy lift to get other people to change because it helps them be who they want to be simply by you being who you are.

In sum, trying to control what other people will think about you by seeking their acknowledgment, preventing their criticism, or not disappointing them is a detour that keeps you in your "small game." And it's unwinnable. It's a never-ending vicious cycle, where the more you source your sense of power from others, the more you need to keep doing so because you haven't built it from within. It's stressful and exhausting. And it's not what you're *here for*. Focusing on your purpose lifts you from an out-of-your-power state. It reconnects your focus to your true north and connects you to that inner renewable energy source that is your innate sense of purpose.

When you have self-reliant ways of staying connected to your purpose regardless of the challenge, your life will get on a virtuous cycle. You won't need or live for the recognition, but you will get it in greater spades because of the bigger-game contribution you make. Opportunities you have wanted will show up or ones that are even better. In fact, I *did* actually present at the White House 15 years later (to help the team deal with stress and prevent burnout) along with countless opportunities to present around the world. I'm even acting in the service of my purpose and playing my big game right now as I whisper in your ear to get back in and stay in your power.

In order to do that, you need to free yourself from that self-critical story you have for your life, which is exactly what I'm going to show you how to do in the next portal.

In Your Power Practices: Purpose

1. Your purpose is the thing that makes you feel most alive; it can reconnect you to your power on demand. Reflect on what your purpose is for your life, use the 5 Whys exercise as a start. Enjoy living and breathing your purpose.

2. Indirect behaviors are your small game. When tempted to go Indirect, play out the scenario in your mind to its logical conclusion. If it's Indirect, you'll have a clenched response, a knowing that you don't want it to unfold that way (again). Instead show up at your Horizon Point and Go Direct. Note: There are four different patterns of Indirect behaviors, such as seeking approval versus preventing disapproval versus focusing on never being good enough. Each has strategies that will help you overcome

this approach or be counterproductive to it. Learn which pattern you use, and get strategies that are right for your type by taking the full In Your Power self-assessment at **www.inyourpowerbook.com**.

3. Go Direct! Know what your big game is, and act in the service of it. Change your question from "Who am I?" to "Who is my end user?" Pour yourself into serving people who will benefit from your taking confident action. It's not about you it's about who you're here to champion.

4. Help others be who they want to be by you being who you want to be.

5. If you are feeling less than confident within your company or community, think objectively to what extent it's the consequence of ways you are being treated in the culture versus your innate personal confidence level. Drive an approach to require objectivity in the way you're treated, don't internalize it, and use your sense of Purpose to lift above biased behaviors and accomplish bigger things.

CHAPTER 7

Psyche: From React to Reclaim

"Until you make the unconscious conscious, it will direct your life and you will call it fate."

—Carl Jung, Psychoanalyst

I magine you are driving your car in a shopping mall parking lot, and the driver behind you honks his horn. Immediately, without thinking, where do you go in your mind?

- What an impatient and aggressive jerk!
- I must be doing something that's getting in his way.
- Is he warning me about something?
- He's trying to catch the attention of his spouse leaving a store.
- He must have an emergency. I should get out of his way.

You don't really know why he honked his horn, but you create an explanation, or story, about why. That story is shaped by your experiences and will determine your response. If you think he's warning you, you'll scan the area around you to check you're not about to be hit by another car. Think he's a jerk, and you might curse him in the rearview mirror.

This storytelling we all do isn't some sort of pathology, it's part of our distinctive human ability to interpret our experiences and choose our responses, differentiating us from animals who act purely on instinct. But it's important because what endures from an event is not the actual facts of it but the story you tell about it.

Our human nature also leads us to turn our stories into "facts." Chatting on the phone with your bestie as you leave the shopping mall, you might vent, "Some jerk took his stress out on me!" You're not likely to tell yourself, "That guy honked his horn *and what I made of it was . . .*" Your take on the event is now engraved as part of the history of your day.

And the narrative you choose will help you be in your power or hijack you right out.

The Stories You Tell Determine the Quality of Your Life

We all experience a "horn honk" dozens of times a day—your boss dismisses you, a friend doesn't respond to a text, someone doesn't do as you ask. Some of these barely affect you, but others make you react. Why?

You'll react if their behavior re-enacts a disempowering story about yourself that is embedded in your psyche, which I call your lead story. You associate the current experience with a similarly themed difficult experience from your past, particularly from your early life, which led you to tell yourself this negative story. Stored in your subconscious mind, the story is like kindling, and the current experience that reminds you of it is like a match igniting it. In other words, the current experience is a trigger.

Triggers are *a painful reminder of something that's happened too many times in your past that took you out of your power.*

Your lead story rarely shows itself blatantly, but it lurks in your mind and underlies your identity and self-concept. Usually it can be boiled down into a main theme, which might be phrased as a doubting question: "Am I good enough?" "Am I loveable?" "Do I have what it takes?" Or it might take the form of a conviction: "I'm not worthy," "I don't matter," "I'm not good enough." This story is *the hook* that makes you react defensively, take situations personally, and have a hard time letting them go.

My client was vexed by a direct report who was not taking action on a clear instruction she had given for high-visibility marketing communication. She followed up with multiple attempts, but still she was not hearing back from him. She felt totally controlled by him, she felt full of anger toward him, and worried she'd explode. We used the situation to discover this insight: It had triggered her to feel the helplessness she had felt when her father had been violently abusive toward her mother, and she couldn't stop it. Underneath her anger she felt afraid, and her lead story was that she doesn't matter.

As long as you have this place of powerless that you go to within you, other people's actions and external circumstances can send you there without your permission or forewarning.

You will look to circumstances that happen, and what other people do (or don't do) as the information you need to answer your question or confirm your conviction. You will scan through situations seeking information *from others* that confirms your doubt or conviction. This is Indirect. This sets you up to take things personally—making other people's behavior and outside circumstances *mean something about you.* And not just about how you handled that particular situation but about who you are as a person. This is why it seems that other people have their hooks in you.

Getting kicked out of our power seems as if it were a reaction to something happening outside of you, but it's really the activation of this personal hook inside of you. When you react to a trigger, you "re-activate" a prior experience of feeling powerless. This is why your reaction can often be dispropor-tionate to the current scenario. It's an interaction we are having in our day, but we make it a referendum on our worth.

It sets us up to not see all the information that is available. We build up a story in our mind and then misinterpret information through its filter. This was the case with my client the marketing executive who took it personally when her direct report didn't take action (what she later found out is he dragged his feet because revisiting the project would expose his mistake in a prior spreadsheet). In a reactive survival state, all information is routed toward "What does this mean about me?" rather than "How can I bring solutions for the good of all?"

I know the experience well. When I moved to New York City early in my career, I subcontracted as an executive coach for one of the marquee recruitment and leadership firms. I had been introduced to the firm through a friend and was hoping to grow my engagements with them as a bridge to life in my new city. Three months into my first engagement, I received the startling news that my client had been fired. The next day, I got an email from the administrative assistant to the head of the coaching group at the firm, wanting to set up a conference call. I went into reaction mode, immediately deciding my client got fired because of me. I berated myself, "I let things fall through the cracks. My coaching allowed this to happen."

I had spent much of my life monitoring other people's opin-ions of me in order to know what I thought about myself. My lead story was on the theme of "I can't trust myself / I'm not good enough." This led me to fear that the firm would fire me too and stop sending me any future business. I had fitful sleep for several nights. Then the morning of my phone meeting with the "big cheese," his assistant postponed it for three weeks. Ugh! I stayed in torturous anticipation that whole time.

When the head of the coaching group and I finally had our call, it lasted five minutes. What did he say? "I wanted to know if you would be open to coaching a close personal friend of mine who is stuck; I've heard raves about your work." I felt like I could breathe normally for the first time in three weeks. All of that emotional churn was for *nothing*!

Reconnected with my thinking brain, I called the firm to ask why my client was terminated, and I learned it had nothing to do with me. It was a consequence of a public statement she made the year prior, which was turning out to be a liability to the company. I could have found that information out weeks before, but I didn't act constructively because I made the false assumption she was fired *because of my flaws.*

You may be aware of your lead story, and perhaps you've tried to get over it but haven't been able to. Or maybe you know it in a vague way but don't have specific words for it. Because our kindling is stowed away deeply in our minds, it may seem out of your control and that you will always be vulnerable to triggers, draining your energy for nothing or having to expend extra energy undoing your reactions. But there are ways to transcend this trigger point. Being intentional about the stories you tell is the big unlock for you to live your life in your power. The portal of Psyche shows you how.

You Have the Power to Choose a New Story

You can consciously dissolve a lead story and write a new one that will become your go-to story. By staying mindful of how your old lead story has pulled you out of power, you will be able to switch narratives more and more readily over time. The first step is to identify your lead story, which I'll show you how to do with the 'stories exercise.'

You might want to get out a pad of paper or fire up your computer, and create five columns, as shown next.

Column 1	Column 2	Column 3	Column 4	Column 5
Fact/event	Lead Story	Alt. stories	Horizon Point	Action

I'll walk you through how to fill them in using the example of my client Jana, who is Medical Director for a clinic.

Jana works closely with a non-physician administrative lead of the clinic, Valerie, and she shared with me that she repeatedly felt disrespected and controlled by Valerie. Jana had seen on a shared clinic calendar that an interview had been scheduled for a key physician position on their team, and she wasn't invited to take part in it. She was boiling with resentment that she'd been left out.

Column 1: Fact or Event

In this column you simply write down the fact or event that triggered your reaction. For Jana, that was:

I'm not listed on an invite for the physician interview meeting.

Make sure to simply state the fact and not add your interpretation of it. For example, "She's cutting me out of the process" is not a fact. "She arranged an interview and I'm not on the invite list" is a *fact*.

Column 2: Lead Story

In this column, note "where you go in your mind." Write the immediate story you told yourself about why the fact happened, your gut response. For Jana, that was:

"She didn't think I needed to be involved."

Now, to understand what kindling made you see the situation that way, dig deeper. Ask yourself what I call the "dig down" question: "What does [lead story] mean about *me?* Jana wrote:

> "It means: 'My perspective doesn't matter. My leadership isn't valuable.'"

Now dig down again to probe more into something deeper you think about yourself that this relates to. For Jana, that was asking: "What does it mean about me that my perspective doesn't matter?" And her answer was:

> "It means that I'm worthless in my role."

Here we have Jana's lead story. Her colleague scheduling an interview without inviting her triggered her go-to explanation that she was left out because of her worthlessness. Notice that it was only three associations away once you start scratching the surface. In her mind, it was as if Valerie sent an email with the subject line: "Jana, you're worthless, so we haven't included you." Valerie's behavior reminded Jana of past experiences of feeling powerless that led her to doubt her worth.

What happens is **we get stuck in our lead story**, believing we have fully analyzed the whole scenario when this is just the beginning of your understanding. And when you are convinced of your lead story, what happens next? She ruminated about the situation the rest of the day and complained about it to her husband that night. She also sent an email to Valerie asking why she was left off, which was unpersuasive and unconstructive because it reinforced the notion that Valerie was the one in power over whom to invite.

Column 3: Alternative Stories

Column 3 is where you start to come back into your power. You review the facts and the context of the scenario you're in. You want to *require yourself to tell at least three alternative stories* to explain why the event/fact happened.

Jana's alternative stories were:

1. Valerie forgot because she was distracted by her father being in the hospital.
2. She thought I would rather not be there and that I would like her to vet candidates before I spend time meeting them.
3. We have no formal process to follow about interviews, so she didn't know to include me.

Considering these other explanations allows you to see the event as about that day's interaction rather than about experiences from your past. In coming up with your three alternative stories, you want to consider the 3D context of the situation—understand each person's behavior, the interaction between you, and any important context.

As discussed in the portal of Perspective, it's important to consider reasons other than someone's seemingly flawed character that are behind their behavior. And your stories don't have to be positive, just empowering. Sometimes the most empowering story is a seemingly negative one—to recognize that the other person truly is limited and cannot partner with you to make the situation better.

You always want to ask contextualizing questions such as:

- What is the other person trying to accomplish?
- What are the stressors and constraints they are contending with?
- What about their personality is showing in their actions, which has nothing to do with me?
- What's the history between you that is being perpetuated?
- What is the communication or system-level breakdown?

In all future triggering situations, you want to require yourself to come up with three alternative stories before you allow yourself to take any action.

Column 4: Your Horizon Point

In column 4, you remind yourself of who you want to be at your Horizon Point. Jana wants to be a Poised Problem-Solver.

Here's the crescendo moment for you to get back in, or stay in, your power: *You now choose* the alternative story, or combination of stories, that will enable you to show up in your Horizon Point state. Jana chose the stories that Valerie was trying to spare her time and also that she might have been distracted because her father was in the hospital.

Column 5: Your Response

Column 5 is where you decide on your response based on your new understanding.

With her new view of the situation, Jana showed up as the poised problem-solver she wants to be. She followed up with another email to Valerie saying she was excited about the interview and asking for the invite to be resent to her. She also requested a protocol for new hire interviews, taking charge so it wouldn't happen again. Most importantly, Jana got out of her mental swirl.

People only see the behavioral action you respond with in column 5, but it's the processing you do in columns 1–4 that determine whether you are in your power and take collaborative action.

How do we get stuck in a lead story? First, its *personalizing*— you take their behavior to mean something about you. Second, its *generalizing*—not specific to the situation. "Worthless" is all-encompassing as opposed to "I could have done more to put a process in place for hiring."

No one is all good or all bad, a lead story glosses over important nuances of the situation. All your learning takes place starting in column 3 with the alternative stories of actual facts and a closer look at the factors that caused the situation, or even the role you might have played in the interaction. Similarly, when resentful of others we're unlikely to notice their improved efforts. The "stories" analysis is what enables you to grow beyond the unchallenged narratives that kick you out of your power. Otherwise if a similar situation happens a week later, you're going to have the same response. Regardless if their behavior stays the same, *be the pattern breaker*. #Now's your time!

Here's another example:

Fact/Event:

Steve is the leader of an entrepreneurial team, and a team member shows him a customer campaign she sent out with two glaring mistakes in it.

Lead Story:

She is incompetent and unmotivated. (Notice this is generalizing)

Dig down: What does it mean about me? I don't hire people well. I don't set a good culture. I am not a good leader. (Notice he personalizes her behavior.)

Alternative Stories:

1. She didn't fully understand the assignment.
2. We haven't set up communication that creates accountability.
3. She is someone who doesn't currently have a detailed eye and needs to be specifically coached and incentivized to develop it, or else she isn't a good fit to work here and shouldn't.

Horizon Point: Motivator of Excellence.

Action: He communicates a more motivating vision of excellence for the team; he sets the tone by shining a spotlight on those who get the details right and puts processes in place to ensure greater attention on the finished product. He has an active two-way dialogue with his team member who needs to improve.

An important takeaway is that Steve may have played *some* role in his team member's mistakes. It's true he can be better at explaining assignments and creating a culture of accountability and so forth, but this does not affirm he is a bad leader overall. He can just do better in his 50% to prevent scenarios that put him out of his power.

Now it's your turn. Think of two or three most recent examples of when you got kicked out of your power and go through the exercise.

Column 1 Fact/event	Column 2 Lead Story	Column 3 Alt. stories	Column 4 Horizon Point	Column 5 Action

Now examine what you wrote for each example and look for a common thread in the lead stories you had been telling yourself. This should lead you to discover a negative conviction or defeating conclusion you've come to that makes you feel vulnerable or weak and that you want to eliminate or get free from. The next step is to understand where this lead story came from, which will help you stop yourself from getting triggered by it and find more constructive and compassionate ways of reclaiming your power from it.

Why You Chose Your Story

It doesn't seem like it, but *you chose your story*. Stay with me here, we tend to think of this negative story about ourselves as messaging from others we internalized. We'll say, "I grew up with an alcoholic mother" or "My dad yelled at me if I didn't get A's in school" or "The kids at school bullied me about my weight." The underlying thought process is "Important people showed me or told me that I wasn't enough, so I started to believe it."

There is some truth to that. We do internalize beliefs and feelings of people in our lives and adopt them as if they were our own. But if you say to yourself, "My parents thought I wasn't good enough, so I don't think I am," you're falling into powerless thinking. You don't have any agency in this understanding of your situation. It overlooks a deeper understanding of why we developed that negative conviction about ourselves, an understanding that holds the key for freeing ourselves from it.

What we aren't seeing when we think this way is that we *chose* to agree with the story our parents or others in our lives told us. This was a coping mechanism, and I want to show you why it was a *brilliant choice*.

You chose or created your story for the most important of reasons—so that you could preserve *hope*. You wouldn't be who or where you are today without it. Most children understand the behavior of their early caregivers (or siblings/teachers/coach/peers) as "they are right," thinking their caregiver "sees something in me that shows I'm not smart enough," making the caregiver right and themselves wrong. Why? Because if you make them right, then you can still believe they will be capable of being good to you, of providing the security you need, of taking care of you. You can believe that they may become kinder or that one day soon they'll recognize your talents or stop yelling at you.

You are *preserving your hope*. Without hope, we have no motivation. The present moment of difficult experiences is too painful. Hope gives us a sense of agency to choose and create a better circumstance.

Taking on the blame this way for unsupportive or abusive treatment can be *a short-term adaptive psychological sacrifice*. It can be the better of two bad options, because the alternative might be not having basic needs met. Some children who don't take this approach to coping with difficult caregivers instead intuit that they will never get their needs sufficiently met, and they become hopeless, sometimes running away or becoming suicidal.

Choosing to see ourselves as wrong can also be adaptive because it gives us a *semblance of control*. A child thinks, "If only I could be more perfect and please them, *then* I wouldn't be yelled at," "If only I am over-responsible toward my parents who can't take care of themselves, *then* I can prop them up enough to get my basic needs met." This is the source of Indirect behaviors to get that confidence and self-worth via others. The sense of control helps cope with the fear of feeling helpless.

As we continue through life, our lead story may be reinforced by additional difficult experiences. If earlier life experiences led you to create a story that you are not good enough, and your first manager is highly critical, you may see that as confirmation of your story rather than possibly as a reflection of your manager's perfectionism or lack of feedback skills. In this way, we may unwittingly strengthen the hold of our lead story on us.

Change Your Lead Story into a Life Story

To break that hold, you want to create a new life story for yourself, a story that reflects who you want to be.

You begin by reflecting on how you developed your lead story. Slow it down and take some time to build awareness of yourself on this one, maybe pull out a journal or mull it over a leisurely dinner with a long-term trusted friend. Whose voice did you take on, whose eyes have you been looking through to see yourself that way? What cultural messages have influenced your story? How was your story adaptive for you in your life? How has it led you to go Indirect, looking for others to validate you? What adaptive behavior pattern did it set you up for?

Now you can say, "Not about me!" I'm going to decide my own life story.

Your life going forward is an unwritten book, and *you* are its author.

Now write below, what is the life story that you choose to take the place of your lead story? Think of a recent example where you got emotionally hijacked and stuck in a lead story. Now insert your new life story about that situation. Does it put you back in your power?

_____

_____

_____

You Can Own the Narrative of Your Life

You can leave behind your lead story because with all of the tools the portals provide you, you no longer need the protection it gave you back when you were young. You have new forms of protection, and one of them is that you can now override your subconscious mind to tell an accurate story about yourself. And now you know how to move emotions through your body, so there is no need to be afraid of feeling them.

You will no longer take things personally, so you will feel less need to control how others act. You will have a greater ability to respond with intention. *You'll be free.*

Here's some examples of how I do this: I used to genuinely believe that "who I am" was objectively "not good enough," which would cause me to easily react and take things personally. I've come to see this as a belief I was having about myself in that moment, but I no longer see it as an all-encompassing truth. I started by accepting myself however far away I was at the time from the ideal of who I wanted to be, and I could love myself for where I was, even knowing that I wanted to develop so much further.

Now when I start to feel defeated and self judgmental, I have a repertoire of strategies to get back in my power in the heat of the moment. Sometimes I connect with the rays of light of my Horizon Point, and I use those rays to surround my anxious perfectionist energy until it dissipates. If I believe my lead story, I might ask: "What would Dr. Melnick do?" and invite her to the party of how I'm going to react to that frustrating event! Or I reclaim ownership of "all of me," changing my tone to how "adorable" or "amusing" I can be when I fall back into this same old pattern again. Other times I think of my best moments as a coach or while doing my sexiest dance, and I overlay those experiences of myself onto my lead story—that reminds me who I am and brings back the twinkle in my eye.

When other people project fear-based stereotypes onto me, I neutralize the effects by enjoying those aspects of myself even more. Then there are moments where I don't feel very emotionally resourceful. I throw myself some compassion, give myself a break, and don't force myself to act on the situation until I can reconnect with my power. That old story is no longer the only and loudest voice, it's an aspect of my being that can get activated sometimes, but it's not in control. We can take the wind out of our sails of shame, we can rewrite our lead story, we can own the narrative for our lives.

I once had a client who after our work together said, "I am who I am, and I'm *good* with that." I get that now, and want you to as well.

What are strategies you can use in the heat of the moment to get back in your power when you get stuck in the swirl of your lead story? Take some time with your reflection on this, it's how you own the narrative for your life and build a new experience of you in your power.

_____

_____

_____

A negative lead story can also be the result of harmful discriminatory messaging in the ways that society can make us feel bad about ourselves and that we don't belong. We are made to feel ashamed of who we are, our circumstances, or who we love. We are barraged with demeaning media and social media images, we're slighted in daily interactions, and we're shamed if we don't conform. Because of the ubiquity of these messages, we often subconsciously internalize these stereotypes that we are less than or unworthy. And this internalization can layer onto our personal lead story.

But we can take our power back. Zooming out to understand these messages as derived from other people's fear and blind spots provides us with an alternative story and helps you not reinforce your own lead story by taking other people's actions personally. It helps you separate from the narrative that is being put upon you so you can say, "Not about me."

This conscious intention to not internalize is demonstrated by Minda Harts, author of *Right Within: How to Heal from Racial Trauma in the Workplace*, describing how she didn't internalize the microaggression of her white luxury building neighbor mistaking her for a delivery worker: "I had to make a decision if I was going to internalize this situation and let it take up space in my mind, which would only cause me chronic stress. I also decided not to blame myself for her offense. I am no longer allowing anyone's ignorance to break my peace and my healing process. I am actively choosing to move forward."[1]

By not internalizing these messages and moving the emotion through, you set yourself up to be a person who knows your worth, speaks your truth, and sets boundaries in your own life. This is how you keep your energies for yourself and be a change agent, simply by the way you show up.

You can do a similar exercise to the previous ones where you created a new life story for ways you've been *made to feel bad about* yourself. Instead, list the ways you are proud of and enjoy yourself and your identity? What strategies help you get out of your lead story? Become too busy living your own new life story to help you as Minda Harts writes "actively choose to move forward."

_____

_____

_____

Assign Your Story to a Part of You

If you find crumpling up your lead story and tossing it away too challenging, another way of loosening its hold over you is to conceptualize it in your mind as a protective part of you. With some distance, you can collaborate with rather than be hijacked by it. We often use language that "part of me" wants to go away this weekend, but "part of me" wants to stay home, for example. When you hear the internal thought "You're not good enough," you can better understand this as a physical sensation and voice that make up a metaphorical "part" of you that carries the feelings and reminders of being not good enough.

Lauren is the head of digital transformation at her organization, a role that is important to her and to the future of the organization. Her lead story was that she didn't know enough and wasn't enough. She was in a leadership position but wouldn't trust herself to make decisions and would barely speak up in meetings for fear of saying or doing the wrong thing. Yet every time she didn't speak up, she'd criticize herself as well.

I walked her through an exercise that's inspired by the work of psychologist Richard Schwartz. He has developed a theory that understands humans not as having a "mono-mind," but a mind made up of multiple parts. Though you may not like a part of yourself (e.g., that self-critical "part"), you want to appreciate the concept captured in the title of Dr. Schwartz's book *No Bad Parts*: that every part of you serves a purpose.[2] Each part, Schwartz writes, "has a secret, painful history to share of how it was forced into its role and came to carry burdens it doesn't like that continue to drive it."

We reconceptualized Lauren's lead story as being the voice of a "part" of her using the following metaphor: She is the CEO of her life and this part of her is like a mid-level manager who works in the "risk management" department. This part sees it's job to monitor her behavior in every meeting, escalate criticism, and shut down her speaking whenever it was concerned she might say something that would cause humiliation.

Making this voice concrete and seeing it as a metaphor overcame her sense of powerlessness regarding her own self-critical thoughts. Then she could bring more playfulness to her inner dialogue and reassert her leadership of herself. She told an alternative story about this direct report—seeing it as a manager who was earnestly trying to protect the company but was so dedicated to doing so that it didn't know the difference between a true risk to her reputation vs. a false alarm. The natural solution to this felt authentic to her—together they came up with criteria to determine the degree of risk she faced. She educated this part how to make her aware of its concerns but not make the decision for her, so she could be the one to determine when she was willing to stretch her comfort zone.

Lauren also explained that as CEO she has a bigger-picture perspective on her whole life goals than a mid-level risk manager has visibility into. She set the priorities for her life as leadership, mentoring her team, and making a difference—and stated that these are of a higher order than the goal of not saying anything supposedly stupid. She held an inner "negotiation" between her and this part which yielded an approach where she could get information from this part but be the ultimate decision maker.

She found this mental exercise very helpful. This new way of working together involved more self trust and allowed more risk. She tells me that she and the risk manager have some knowing glances in high visibility meetings where she doesn't know everything, but she no longer gets clamped up. She makes decisions more quickly and is leading meetings that are not always within her subject matter expertise but are taking her organization into the future of digital solutions. Her life story is now her chosen one.

To understand and bring healing to your parts it's best to work with a counselor or coach trained in this kind of work. Some of our parts can contain strong levels of emotion that you may or may not be aware of, and it's helpful to have someone outside of yourself who is skilled in holding the space for you and your part so that both get their needs met in the negotiation.

But you can start to develop a more conscious connection with the part of you that is associated with your lead story. Maybe call to mind a recent example where you told yourself that lead story, and start by putting your hand on the part of your body where this critical part lives. Start to notice the situations in which it gets activated. Honor and appreciate this part of you for the role it has played in protecting you to date. You can even make an inventory of the ways that part has helped and how it was right to protect you in the ways it did. You can appreciate all the success you've accumulated as a result of that protection and all the possible what-ifs had it not protected you. Tell it what a genius it's been. Think of surrounding that part of yourself and bringing appreciation and loving energy toward it.

See yourself as bigger than the reactions of that one part, and be able to hold space for all the different parts of you—"all 88 keys of your emotional piano." Bring the clarity you've developed about what you really want *now*, and begin to message that consciously so that parts that are helping you fulfill basic needs of protection can start to help you act toward your bigger-picture purpose.

You Can Move beyond Your Storyline

As you are coming into your power, at a certain point you become aware of the repetition of your lead story, and you become sick of it, ready to move beyond it and live your chosen life story. You can do this by bringing a greater sense of ownership to the way you assign meaning to situation. Just as we changed our question in the portal of Perspective to "How might this have happened *for* me?" you can change your question from "What does this mean about me?" to "How might this have been made *for me*?"

Taylor is part of a community of entrepreneurs whose leader launched a book. The book includes names of all of the people in the community in the acknowledgments with the exception of one: hers. I can hear the upset in her voice. "Did she do this on purpose?" Taylor started to catalog all the things she's done for this leader, never asking for anything in return. "I even helped her plan the book launch party."

What was more important than whether this was a clerical error or deliberate intent is that upon realizing that this scenario teleported her to that place again, she came to the point of "You know something? Regardless of whether my name is in the book, I AM worthy. And I NEVER will allow this to happen again." She saw the opportunity to make this situation the watershed moment where she reclaimed her power.

After you've become practiced at making accurate meaning in situations, there comes a time when you are ready to move beyond trying to figure out why people are acting the way they do and create a post-story life. Figuring other people out becomes a waste of your energy. The catch-all phrase "They're limited" captures the explanation enough. You're here for bigger things.

When you signal you are ready, the universe will present you with an opportunity to once and for all work it out. That's what I hypothesized as soon as I heard Taylor's story—how it might have been "made for her." Even though upsetting in the moment, the hurt was of such a magnitude and in a community that she so treasures that it's as if it was orchestrated to be the breakthrough where *you yourself see and believe* the story you've been telling yourself isn't true and you declare the life story you want.

My secret metaphor for this is: When you are ready to reclaim your power at a deeper level, your "angels" get together in a meeting and say something like: "Taylor is so gifted and has so much more good to bring, but she's still in this 'do for everyone without return and then get taken advantage of so I feel unworthy and invisible' pattern. Which means she'll never lead her company to its important mission or find love that truly matches hers. So let's devise a plan to *make sure* she takes the lesson this time."

They brainstorm and scheme together. Angel #1: "We could make it affect her in her entrepreneur community because she really cares about that, that will get her attention!" Angel #2: "Great idea, the hurt could come from the leader." Angel #3: "Well, the leader has a book coming out. How could we use that as a prop?" And so on until the plan is perfectly constructed to help breakthrough and get her to own her life at the next level. Warning: It's not always pretty, and if you haven't followed through on prior intentions to be in your power from previous challenges, your "angels" will likely add in an extra layer of pain to ensure *this time* you're going to own your life. But you'll get the net result.

Leaving behind an old story doesn't have to come with the slog of emotional drain. You might have heard the saying "Difficult people are brought into your life to be your teachers." Just so, you can choose to see a learning story in any difficult experience you go through. A good friend of mine did this brilliantly regarding her marriage to a malevolently narcissistic man. She ultimately divorced him and has gone on to become a world-renowned energy healer.

The stories she told me about the behavior of her ex are among the most manipulative I've heard about. Beyond a deadbeat dad, he was malevolently critical, falsely accusing, and she had to get the legal system involved to end the harm.

> I got myself into a relationship with someone who was SO unbelievably uncaring of me, that it required me to learn how to take exquisite care of myself. I *had* to live from my own intuition and learn how to access a higher wisdom in order to know how to make it through. I had to develop the intuitive skills to read him and know when he might be dangerous. I had to systematically believe in myself and make myself whole as the opposite of everything he said to me. These skills became highly valuable in my profession and contributed to who I am today.

When she thinks of him now, she *thanks* him for being such a good teacher. She learned from all of that hardship and work she had to do with herself that she could be someone with a vast spirit and enough energy to help many other people heal.

When you reach this point in your power, you start to become untouchable. Difficult situations don't feel senseless; other people being limited can take you *even higher* and strengthen your preparation for a mission you're being readied for.

When events don't teleport you back to that place of powerlessness based on your lead story, then you can walk boldly in your power in the world. Regardless of what happens *outside* of you, you can always flip it to be life's way of serving you. **No person or circumstances will be able to put you out of your power when you have this kind of sovereignty within yourself.**

In Your Power Practices: Psyche

1. We each have kindling inside of us that can get reignited in a current-day interaction with a similar theme. What's your lead story?

2. You can choose the story you tell based on the facts and context of the situation. Whenever you find yourself reacting with a lead story, require yourself to tell three alternative stories before you allow yourself to act.

3. You chose your lead story for important adaptive reasons, and you can unchoose it. Journal about why you may have chosen this story. How did it help you have hope? What new life story do you choose?

4. You can assign this negative voice to a "part" of you, and then try to understand its protective function. (It's best to work with a trained counselor or coach when it comes to this deep work with your parts.)

5. You can get to the point where you move beyond stories and see all that happens as serving your life intentions. With the challenging scenarios you have in your life now, what do you think your "angels" are trying to prepare you for?

(Go to **www.inyourpowerbook.com** to learn personalized strategies to free yourself from your lead story and step into a life story you choose.)

CHAPTER 8

Proficiency: From Invisible to Invaluable

"There is only one corner of the universe you can be certain of improving, and that's your own self."

—Aldous Huxley

"Although you are respected within the company and have done a great job over the years, your name hasn't come up." Melanie was VP of business development at a $4 billion health care company, and that's what she heard from the CFO about the senior leadership role just vacated by her boss.

As you can imagine, this news was like a gut-punch and she spun out of her power for some moments. She felt extreme disappointment and embarrassment: "How am I not the obvious candidate after 18 years here in this department?" and self-doubt: "I don't have what it takes. He doesn't think I'm capable. I know they are looking for someone similar to the previous leader with a financial background, and I'm more a relationship-based leader." Given this swirl, she had to soul-search to determine if she really wanted the job. But of course, to tell someone in her power that she can't do something is the surest way she'll prove you wrong. She reached out for my coaching saying "I'm going for it!"

Melanie had the opportunity to prove that she was the right person for the role, but it's clear that influencing the CFO was not the way forward. Rather, she was going to have to demonstrate her capability to be in the next-level role through her own means. There are times when you can use competence you already have to transcend an out-of-your-power situation simply from your ability to get a result. Your proficiency is your "special sauce," a blend of your knowledge and experience.

Proficiency gives you power. It gives you leverage that makes you valuable and worth listening to. It compels others to buy into your ideas and accommodate your requests. In the portal of Proficiency you will learn to solve as much as you can on your own before you have to recruit others to be a part of the solution. You'll develop and deploy your unique talents to ensure that your contributions are respected and you—and not others—have the power over your career path.

Melanie conducted a listening tour of 11 stakeholders both within her department and in adjacent functions. She packed with punch a presentation with her go-forward vision and strategic map for the department that reflected key stakeholder input as well as her own observations from her years of experience. She started exemplifying the company's values of "stronger together," not maintaining siloes.

From doing all this, she deepened her sense of ownership in her own value. Three months later at the end of our coaching (after the interviews but before she heard the results), she told me, "Regardless of the outcome, I've become my Horizon Point, a Knowledgeable Confident Leader! I see *myself* that way." And the entire executive team then did, too, voting unanimously and enthusiastically to offer her the role. She put herself back into her power (and to this day the CFO enjoys joking how wrong he was in his skepticism!).

***

When it comes to your proficiency, you don't want to over-rely on it and not take advantage of all of the other approaches outlined in this book. At the same time you don't want to underutilize it. Often we devalue and underplay skills precisely because they come easily to us. For you, public speaking might be a breeze, while for others it's a terrifying affair. You want to be proud of what you know how to do, and you want to let your capabilities lead you out of a crunch. Plus, cultivating your own abilities is something that you can do on your own time, in your own way, in your own home, from your own computer—no one else has to change in order for you to come from a position of strength with your proficiency.

There are so many ways you can use your know-how to move people in the direction you want; for instance, ask questions based on your knowledge that challenge assumptions. Introduce information that is consequential to making a decision. Provide innovative or strategic perspectives that make everyone want your voice at their table. When you are someone who knows how to get it done, you find yourself more on that virtuous cycle where people want to follow you.

Manisha was interviewed for a CEO role at a private equity–owned tech company, and the process was fraught with thwarting circumstances. As an Indian American and Black woman in her mid-forties, she didn't fit the prevailing discriminatory image of a tech company CEO. What's more, the firm was already in the process of writing up an offer for another candidate. In addition, one of the people who gave her a recommendation also threw her under the bus, so she had additional power eject buttons. But rather than reacting to these distractions, she leveraged her experience and insight about problems the company was facing, making a compelling case for her to steer the company through a turnaround.

The company's revenue had tanked in the previous year, and the hiring team thought a CEO with a long history of sales and marketing was the best fit. Manisha saw the needs of the company differently. She had worked in the field for years, launching products and talking to customers, and she believed the problem was that the company had targeted the wrong market. Trusting herself, she put herself out on a limb in the interview process, making a bold presentation that the firm should pivot to a new market.

She led the hiring committee on a journey of discovery, showing them she was a leader with the broad expertise they needed—able to drive the launch of new products as well as find strategic partnerships and improve the company culture. Because of her proficiency, she changed their hiring criteria. She was offered the CEO role, and since then she has created a culture of belonging and led the company into a better financial position.

If you are not seen or heard and it's putting you out of your power, you can use your proficiency to create a perception you are ready for a next role or even create a role for yourself. You might think if you're in your early/mid-career you can't have that much control with only the abilities you have now, but if so, let me blow your mind.

Jessica, who worked at a biotech company, had prior experience in medical devices, but her current role had no use for that expertise. She was stagnating and frustrated. In our strategizing about what value-add she could bring, she had the out-of-the-box idea to *start* a medical devices unit within the company to bring forth her innovations. We strategized the business case in a proposal, and her idea for a new medical devices unit was accepted. I love this story because we typically conclude that the role you're in is all there is when infinite opportunities await you once you exercise the creative force of your proficiency. "If the company doesn't need my talents right now, I'm going to start a new business so that it does!" That's an "in your power" mindset!

In order to own your power of proficiency in this way, you must have clarity about both your strengths and the areas you may want to work on. This is a good time to see how your proficiency can help you get back in your power, stay in your power, and use it. Start by taking an inventory of your proficiencies. Ask yourself:

What can you do really well, or better than most other people?

What result can you reliably get for other people that people need?

What distinctive points of view do you have to offer? And how might it build on or differ from the common view?

How could you use your insights and experience to make a case for a valuable contribution?

What talents will be helpful to develop further?

As you consider talents to leverage, think about interpersonal skills as well as more procedural skills such as strategic planning and product development. I was able to come more into my power, both in my work and my personal life, by developing the ability to manage my emotional responses so I can hear what others have to say without reacting—even if they're being critical of me. This skill prompted an ex of mine to comment with this memorable line about how I was able to defuse tensions between us, "Thank God there were always three people in the room: me, Sharon, and Dr. Melnick. And Dr. Melnick always knew how to guide us to understand each other and have a good outcome!" Developing this skill has also enabled me to establish the psychological safety to bring up awkward topics. Now I don't shy away from difficult conversations in my personal or professional life, so issues are addressed swiftly instead of me staying in the swirl.

Finally, your proficiency protects you from the long list of ways in which people may kick you out of your power and undermine you, whether intentionally or not. One of my "soul sister" friends, Teri Cochrane, is a disruptor in the field of integrative health and has developed and validated new treatments for common and especially mysterious health conditions. She consults with clients to craft "bio-individual" regimens scientifically matched to their needs. Her results are so impressive that she is consulted by elite athletes, doctors, government leaders, and other health influencers.

She faced a slew of potentially sabotaging challenges many business owners and rising stars commonly face: People enter into partnerships with promises they can't keep or try to take advantage of one's services and connections. Trolls abound on social media. Team members lack alignment with the mission, while past employees "borrow" intellectual property without giving due credit.

As an immigrant from Cuba, Teri has built resilience and perseverance to problem-solve in the face of obstacles and stay the course. She did the same to stay connected to her proficiency and just kept "doing the do." She showed up authentically every day focusing on treating her clients, sharing insights with other health care providers, and spreading the word of her findings on podcasts and through her writings. She has the "goods," so she can always stay connected to her power. Not having given attention to the noise of those seeking to pull her out of her power, she is having widespread and growing impact in her field.

Be Confident—and Objective—about Your Proficiency

As you go through this evaluation process, keep in mind how difficult it can be to be make objective assessments of ourselves. Our natural tendency is to interpret situations through our subjective filters. Those include the messages we internalize from others as we're growing up. A teacher might have told us we're not a good writer and it casts a long shadow. We also tend to compare ourselves to others in order to evaluate our talents and too often decide we just don't measure up.

You might be excited to use your proficiency but then come up against a ceiling inside yourself. It's helpful to sort out where your proficiency is and isn't—and to be reality-based about this. When you don't have a strong proficiency it can lead you to question your abilities, and that kicks you out of your power.

Its natural when entering a new role or launching a new program to be concerned about whether you know what is needed to succeed. However, often we pressure ourselves to be perfect, expecting we should already know everything before we are even in the role! We are so focused on predicting we might fail, we lose our objectivity.

Nina was a senior leader in a consulting firm. She wanted to be more strategic and be a change agent, but her lack of perceived proficiency caused her to constantly beat herself up. In this case, there was some objective truth to her concerns. She hadn't had prior roles or education that emphasized strategic leadership, and she now leaked her power with that regret.

Here's where having clarity can take you out of your mental spin. If you are vague about the proficiency you need, you will always fall short. What does "I'm not smart enough" actually mean to you? Define it. To Nina, it specifically meant: I don't know how to make a strategic plan, get buy-in for a strategic vision to the board, or answer board member questions to her satisfaction.

Once you have a clear idea of what enough would mean for you, then you can move forward to problem-solve using your abilities. The next step is to require yourself to make a decision on how to do that. Here are the choices you have: Either *Accept* the capabilities you have now or *Accomplish* new learning to improve them. Choosing to accept means that you can make peace with your current level of ability and not beat yourself up for it. This approach accepts that the strengths and proficiencies you have now will enable you to fulfill the functions of your role. It includes finding workarounds or bringing in additional expertise where needed. Choosing to accomplish acknowledges your estimation that you *do* need to learn certain proficiencies in order to have the impact you want. And it means making a plan to upskill through coaching, training, mentoring, certification, and so forth.

Nina chose a hybrid. She accepted that her strengths were in leading the culture, not in leading strategy, and sculpted her role to reflect this. When she did a town hall for the firm, she partnered with another executive who excels at strategy so she didn't need to know everything. At the same time, she accomplished growing her skills enough to be an important voice in their strategy initiative. She took a course on strategy, used templates from colleagues who had done this kind or work, and reached out for some consulting to plan the upcoming retreat. Once she did this, she was able to lead the team through a highly successful strategy retreat. Instead of beating herself up about it, she maximized what she could already do and then developed the proficiency she needed. Now she is able to make the contribution she wants and has more credibility and say over the direction of the company. And she's not putting herself out of her power all the time.

Now your turn. What is a perceived weakness that has been holding you back? Let's do the exercise. What are the components of that perceived weakness?

Now decide, for each component:

I choose to Accept:	I choose to Accomplish:

Finally, an example for solo entrepreneurs or business owners. Have a nuanced understanding of what proficiency you need to develop. For me, earlier in my career I was grateful that I had the proficiency to get clients the results they wanted from coaching. Yet too often I worked hard on a program offering, I'd offer it online, and then . . . crickets. It was devastating. It felt like my prospect had all the power as to whether they would answer my phone call or enroll in my programs.

For me to overcome the confusion, I learned that the proficiency I needed to develop was not in my coaching craft, it was the marketing ability to connect with those I could help.[1] What I needed was to better describe their pain points and the outcomes they could have after working with me. Since that shift, it's been easier for people I can help to see themselves in what I describe and know when it's right for them to reach out to me.

Years later I'm realizing the proficiency I *really needed* above all was the one to come into my power. It's a quantum difference to use your proficiency from within your power. Today I see that it's less about marketing tactics per se and more about the energy of how I show up in every situation—when I show up in my power it creates magic and doesn't if I don't. Consider this a heads-up to not over-rely on your proficiency alone—combine it with the other approaches in this book because your proficiency in the context of your power creates an energy that makes others say they want to be a part of what you're doing!

Where you have proficiency, value it and make it a go-to part of your approach to staying in your power and bringing people along to a better result. If you don't have the proficiency you need, don't stay spinning out of your power around it, go develop it!

This concludes the section of the book where I share strategies to help you be *in your power*. Take a look at the chart I suggest on the next page in order to know which tools you want to reach for the moment you get kicked out of your power. These are your first responder go-to strategies. Each of these is a high-level reminder of what you learned in each portal and can signal whether it will help you to revisit the tools in that portal again.

I'll also wrap up the "be in your power" portals with two case studies to show you how one person can make use of strategies from the different portals. Then in the next section I'll go into great detail about how you can use your power to get the results you want for your life and for the good of all.

In Your Power Practices: Proficiency

1. You have a special sauce that uniquely enables you to get a result—this superpower is your Proficiency. Take an inventory of your proficiencies.

2. What can you do on your own—before you ever ask for support/advocacy from others to drive the outcome you want?

3. Allow focus on your Proficiency to drown out saboteurs.

4. Don't stay stuck in believing you're "not enough." Decide between whether you can accept the skills you have now or need to accomplish building new ones in order to make the impact you want.

5. If you're not getting the outcomes you want from others, think critically about whether you are developing the *right* proficiency. Combine your proficiency with skills to show up in your power—it creates a powerful energy that raises others.

In your Power Emergency Toolkit:

- **Precision:** Upload who you want to be at your Horizon Point.

- **Perspective:** Ask how the situation might be happening *for* you, not *to* you. Check if you are bringing an abundance mindset and seeing infinite possible solutions in which you can thrive.

- **Physiology:** Move your emotion through, reconnect with your thinking centers through slow breathing, and then refind pleasure and joy.

- **Purpose:** Reconnect to your Purpose. What's your big game in this situation, and how can you act in the service of it?

- **Psyche:** Are you stuck in a Lead Story? Tell alternative stories in the service of your Horizon Point.

- **Proficiency:** What can you do from within your own Proficiency before you have to deal with anyone else to make this better?

Case Study #1: Being in Your Power in the Face of a Bully Boss

Christine was the Deputy Communications Officer for a fast-growing commodities company, and there was always a *ton* of communication needs. She was being considered as the successor to the Chief Communications Officer (CCO). She had the opportunity for coaching to develop her executive presence and groom her for the CCO position, which she was competing for with other internal candidates. She had to contend with a bully boss.

Christine started off with an Indirect approach, worrying about what her manager would think about her and monitoring her peers' communication to determine how much she should speak in the senior leadership meetings. This hesitation was interfering with the executive presence needed to represent the company and be considered for promotion to the top job. Now, she steps into the purpose she's there for as the communications officer—Go Direct! She told me, for the first time in her life she's not worrying about the other candidates for the next role, just about acting as a Confident Leader at her Horizon Point.

Though she's praised for her writing and interpersonal skills, a volume of merger activity required a lot of technical communication she didn't have experience with. She'd get out of her power whenever she'd have to write one of these memos or even think about doing so—doubting her ability to be the CCO. She deconstructed "I'm not good enough" into "I'm not experienced enough yet in these technical terms." So she did "Accomplish"—she took a course in this specific communication and got mentored by her former boss and now isn't susceptible to getting kicked out of her power.

Her manager's dismissive comments kicked her out of her power. To stay sane, she started doing a daily let-it-rip car scream to move her anger through (so she wasn't carrying the effect of her boss's insecurities inside her own body).

At the end of meetings, her boss would typically say, "I need to talk with you later." Christine would get a pit in her stomach and feel paralyzed and distracted until she had a chance to talk with her boss. Her lead story was "I've done something wrong, I'm going to get in trouble. *I'm not good enough.*" She became accustomed to telling alternative stories, such as "She's in a mood for reasons that have nothing to do with me," "We have lots to catch up on since she was out of the office and a lot of communications have been updated," or "She wants to discuss something that could be for my benefit, since I'm up for a promotion."

Now she bypasses the stories and just goes straight to who she wants to be at her Horizon Point, which is now updated to be simply "I'm the CCO!"

Case Study #2: Being in Your Power When Ending a Relationship

This case study is about . . . me. A few days after I submitted the manuscript for this book, my partner and I had a candid set of talks and decided to move forward in separate directions.

Background: We had a magical connection. Unconditionally loving, generously communicative, and irresistibly fun—we wanted it to last "forever." Yet, we are in different phases of life and want different things. She sold her company and wants a full-time companion with whom to travel the world. She would say, "Come sail away with me!" to hang out in fishing villages in foreign lands. (I know, it's tempting, isn't it?) I loved being on the water together, but I'm more of an "I'm here to change the world" kind of person. I'm still happy when I'm speaking/coaching/connecting.

She shared her truth that she felt we couldn't find a common enough purpose to make our day-to-day work. I was heartbroken. And I also went through it in my power.

Bereft at first, I allowed oceans of grief to wash through me even when all I could do was surf their wave. And then I moved it through. In the moments when I didn't want it to be true, I trusted that this separation was happening "for me," not "to me." I knew intuitively that both of us would otherwise have to compromise what really filled our souls and that this separation could be a release for each of us to live more deeply into what we desired.

This experience brought up a lead story in which I can feel powerless. Rather than react (reactivate this kindling), I had "Dr. Melnick" whispering in my ear to respond instead with the life story I've chosen: I am a powerful Creatrix! I can tap my power in every situation to create the experiences I want. This "part" of me doesn't fully take me over anymore, so I don't feel afraid walking forward on my own. I started to tell an alternative story that the reason we came into each other's lives was to experience unconditional love so we could each grow and heal (which we did beautifully). I've seen from my own experience and in that of thousands of clients, when you release yourself from an old storyline you are being readied for an uplevelling to get more of what you want in your life. I'm more able to walk through the world with a brave heart, not closed off from experiences I fear might break my heart.

Rather than feel powerless that "she was doing this to me," I viewed our relationship with a 3D perspective. I understood and honored what she needs, and as incredibly sad as it is, I feel a sense of ownership that I'm going in a direction that makes me feel "on purpose" and lights me up. Rather than look at the finite problem of "being on my own," I stay tethered to the infinite possibilities of how my life can unfold in ways that excite me.

Throughout our interactions and subsequent re-consideration of our possibility together, I was intentional about showing up at my Horizon Point, which supported us to continue to bring love and grace toward each other.

In short, even as I had moments where I went in and out of my power, I owned all of it—what I felt, what I chose, who I was, who I am, and who I want to be.

Being in your power doesn't mean that hard things won't happen. It means *you* determine who you will be as you go through those challenges and how they unfold for you—this is what I have been doing and what you can do, too. I didn't require myself to be perfect, just in my power!

PART III

Portals to Use Your Interpersonal Power for the Good of All

CHAPTER 9

Persuasion: From Unheard to Undeniable

"You don't rise to the occasion, you sink to the level of your training."
—Navy Seal saying

Now that you're in your power, you might be fired up and ready to march up to the powers that be to boldly ask for what you want and tell them how things need to be done. Yes! But before you do that, let's think through your approach and set you up for success.

One of the most common catalysts to being out of our power is the frustration that we can't get other people to act on our ideas or requests. How many times have you had an experience broadly similar to this one with a manager, peer, or family member?

You've suggested to your boss that your apparel company work with a reverse commerce service, which facilitates customers selling their used purchases to one another. It would give a sizable lift to revenue, customers love the option, and it would support your company's sustainability goals. You even provided compelling data graphs. When you broached the idea enthusiastically with your boss he expressed little interest.

To you, it's a slam dunk. His response makes no sense. How could he not see the merit? It feels as if the decision-maker is willfully devaluing your ideas or trying to subvert you. You take it personally, and you're down the rabbit hole out of your power. It makes you want to say, "Why bother."

In my experience many times what you take to be active thwarting is rather the case that you haven't been as *effective* as you can be in your 50% to *influence* the person. Consider there may be an element of *your approaches* that are keeping you out of your power, *not* the other person blocking you. (This is actually good news because then you can do something to change it.)

All of your communication, whether in the form of spoken word, written report, email, or slide presentation, travels across the 50% line from what you control over to what you're not directly in charge of. It is then filtered through the minds of those you're communicating with. The way they see and hear you depends on their priorities, their motivations, their beliefs, their mood, and their prior experiences.

You have the power to make yourself heard, to move people to support your ideas and follow your leadership, but you must be intentional and strategic in your approach. Remind yourself to start with a 3D understanding. Focus not on how right your case is but on how you can move others to see how right it is for them. Your power will come from your ability to unlock others' energies in the service of your vision or request.

In the portal of Persuasion, you will learn a series of ways I've helped clients get a *yes* where they previously had been getting a *no*. I'll present the pitfalls I've seen followed by the persuasion strategies that overcome them.

Persuasion Pitfall #1: Asking, Not Aligning

In my discussions with clients about these frustrating situations, I often hear, "I said something, but they didn't listen," "I emailed them about it, but I didn't hear anything back," or "I asked for the resources my team needs, and they said we just have to do without."

We tend to focus on asking for what we want based on how we see the situation, rather than on how the other person sees it and what they want. If you were to do an "after action" review of how you approached making your request, or pitching your idea, you'd likely find that you started by making the case for it in your own mind. You tell yourself why they are wrong, why what you're asking for would be better. You repeat your argument in your mind, while on a walk or having your morning coffee or on your commute to work. You might also have looked for validation of it by sharing with your partner or with friends. Then, when it came the time to talk to the person or hit "send" on the email, you probably presented your ask in just the same way you formulated it in your own mind. The case couldn't be clearer—to *you*.

What you might not have considered is "what's in it for them" (which I call their WIIFT). You want to get out of your own mind and *see the "ask" through the eyes of the other person*. By identifying a WIIFT for them about what you're proposing, you can reframe your request in a way that will make them see how you're helping further their own goals. You align your goals with their goals. Always start your influencing with the point of view of "why should they care?"

I'm sure you prepare a business case to support your idea, so you may ask why appeal to their WIIFT when the logic of your request should be obvious. For most people, our lives are like a rapidly flowing river of demands to be met. We're so busy just trying to stay afloat, to keep things moving forward, that any demand on our time or attention that isn't contributing to advancing the onrush is seen as going upstream against the current of our concerns. This approach is weak leverage. If you show others how your request does in fact help them advance their own motivations, you harness the energy they are already directing toward those outcomes. It's like entering an already flowing river. This is strong leverage.

For instance, in Chapter 1 I gave the example of my client from a Fortune 100 organization who for six years had been asking her sales manager for resources and plum assignments, but she had only been told "no." She described that he only managed up and didn't care about her. To her, this spelled a dead end, but in my experience, where someone has strong motivation, it can be leveraged.

We scripted how her requests would make him look good in front of his superiors, make him seen as a leader who developed his people (and supporting their DEI—diversity, equity, and inclusion—initiatives, especially because she was the lone woman on the team), and as someone who was resourcing innovative approaches that would reel in big clients for the whole enterprise. She got a "yes" for the first time! Now supported, within four months she brought in her career's best deal and was promoted to head her own sales team.

This idea works for leaders motivating a team member as well. Find out what really makes them tick: Is it getting promoted, is it success/money (e.g., the new house they want to buy), is it getting the work done efficiently so they can maximize time with their family? For many, it's a sense of mission or pride. My client Tom has an executive assistant who prides herself on controlling the details, especially doing things her way, which is different from his way. He felt controlled by her and didn't know how to say, "Do it this way." It would be received better by her if he appealed to what drives her: "I really appreciate your dedication to client service; you've been an important part of contributing to the reputation we have here.

What I've heard from our clients is that they feel very supported when we do _____ [his way]. Could you set it up to try it this way and see the feedback we get, and then we'll know more?"

Appeal to Both Their Business and Personal Interests

As you consider the WIIFT for whomever you want support from, identify both their business interests and their personal interests. You can consult the WIIFT wheel to put your thinking cap on.

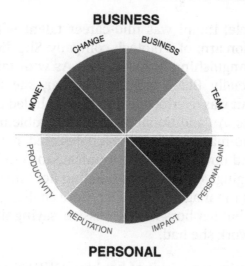

To identify their business WIIFT, what are the business interests they are paid to deliver, the metrics they are focused on, the career development goals they've been given, and the corporate initiatives they are tasked with furthering? They will see any request you make of them through the lens of "will this help me achieve my goals?" Categories include (1) money: increasing revenue or saving costs; (2) change: supporting a change they champion; (3) business: something that helps the overall business or their business goals or improve innovation; and (4) team: something that elevates or improves the team.

People's personal interests have to do with their motivations for themselves, as a person, as reflected in their personality. Personal categories include: (1) personal gain: the decision maker personally benefits by showcasing a win, having more control, taking ownership of a good idea, and so forth; (2) impact: it furthers their mission and they are seen as a leader who develops others; (3) reputation: makes them look good; and (4) productivity: helps them be personally more productive, reduce overwhelm, or do only the work they want.

It's best if you can appeal to both business and personal interests in your framing of your request.

For example, Imani was mid-career talent who worked in the investigation arm of a biotech company. She did great work, but she was languishing in her career. As with many qualified women, especially Black women like her, she wanted more opportunity but was overlooked and pigeon-holed in her current responsibilities. An additional layer to the problem was that her Manager micro-managed her. She felt defeated, neither seen nor supported. And how do you communicate to your boss that she is micromanaging you without offending her? Imani had previously asked her manager to give her more challenging and stimulating work, but her boss was dismissive, saying she should just focus on the work she had.

We dived into an analysis of her boss's WIIFT. Her boss had a big job, and she was probably somewhat overwhelmed and would appreciate things off-loaded from her plate. She was intent on having the group shine in presentations to the senior leadership team. She prided herself on being seen as a champion developer of people. We considered all of that and scripted a new approach for Imani's request.

> I know that you have a lot of responsibilities and I want to be in a position to take things off your plate. What could I do to earn your trust so I could play more of a role on our presentations to the senior leadership team and you could spend less of your time managing me?

Imani told me later, "I was so nervous about that conversation, but the way we scripted it made it really helpful and very productive!"

What happened? Her boss thought for just a moment and right away suggested areas where she could manage Imani less. She offered her the opportunity to work on a high visibility project with colleagues across the globe and then present the results to the entire leadership team. She also gave her more opportunities to expand her skills and work on projects outside of the department. Not long after, her boss supported Imani when her view contradicted group-think on how to handle a matter, which resulted in fending off a prolonged investigation. Shortly after, she was promoted.

Imani's appeal targeted both her boss's interest in her team's reputation as well as her personal interests in lightening her crushing workload and being seen as a developer of people. That one conversation, crafted strategically, was like a slingshot propelling Imani's career. (It also solidified a relationship of open communication between them, which was important because after two years of great relationship her boss made microaggressive comments, but Imani had a relationship context in which to educate her about it. You'll learn more about graceful responses in a later portal.)

It's not natural to "take off your own head" this way and see what's in a situation from the point of view of the other person. You have to *train yourself* to never approach a decision maker without identifying their WIIFT first. If you don't, you are not being impeccable for your 50%.

Think about a project or idea you haven't been able to get support for. Who's the decision maker(s) and what's their WIIFT? Then reframe your request in the service of their WIIFT. A great way to get started is to consult the WIIFT wheel.

_____

_____

_____

Persuasion Pitfall #2: From Single Conversation to Stakeholder Campaign

Another common mistake I've seen in my clients' influencing is putting all their eggs in one basket. They prepare for a *single conversation* with their decision maker, which they see as make-or-break. And if that one person is a roadblock, you're popped out of your power. Instead, you want to engage in a *stakeholder campaign*.

Think of your approach to getting a yes as an influencing campaign in which you enroll multiple influencers over time.

You want to make a stakeholder map of all the decision makers with a potential interest in the outcome you want. Some of them will immediately come to mind, and then you want to expand the map to take into account people whose interest is less obvious. Who whispers in the ears of your decision makers? Who else has a vested interest in the outcome you advocate for, even if they are not a direct decision maker? Include these as stakeholders.

Then fill in customized messaging for each person so it aligns with their motivations.

Take the case of Ama, whom I coached through the "Next Level Leader" mid-career professional development program. She's a PhD scientist at a pharmaceutical company with an idea for how to improve the way they conduct basic chemistry research. She'd been suggesting the approach to her manager for two years without getting any traction, and she was ready to leave.

We crafted a stakeholder campaign. Who would benefit from this research innovation and could form a coalition to support it? She talked to the point person in the clinical development group to show him how this new research approach could speed time to market for new drugs. She talked to other research scientists about how the innovation could help them do their work and also to a leader of the sales team, who was concerned with all the ways for the company to stay ahead of competitors.

These conversations helped her understand how to convey to her boss how her idea would help him be seen as a leader of innovation. He asked her to present the idea to the executive team, and that led to approval for her to lead a pilot project. It was so successful that she was then put in charge of leading the transformation across the whole company.

You can also use this approach when asking to be promoted—who are all the stakeholders that care about that outcome?

Now's your turn: Put together a visual of a stakeholder campaign (it can be quick and dirty—just boxes on a page). Who's on your map? What customized WIIFT can you identify for each? In what order would you approach them?

_____

_____

_____

Persuasion Pitfall #3: Not Clearly Providing a Framework

One of the big impediments to getting support for change is that you don't have a specific enough vision of what will be better once the change happens. You want to develop a pithy framework that helps people to contrast the old way versus the new way to help them embrace the new way.

A great approach is with the "before versus after" exercise. Require yourself to describe the before of how things are now with your observations about what is wrong. Then contrast the painful before with a vivid description of the after, a description of how things will be at their ideal. This description should also again appeal to both the business and personal interests of those you're seeking support from.

This exercise helped my client Karina gain support for culture changes at her global nonprofit organization with the mission to help people in war zones gain safety. Unfortunately, many of the staff were suffering from burnout and mental health struggles. Karina was in a mid-level position, and she felt helpless to bring about the change in culture she knew was needed.

We started by having her describe the "before." She told me that the organization's leaders weren't showing empathy to workers about how physically and emotionally punishing the work is. "There's little room for us to be vulnerable," she said, "or to say, 'I had a rough day, I'm not digesting this well. My family and I are struggling. I need a break.' Our success metrics only measure cash spent and number of people who received services, but not the well-being of our employees or the survivors they serve."

Make your observations of the "before" act as a mirror that vividly reflects their experience so they see themselves in your description. The more empathy you show to describe the "before," the easier you will engage others. And the more you are implicitly positioned as the one with the solution.

I next asked Karina to describe the "after" she wanted to promote. Often, you'll start with answers that aren't yet fully fleshed out; just keep talking it out, and you'll find your words (a peer or coach can help you package your ideas). "We would be better at our jobs," she told me. "Instead of only debriefing the data, we would have a culture of caring in which we debrief our sense of helplessness from having to keep telling refugees we can't do anything. Rather than complaining how frustrated we are, we could start to create a more positive work environment. We could start by changing the contracts of our employees."

That was a great deal to digest in the abstract, and I prodded her to state clearly and concisely the bottom-line changes that were needed and to see whether there was a natural way to group them. "We need a different kind of leadership," she responded. "The mindset we have is that we are the 'heroes' brought in to save the people we serve, but we fail to recognize the needs of the people who work here. The job of a leader," she continued, "is to see their people as their biggest asset. They need to understand what motivates the staff, appreciate they heard gunfire all night. We need a leadership style with a humanitarian mindset."

There it was! A simple, compelling statement of the "after."

Once you have clearly articulated the problems of the "before" and the vision for the "after," it's powerful to boil them down into the simplest phrasing you can craft, like you did for your Horizon Point. This catchy phrase makes your message relatable, helping others to grasp at a glance the nature of the change you're advocating, and to spread the word about the mission. Karina's phrase was that we need to go from a *"hero to a humanitarian"* mindset.

As she began discussing the need for change in these terms with colleagues, she found that they could readily relate to what she was saying. She started holding meetings with staff to discuss the culture change she envisioned, asking them to reflect on the kind of culture they wanted, hero or humanitarian? These conversations led to a movement for change within the organization, and HR allowed her to start giving trainings on how to lead with empathy. Leaders began reviewing the required working hours and terms of contracts with their employees.

The pithy phrasing of the problem and solution was catchy and intriguing, and it allowed her to avoid the trap of burying her vision for change in a long list of grievances that leadership didn't want to hear.

What is a framework you might develop to rally conversation around?

Persuasion Pitfall #4 Focusing on Past Achievements to the Exclusion of Future Ones

This pitfall is especially pertinent when it comes to persuading others that you have what it takes for a next-level opportunity, whether this is for a next-level role, to have your start-up funded, or to be elected for a position you haven't held. A known gender and intersectional bias is the "prove it again" bias, in which men are more often evaluated based on future potential and women based on current and past accomplishments.[1] If a person without relevant experience is applying for a next-level position, the decision makers' view will depend on the gender of the applicant: If it is a man, they will tend to say, "He'll figure it out," but if it is a woman, they will most likely say, "Let's put her in a lateral role for two years and have her get more experience." Similarly, women entrepreneurs seeking funding are more often asked questions about protecting their downside rather than growing their upside, making their pitches less attractive to investors.[2]

So often we make the case that we are right for a job by reciting our past accomplishments. This reinforces the focus on seeing you in the box you are already in. Instead, require your decision maker to see you inhabiting that next-level opportunity. In addition to describing your current and past accomplishments, *describe your future contribution.*

Create a mental movie in the mind of your decision makers so they *see you* carrying out that future vision. How do you do that? Describe the actions you'll take and results you'll get as if you were the director of a movie who is setting a scene. "The first thing I'll take on is _____. The next thing I'll do is _____." Then paint a vivid picture of the results you'll achieve. For example, "Customers will be posting product pics."

One client I coached about how to approach a job interview this way told me that at the end of her interview, the hiring manager said, "I can *see you* in that role." (Wink, I wonder why.) Sure enough, she was offered the job!

What is the mental movie you want to create?

Persuasion Pitfall #5: Not Making It Easy for Your Decision Maker to Implement Your Idea

To get support for your idea, your decision-maker might have to reverse a prior course or undo a situation that's not working. If you don't address this resistance, you may have a perfect idea, but they won't be in their power enough to help you implement it. Make it easy for them to follow your good idea. This will often involve them saving face, that is, not having to admit they were wrong. That's what my client Rana did in persuading the founder of the start-up she was working for to step aside as CEO and put her in that role.

As is common with start-ups, most of the employees who joined at the beginning were friends of the founder, but she was a later hire. She could see that some of the team were doing great work but others were dead weight and that it was time for the founder to step away from the CEO role and appoint someone with the experience to take the company through its next stage of growth. Rana was well qualified for the role, and she had already been taking the lead in setting the company's strategy, running the meetings, and even in selling their first few accounts. She had asked the founder for the CEO's position, and he had said it would be hers. He'd also said he would remove the underperformers from their roles. But months of inaction had followed, and she was fed up.

In terms of his WIIFT, a key concern of his was he wanted to maintain good relationships with his buddies and not have the hard conversations about why they had to go. Another was to get the greatest valuation possible for the company and secure a next round of funding to keep the company growing.

To make it easier for the founder, Rana scripted a way of helping him make the changes without having to admit he was wrong. She did this by framing the discussion using the idea of "phases." She congratulated him for being the founder that succeeded in phase 1 of the company by having the idea, securing funding, and bringing in the right people to get it off the ground. She introduced the idea that they were now entering phase 2 in which different skill sets and talent was needed. The next phase of the company evolution was about leadership and executing on the strategic vision that had been put into place, and this was especially the point at which future valuation of the company would be cemented or get erased. She painted a vivid picture of the growth and valuation the company could achieve with this stronger team in place and her at the helm. Then he had no more barriers to keep him from saying yes. She's now the CEO and leading them into the success they want as a start-up.

***

You have the power to unlock infinite energy to support you and your ideas. X-ray vision into the mind of your decision makers is the key. To stay away from the utter frustration of not being heard, just be intentional and strategic in your approach. Now that you know how to identify the other person's WIIFT, you can leverage it to resolve sticky scenarios that put you out of your power, which you'll learn to do in the next portal.

In Your Power Practices: Persuasion

1. You must always frame your idea or request in terms of "what's in it for them," their WIIFT. Use the WIIFT wheel to help you identify your decision maker's business and personal WIIFT.

2. Approach influencing as a stakeholder campaign, not a single conversation. Start with a stakeholder map that includes each person's WIIFT.

3. Provide a framework that captures the "before" and "after" to make your idea compelling and memorable.

4. Create a mental movie in the mind of your decision maker so they "see" you doing the future role.

5. Make it easy for your decision maker to implement your idea or request.

CHAPTER 10

Partnership: From My Problem to Our Solution

"If you want to go fast, go alone. If you want to go far, go together."

—African Proverb

Keisha is a finance leader at the end of her rope because her manager would regularly call her in a crisis, at any time of day from 7 a.m. to 11 p.m. He'd plead with her that she was the only one who could fix the problem, kissing her ass so she'd once again save his. When I asked her, "Whose problem is it that he's coming to you with these last-minute emergencies?" she responded, "It's his." I asked her to think about the question again, and she paused and then had an aha moment: "It's *my problem!*"

She is the one who is experiencing the frustrating effect of his behavior, not him. How much incentive does someone have to fix a problem that they are not experiencing?

Because we are so intent on solving the problem, we have inadvertently taken possession of it. We're still taking behavior that's going on in the other person's 50% and trying to control it in ours. This is why we spend so much energy ruminating without reaching resolution. Let's get off this stairway to nowhere!

What *is* your problem is that you are conceptualizing the problem as "They are wrong; they should change their behavior." This approach gives them all the power to make it better and keeps you small. Time to take it back. See yourself as the steward who brings everyone along in a solution in which everyone is in their power.

In the portal of Partnership you will learn to bring the issue out in the open and have a conversation with those causing difficulties so you can build understanding and reach better solutions. These kinds of conversations, whether with a manager, peer, team member, friend, or family member, can be fraught and seem daunting. You often don't know what to say or how to say it, so you might avoid saying anything and stew in your mental swirl. *I believe you can say anything constructive you need to say to anybody as long as you say it in a way they can receive it and have a clear path to respond to it.* You'll learn how to not make the other person defensive and instead create a spirit of mutual appreciation and collaboration. You won't make them wrong you'll make them a partner.

A core principle is that you help everyone understand their part in the problem and in the solution. You use your power to create an environment that is the world according to the way you think it *should be*—everyone has a clear understanding, takes ownership of their part, and is respected. You're made for this—let's get started!

You Want to Transfer the Ownership of the Problem

First order of business is to create a *shared* sense of the problem. You want to start with looking at the situation with your 3D lens—what's your experience, their experience, and the experience between you, as well as contextual factors that are playing a role. Building on this foundation, you can help them see that the way things are now is interfering with what they want. That's when they start to share ownership of the problem.

I've put together a framework using the acronym "POWERS," which offers the elements of an intentional way of communicating with a seemingly uncooperative party to resolve it. This is a structure for you to initiate the awkward conversation. You can draw from it only the pieces you need, or it can serve as a template to go through in order. I'm going to share the part of the conversation that *you* can initiate. At any juncture you can invite the other person to share how they see the issue and what they need from you.

I'll illustrate it with the case we considered in the portal of Perspective, of the finance executive, Elisa, who was struggling to get the head of IT to submit his departmental budget. Recall that from his perspective, he shouldn't have been expected to deal with budgeting, believing the systems transformation he was leading to be so crucial that his budget shouldn't be constrained. She rarely heard back from him, and when she did, he criticized her and her team. She had taken on the problem as her own, feeling the heat because the CEO was now prioritizing meeting with department heads about their budgets and she felt hampered from doing her job well. She approached the conversation in the following way to avoid sparking fireworks, and she got the resolution she hoped for.

Pre-Frame

The seed of a plant or tree has within it the blueprint of how it will unfold and grow. The same is true for partnership. You have immense power in the "pre-frame," the way you begin any interpersonal interaction.

Pre-framing is a method of approaching a conversation with someone to immediately reduce defensiveness and entice partnership. It's crucial that you offer a neutral pre-frame, clearly expressing you are interested in surfacing all perspectives and moving forward in a mutually beneficial way, not in making them wrong and you right. I've placed in bold text helpful scripts for introducing a neutral pre-frame.

Elisa started her conversation with: "**I wanted to see if we could discuss how to get our budgeting project done with fewer back-and-forths.**" Or, "**I want to hear your perspective about how the process is going,** and what you need from my team. **And then I'd like to share with you my perspective** of what we're trying to accomplish, what we're putting into it, and what we need from our business partners." She could also use alternative neutral language, such as: "**I think it could be helpful to take a step back and talk through what you see as your role and I see as my role; we might be able to come up with a better way of working together and take things off each of our plates.**"

This part of the conversation can be done when inviting the person to a meeting, as well as to start the meeting. This engaged the IT leader Elisa was talking to and motivated him to participate.

Own Your Part in the Problem

Take responsibility for your part of the situation, anything you might have contributed to communication breakdown, lack of understanding, or escalation of the problem. This is being impeccable for your 50%. Being the first person to do this creates a lot of goodwill and also role-models how to take responsibility. It inspires the other person to rise to the occasion and reach for higher ground.

Elisa acknowledged, "**I haven't had a chance to share** that in our finance meetings we've been hearing how important the CEO believes it is for department heads to own their budgets."

Or, "**I should have prefaced my outreach with that context** and indicated how we could help."

A more generic way of doing this might be to say, "If you haven't been receiving the information or guidance you've needed, **I want to take responsibility for my part in that.**"

Work their WIIFT (What's In It For Them)

You now want to motivate the person to engage in participating in the solution with you. Leverage the ways you've thought about their WIIFT—why they should care about the problem and how a resolution will benefit them.

You might immediately think the other person is obstinate, like in this case she attributed his behavior to his ego. At first blush, this seems like an answer that shuts down your ability to engage the other person, but as discussed in the portal of Persuasion, where there's a motivation, you can appeal to it! She had to stop focusing on how he was wrong and instead on what motivates *him*.

Motivate someone with a big ego? Easy, help him look good to the CEO. Or make them the ones to have your idea.

She could say, "One of the CEO's priorities is to have department heads own their budgets, and he has started meeting with each to do a formal review of their budgets. I want to be able to prepare you for your review so you can justify your requests, and show your knowledge of your numbers." This would get his attention!

Enumerate the Effects

Here's where you start to transfer the ownership of the problem. Help the person become aware of the behaviors they are doing that are contributing to the problem. In these seemingly intractable situations we have an implicit assumption that they don't care about the effects on you. Or worse, they're intending to have them. This may be the case with some people, especially those that are narcissistic like him. But the truth is, many of us are inadvertently unaware of our effects on other people. We blithely go about our behaviors, without having considered the downstream effects. (OMG, that was a memorable moment when I heard from my family members what it's like to wait for me when I'm late for dinner, when of course I had no intention of being disrespectful. Now I hustle to be on time!) Just like we benefit from changing our own perspective, we can help them connect the dots to change theirs.

The first step is to describe their problematic behavior and articulate the effects of it. Do this by observing their behavior and describing it to them, using neutral rather than judgmental language to defuse their defensiveness. Be specific, and factually describe their actions rather than characterizing them. Say, "When I don't hear back from you after three email messages," as opposed to, "When you blow me off . . ." (because in their mind they may not be blowing you off). The person has to be able to objectively evaluate when they start doing it differently. Other examples might be: When you . . .

> "started adding your thoughts before I was finished answering the sales director's question in the meeting . . ."

> "get the materials to me only 30 minutes before our presentation . . ."

> "present the ideas we formed together without putting my name on the presentation . . ."

Next, help them see the downstream effects. Specifically, what you need to do is help them understand how their behavior is interfering with *their* WIIFT.

> **"When** I don't get a chance to walk through a budget with a department head before those reviews, **what happens**

is I don't have time to catch mistakes. And then the CEO can give a good grilling to the department heads about expenses."

"What happens is you present brilliant ideas that are game changing for the organization, but if you talk for most of the meeting, people see you less as a strategic thinker and more as someone who's about himself. And they start to lose interest in implementing it."

Warning: You'll be tempted to launch into a litany of woe about all the ways they've caused *you* harm. Keep in mind that because of human nature the other person will care much less about the impact on you and your role and much more about how the problem is affecting outcomes that *they* want. Start with your focus squarely on their WIIFT. After you see they've really absorbed how it affects them, you can concisely walk them through how their behavior affects you.

Respect Them

You want the other person to feel respected, heard, and empathized with. You want your "come from" to be one where you make them right. Take the perspective that everyone's behavior is understandable, and have that inform your tone. When people feel heard, they come up with better problem solving and are more willing to engage with you as a partner. This might sound like: "I know you are probably responding to the pressures from your leader." For Elisa this might sound like: "I appreciate you have a huge lift on your shoulders to change over our IT systems . . ."

Say What You Mean, and Mean What You Say

Here's where you make your request, or set your expectations, or suggest a better way. Often, we want to sugarcoat what we say so that we don't hurt the other person's feelings or make them uncomfortable. But that can lead us to dilute what we are requesting of them, using vague terms that you can bet don't have the same meaning to them as they have to you.

In her prior effort, Elisa had said something vague and unactionable like, "Let's try to work this out." You don't want to tiptoe around the call to action. Instead, you want to be clear and specific about what you are asking, requesting, or expecting. Own your power! Saying what you mean might sound like:

"I'd like to have a follow-up conversation where you come prepared to talk about what you want, and I'll talk about what I want, and let's see if we can find a common ground on what our relationship looks like going forward."

You *will* be tempted to jump in, tell them what to do, and make all the plans for them. You might say, "Let me send you the materials again and take a look at X and Y." But if you do this, you will be maintaining ownership of the problem!

At this point in the conversation you have connected the dots, and the other person should be clear what they are doing and why it's a problem *for them*.

Ask them with respect and genuine interest, "So how would you like to proceed?

You've now changed the problem from being between you and him to it being his problem if he wants to get his WIIFT. Challenge yourself to take a deep breath and do what comes unnaturally to you: give up full ownership of the problem. Let the other person initiate the go-forward plan, and *then* you can add the specifics of your input. This helps to complete the transfer of ownership from *your problem to our solution.*

And mean what you say. Since you've given the person the clarity they need, allow there to be a natural consequence if they continue their behavior.

Make Them an Active Part of the Process

If you repeatedly tell the other person what to do or continuously hope against hope they will change, you think you are working to make it better, but you are keeping yourself out of your power. The way to get someone to partner with you is to make them an active part of the process.

Make it a practice to do a check-in about how the other person understands what you've discussed, especially if you did most of the talking. You can ask, "We've talked about a lot of things. What is your takeaway?" Or you could soften the phrasing by putting the onus back on you: "We've just said a lot of things, and I'm not even sure that it all came out the way I meant it. What are you taking from what I'm saying?" Get *them* to put it into words and tell you their go-forward plan and their commitments. That gives them a sense of ownership.

This is a great practice any time you're giving direction to someone else, whether manager to team member, parent to child, peer to peer, or coach to client.

Your responsibility in your 50% is to infuse every situation with clarity. *Clarity is love.* Play your part, but don't go over the line to carry the problem as yours because then they have no incentive to partner with you. The POWERS approach and making the other person active gives them their best shot at rising to the occasion.

You have considerable power to set these situations on a course that will end up with more grace—reducing friction and wasted energy and coming up with better collaborations to carry out better work in less time. That's using your power for the good of all.

Try filling out the POWERS framework with someone you have friction with and who is putting you out of your power.

The POWERS Framework

P = <u>P</u>re-frame: provide a neutral context and structure for the meeting that invites all perspectives to reduce defensiveness.

O = <u>O</u>wn your part in the problem: take responsibility for anything you might have contributed to the escalation of the problem. Create goodwill.

W = <u>W</u>ork their WIIFT (what's in it for them): motivate the person to engage in participating in the solution with you.

E = <u>E</u>numerate the effects: observe their behavior and describe it to them using objective language that makes them aware of it; connect the dots on how their behavior interferes with *their* WIIFT.

R = <u>R</u>espect: show empathy for the person's circumstances that might set up their behavior; make them right, saying, for example, "It's understandable."

S = <u>S</u>ay what you mean, and mean what you say: be clear and specific about what you are asking; Then transfer the ownership—ask them *their* plan to participate in the solution.

See Yourself as the Steward of the Whole Scenario

Are you in a situation where you micro-track what other people are doing, react with aggravation to each new limited behavior they do, or tiptoe around one difficult person sacrificing the welfare of everyone else?

Here's where you can press a different button on the remote control of your mindset and instead of feeling powerless, you can come from a place of power to make it better. *Think of yourself as the steward of the situation*. Be the one who initiates a process of problem-solving that makes the whole situation better for everyone. Lift your attention up from blame and keep your sights on the good you can create for all involved.

The more you keep in mind all the people who are affected by the problem you want to solve (e.g., other team members, cross functional colleagues, clients/patients/customers), the easier it will be to practice the nonjudgmental, constructive partnering that will solve the problem. That's your big game!

This was a helpful reminder for my client Ali who was the Executive Vice President of a company. She had a regional director who wasn't putting together his goals, let alone fulfilling on them. Each time she had an interaction with him, she'd get into a fit and out of her power because "again" he didn't meet her expectations. She was draining her time and attention micromanaging him instead of remembering that she's the head of the division with *all* the district managers, retail sellers, and product producers. She instead needed to work out a process that would determine whether he was the right fit (or not), and also to bundle her interactions with him into once a day or week. Then she could be the steward for the hundreds of other people under her leadership. What a relief!

Being the steward might also look like being the one who smooths out the emotions for yourself and others.[1] Mia is a chief of staff in a meeting with John, the owner of a small company, and their team of designers. He's riled about his discontent with the first draft provided for his new idea pet project and criticizes her and the team. She and the team get immobilized by his outburst. No one—not you, not her, not the team, should have to be subjected to this kind of behavior, but if this is the reality for now, you have the power to lead this kind of stuck scenario into a better place.

One way of being the steward is to translate what is happening emotionally into a useful frame that helps everyone move forward. I suggested she start with a re-frame that makes everyone right: "At the beginning of any innovative initiative, we're often shooting in the dark to figure out what we want."

Then she could empathize with each of the constituents' emotions, which might sound like: "John, I see how important this project is to you and how much you want it to work at warp speed. We're not always able to understand a new concept on the first try so I'm glad we're having this check-in meeting to course correct. We're learning here that the team didn't understand exactly what they need to do. So, John, can we hear from you again what your vision and any updates or anything that's become more clear to you since we first talked? And also, let's hear from the team what they were trying to accomplish with this first round and see if they have questions you can help them answer. That will help us get crystal clear on how to move forward."

As the steward, you have considerable power to be the thermostat. Even if other people are emotional or frozen in their patterns, it doesn't mean you have to be. By unhooking yourself from taking it personally, you can set the tone and harmonize the elements. By having a 3D perspective you can take in the hologram of what's happening. You automatically elevate yourself into being the leader, people will look to you for guidance, and you have the most influence to create the weather on the team (or in your family).

This idea of being a steward of the whole situation has been very helpful for me when I am in danger of getting into a state of pulling-my-hair-out reactivity with others. You want it to become a commitment to yourself, a philosophy of your approach to your life, an approach that becomes second nature in any situation you're in.

I reminded myself to be the steward in an impasse with a marketing writer I hired to help me with a new website. After multiple rounds of edits and hours spent providing detailed examples for the writer—and the deadline approaching—the website copy samples delivered were still a far cry from what we discussed. I was roiled that I had wasted my time, my money—and yet I really *needed* help.

When I talked through the problems with the copy, the writer didn't take any responsibility for anything being wrong with it. Rather, she blamed me, criticizing my language for being imprecise and maintaining that the copy she had written was better for website viewers. I saw the problem as her defensiveness and incompetence. I was ready to fire her. I went to sleep that night with anger pinballing around my head, lacking a path to control an important outcome for my business.

But I'm committed to being the steward. The next day I approached her with a neutral pre-frame to partner on finding a solution. "I want to ask you your perspective and share mine with you and see if we can come up with a way to get a product we're both proud of in the most efficient way possible."

I started by owning my 50% that I could be more precise with some of my language and that if I boiled my points down to fewer, it would help her write them more clearly. I led us through examples in which her phrasing changed my meaning. She said that she now understood how she had been off base from what I wanted to say and pledged to get more on target. My goodwill led to hers.

I proposed a new process for working together built on these insights, producing the outcome both of us hoped for. It was a win-win. (She even said that the approach we came up with was so helpful she was going to start using it with all her other clients.) When you are in your power, you create a ripple effect, leaving the situation better than when you came into it.

Infuse the Situation with Light

Staying in the consciousness of being the steward can be challenging when you are out of your power. So I want to share a practice that always helps me make this my stance.

Recall that when I am at my Horizon Point, I feel surrounded by a powerful ray of white light. My intent is that my participation *uplifts the consciousness of any situation.*

A practice that I have used to get back into this energy is that I "surround the situation with light" through the ritual of reciting a "Prayer of Light" that I learned through Naam Yoga. Before I hit "send" on any message about any delicate issue or initiate any important personal conversation in which I know sensitivities are high, I *always* say this prayer. I say it first for myself, and then I say it using the name and a mental picture of the other person(s).

> *Light before me, Light behind me;*
> *Light at my left, Light at my right;*
> *Light above me, Light below me;*
> *Light in me, Light in my*
> *surroundings;*
> *Light to all, Light to the Universe;*
> *Light in the eyes of those who see me;*
> *Light in the ears of those who*
> *listen to me;*
> *Light in the hearts of those who*
> *interact with me;*
> *Light in the hearts of those who*
> *speak of me;*
> *May the Light restore me to health,*
> *be always in my heart,*
> *be before me and lead me,*
> *establish me and preserve me,*
> *surround me with wisdom,*
> *be near me and fortify me;*
> *May the Light be amongst those*
> *whom I have offended knowingly or*
> *unknowingly, May the Light be With*
> *Them. And so it is.*

Having thus surrounded myself and the other parties with light, I put my hands out in front of me with palms facing toward each other. With the space created between my hands I imagine the outcome I want—a win-win that resolves the matter for the good of all. I then bring *this* energy into the interaction. This brings a palpable grace to any conflict and helps to move the energies toward a harmonious outcome.

It's within your power to break any escalation and to infuse a higher level of consciousness into any situation. As you live more and more in your power as the steward, you will know how to "raise the vibration" in any situation that has devolved.

How can you be the steward in a situation that's putting you out of your power now?

***

One reason we become so focused on how "wrong" the behavior of others we're having difficulty with is that we have expectations about how they should behave. *The fastest path to disappointment and anger with others is having expectations of them in your mind that they have no idea about, didn't necessarily agree to, and then don't live up to!* Here you've set yourself up to be kicked out of your power by focusing on how they are not matching your expectations of them.

Being in your power means being able to be "good in you," to take care of yourself, regardless of how evolved other people are around you. (If they need to change in order to fulfill a responsibility like a work deliverable or childcare sharing, use the incentive of their WIIFT to motivate their cooperation.)

Otherwise, people are where they are on their journey at this moment in time. *You get angry because their limitations reactivate your lead story or bring up your own disappointments.* As you know how to move through these derailing moments, they will cause less drama for you. The more you know how to stay "good in you," the less you will be hijacked by others. On the other side of those hurts, you can objectively think through whether this person may or may not be a good fit for you to be close to at this time.

Accept where others are on their journey, and further yourself on your own.

In Your Power Practices: Partnership

1. Create a shared sense of ownership of the problem by helping the person see their behavior is interfering with "what's in it for them."
2. Use the POWERS framework as a guide to approach conversations with people who have been difficult to deal with. It will help you reduce others' defensiveness and engage mutual problem-solving.
3. Instead of feeling powerless, think of yourself as the steward of the situation, the one who looks after all involved and proposes solutions that keep everyone in their power.
4. Before you have a conversation you anticipate will be difficult, always surround yourself and the other person with the Prayer of Light to enter it with a sense of grace.
5. Accept where others are on their journey, and further yourself on your own!

CHAPTER 11

Protection: From Silent Suffering to Sovereignty

"Boundaries are not a wall or moat around your heart, they are the path to self-respect. They say, 'I choose self-love and self-respect' over the possibility of disappointing you"[1]

—Brené Brown, Author and TED Talk speaker

Sometimes the cause of the continued problem really does lie on the other person's side of the street, and you can't make it better, at least for now. Or you've tried to use your power, with little effect. But you can *always* protect yourself. They might be dishing it out, but you don't have to *take it*. You don't have to wait or hope for other people to change in order to stay in or get back in your power.

Protecting yourself gives you ownership of your life. It says, "I decide what I allow into my emotional airspace. I prioritize me and filling my needs. I make choices to have the life I want. *Your* behavior will not determine that!"

The ability to protect yourself comes from knowing your *yes* and knowing your *no*.[2] How do you even know these, especially if you feel so taken over by the overwhelming force of someone else's personality or demands?

Try this experiment. For the next 20 seconds or so (no need to count it out, just give yourself enough time to get a clear signal), say in your mind or out loud the word *no* emphatically and repeatedly. Notice, where did you feel the signal of *no* in your body? Now try the same experiment for *yes*. For about 20 seconds or so repeat *yes!* in your mind or out loud. Where does your *yes* live in your body? What's the sensation like? For me, my *no* is like a forceful sensation of pushing someone away, and my *yes* is like a streaming of light and energy up and down.

Now you know the language your body signals when a boundary has been crossed. If you are suffering in a *no* situation, *it's a sign that there is something that is not right in the system.* Which means that it's not serving other people either, even the people who are supposedly benefitting from the overreach, like Keisha's boss who calls her 7 a.m.–11 p.m. He's not thriving if he has underlying problems that are causing him to be so reactive all day and night. By relying on her, *he* is missing out on ways of improving his business problems. It's a sign there isn't open communication and negotiation about needs. If you avoid it, it will eventually blow up, but this passive approach doesn't give you much control. If you keep thinking, "They are doing this *to* me," you are missing the opportunity to be the steward of the bigger-picture solution.

And if you don't do anything to protect yourself, you'll get put out of your power. You'll feel taken advantage of or muzzled. Ask yourself, who really benefits? Is it sustainable? Are people getting the best of you? Is it worth it? *Protecting yourself is not self-ish, its self-first.* It's up to you to do something to keep yourself in your power.

Remember that when you are in your power, you raise everyone around you simply by the way you show up—so if you are not putting yourself first to get good in you, you can't help anyone else and your presence is not uplifting others.

Protecting yourself comes in many forms. Setting boundaries is a hallmark of protection. A boundary declares to the world what you are willing to do, willing to put up with, willing to engage in, or not. It gives you self-trust and makes you impenetrable to the effects of others' limitations.

You can also push back and make the interaction more on your terms. You can remove yourself from the situation, not put yourself into the situation to begin with, or engage in a way that isn't unhealthy for you. In some cases you may never need to fix the problem, as long as you can protect yourself from absorbing its negative effects. Declaring what you want and acting in the service of it is part of being impeccable for your 50%. In the portal of Protection, you'll learn a Swiss Army™ knife of approaches to stay in your power despite people and outside forces that conspire to take you out of it.

I'll share about a number of types of boundaries here including protection from intrusions related to your workload and the expectations at work. Then I'll share how to create barriers of protection to deal with the most difficult people, such as outright bullies and narcissists, who may be unresponsive to all of your best efforts to deal with their behavior.

But first, it's important to acknowledge that setting boundaries, of whatever kind, can be intimidating, even highly anxiety provoking. We worry about how people will respond, particularly regarding those in positions of authority over us or who might act hostile. Or worry about what others will think about us, not wanting to come off as rude, or uptight, or not a team player. A few things to keep in mind will help you proceed with boundary setting despite any worries.

Think of someone in your life who is skilled at setting boundaries and holding firm to them. Don't you respect them? Those who are strong in their boundaries give themselves the bandwidth to do big things. And if I haven't made my case yet, let's see if this one finally convinces you: Noted researcher and author Brené Brown found in her research that the one trait the most compassionate people shared in common was . . . they had the best boundaries.[3]

You can develop judgment to determine how much capacity the person you are interacting with has to respect your boundaries—the answer will determine the kind of boundary you need to set. The first time you bring up your needs, pay attention to whether they are defensive versus deferential in their response. If they are defensive, they deflect your needs and focus on their own, or they might frankly criticize or attack you and tell you to "stop overreacting." If they are deferential, they will accept responsibility for their actions and be interested in knowing more about how they can do better: "I didn't realize I was doing that; thank you for calling it to my attention." If the person is deferential, it indicates to you they value your emotional needs in the relationship—this is someone who it is worth continuing to try to make it better with. If their response falls in the range of defensive or deflecting, then follow the immortal words of Maya Angelou: "When someone shows you who they are, believe them."[4] Accept these conditions as reality and release all hope the person will change. It's *not your job* to try to heal them. This is when you want to go beyond setting a *boundary* and instead put up a *barrier*. I'll show you how to do this without getting blowback.

Boundaries to Protect Your Time, Attention, and Energy

Intrusions on our time and attention, both while at work and at home, have become a culture-wide problem, with the implicit expectation that we should be always available to receive and respond to emails and texts and respond instantaneously whether the matter is urgent or not. We're all operating in a culture of immediacy.

Excessive working hours and demands have become standard. Whether in the office or remote, managers interrupt at any moment, slap on a new assignment, call a sudden team meeting. Contributing to the problem is that we pressure ourselves to be perfect as a supply line to our validation.

The "always available" expectation contributes to resentment and feeling you don't have control. It's recognized as a contributing cause of burnout, prompting a rethinking of how to prioritize employees' mental and physical health.

Proactive Boundaries to Prevent Overwhelm at Work

Whatever the situation you're in, you can be proactive about communicating to others about your boundaries so that you set forth the mental and physical space to do your best work and take care of yourself. Don't wait until people intrude on your time or attention to try to fend them off. That's like playing a game of whack-a-mole.

I advised an HR team on dealing with stress and overload to include setting boundaries. I heard, "We don't have good boundaries, everything feels like an emergency. I got an email from a leader at 6:30 a.m. this morning, and I felt like, 'I have to respond *right now.*'" A team member even had a colleague call her while she was at a funeral, and even though she was angry at the intrusion, *she answered the call!*

Here are some examples of the new approaches they introduced, starting with those that address the upstream root causes of their overwhelm. As a team, they talked through their purpose and objectives in order to prioritize their bigger picture objectives over momentary fire drills. They decided on meeting-free times at the team level, so it wouldn't fall on an individual to say no. We also conducted an "ideal day" discussion in which each member of the team gives their collective input on what an ideal day/ ideal week would look like (which usually involves getting the most meaningful work done efficiently while having more sense of control and fun!). Projects were given new timelines. And the new filter for each work project then became "Is this in the service of our ideal day/week?"

You have to train people on how to get the best out of you. They started to introduce a new level of intentionality into communication with colleagues. For example, they educated colleagues about the best way to engage them in a personnel issue. They also replied to email requests by asking for context such as, "When do you need this?" Simply requesting that people think through priorities carefully helps you take charge of your own boundaries and raises others by requiring them to be thoughtful and strategic in their communications.

You want to engage WIIFT to help them see how your setting of a boundary will be to *their* advantage while also trying to respect their work needs. If you're dealing with a boss who works on weekends but you don't, you could say, "I want you have what you need for your work on the weekends. Could we do a check-in on Friday mornings to see if there's anything you foresee needing me to prep for the weekend?"

Or if you've got a colleague who is always disrupting your schedule with last-minute requests, tell them you are only able to give thoughtful input to a presentation deck if received 24 hours before they need to hear back from you.

In this way, setting proactive boundaries helps individuals, helps workflow, and can help a whole team to improve its performance.

Once you set a boundary, holding it becomes the next challenge. This applies in your personal life as well. For example, you may have been in your power to set a boundary with a dating partner (i.e., you won't see them again unless you feel safe, seen, and supported in the relationship), but maintaining it is about keeping a commitment to yourself. It has to come from your place of knowing you deserve better, knowing your energy and attention is sacred and you have a choice where to direct it. It's imagining the magic that is made when two people (or a team of people) in their power come together—trusting you can have that and not settling for less. When you are feeling out of your power and are tempted to loosen a boundary in order to get a quick hit of validation, it can be helpful to remind yourself of your Horizon Point or to act in the service of your purpose and Go Direct!

Set Boundaries to Carve Out Time you Need

Some of us may be contributing to the problems of intrusions on our time and excessive workload because we believe we have to be available all the time for our teams. Many leaders I work with struggle with this balancing act.

My client Jackie is the Senior VP of a mortgage originator team. After she brought on three new team members, her workload and schedule became overly taxing because she felt she had to spend a good deal of time teaching each of them about the ins and outs of the business while also maintaining her high level of loan volume. She prided herself on being available to the new employees, but she could see that she needed to take charge of this situation. Her Horizon Point was to be a Calm, Clear Thinker.

We worked to create a decision tree to set clear boundaries about when they should (and shouldn't) come to her. She outlined the situations in which they should call or email her, and she would hop right on the phone with them. And she educated them on those in which they should first consult the training materials to qualify the buyer or call the operations manager rather than her. This took the excessive load off her and enabled the team to increase their closed loan volume that year from $30 to $80 million.

Many leaders get overwhelmed spending so much of their days putting out fires and rushing from meeting to meeting that they don't do as much longer-term, goal-setting planning as they know they should be doing. If this is you, you can review your schedule to set sacrosanct time for it. My client Kara, for example, has carved out "strategic thinking lunchtime." She protects her calendar and puts an email autoresponder that she is working on a strategic vision. She works remotely, and now two days a week she goes to the living room in her home to sit on a comfy reading chair with a hot beverage, puts on some jazz music, and reviews printed out summaries of conference proceedings in her field, with a writing pad by her side to jot down ideas that come to her.

Take ownership of your days. You have more power over your calendar than you think. Try to have fun with it. You are the Thermostat!

Many people want to set boundaries at work and still be seen as a high performer and a team player. Here's a cheat sheet of guidance to get you started:

How to Say No to Requests and Stay a Team Player

- Acknowledge the request so the person knows you received it.

- Be caring but direct: "I would like to help you, but my plate is full with urgent projects" or "I'm sorry, I can't," or "I am fully committed." (Note if your projects are for a leader you have in common.)

- Convey thoughtfulness about their need and display your generous intention. Offer how you might accommodate with a different deadline, resources, scope, or other change: change- or alternative solutions.

- If responding to your manager or team member, ask if you can look together at the assignment applying the filter of priorities set for the group

- Ask if you can do only a part, or just the part you can readily do (e.g,. attend the part of the meeting they will be discussing your update, not the whole meeting.)

- Think out loud how you would approach the problem so they benefit from your experience even if you can't do it for them.

- Educate people how you are now sculpting your role to include less of what they are asking you to do and more of what you are deeply focusing on now.

- If this is a role clarity issue, offer to meet to resolve it at the team level.

Use Active Questions to Take Back Control over Intrusive People

Most of us have had a client or manager who runs right over our boundaries. I advised an architect at a training who had a client obsessed with getting more from her firm, asking for items beyond his budget, and badgering her, asking why he wasn't getting it. She was overwhelmed, flustered, and afraid that she was going to lose it with him.

Instead, she could use active questions to structure the interaction between them. We scripted a neutral-toned email in which she reminded him of the scope of work that was written into their contract, saying that this was the extent of work that she could do for him within the budget agreed on. She explained that she and her team had already had to put in time for many more meetings than had been planned. Then she offered an active question: "We can do *abc* for the original budget. If you would like the redesign that involves also doing *xyz*, this is outside of what we've contracted for and we can do that for $___ additional charge. *Which do you prefer?*"

An active question structures the intrusive person to contain them. You're giving them a clear choice to make and handing them the responsibility for doing so. You are also showing respect for their needs, conveying that you understand how important the additional work is to them rather than focusing on making them wrong for their expectations. It allows both you *and* the client, or whomever you're having this problem with, to be in your power.

Another great way to clarify where boundaries of your time are being violated is to put together a one sheet of all the projects you have on your plate. This is especially helpful with managers. This allows you to give them a "shock and awe" visual so that they can see at a glance *all* you have going on and agree the load is impossible. Then you can lead a problem-solving discussion by asking active questions about their priorities, such as, "Which is the priority to complete first, *a* or *b*?" or "Would you prefer I finish *a* before starting *b* or could we bring in outside resources to take on some of the load?"

I coached a high performer to use an active question with her manager who gave her 20% less on her bonus despite widespread praise for her work. We were both upset about the way he didn't recognize her, and I thought, "Not on my watch is this going to happen!" So we put together a follow-up strategy. She asked if she could revisit the review to better understand what he was looking for from her. She brought in a one-sheet summary of all the projects she had worked on with their results expressed in terms of their ROI for his high-priority outcomes. She asked, "What aspect of these projects didn't deserve a bonus?" Rest assured, he restored her full bonus!

Reactive Boundaries

You can set a boundary in response to someone who has sparked a No inside you, indicating they have crossed a boundary. A boundary is *not* about changing others. It's about defining *who you want to be and what you want to experience* when you are in relationship to them. A boundary is not a threat to others—it's a statement about you and the rules you set up for yourself: "If your actions look like this, my actions will look like that." It's taking a stand for you.

A basic building block for setting a boundary is to use this frame: "If you do *x*, I will do *y*." I have someone in my personal life whom I love and want to keep a close connection with. Yet in some moments they can become extremely critical of me. Especially if we are talking by phone, with care and calm I set a boundary: "I hear that your intention is to give me guidance on what I need to do differently. But it cuts me down and distracts me when I am committed to staying in my power, so I'm not going to continue to listen to what you're saying. Do you have something new you haven't told me before that you're ready to add to our conversation? If so, I'd like to hear it. If not, I'm letting you know that I'm going to get off the phone now."

Now it's your turn. Where is a scenario you are experiencing a *no*?

Do you now have the mindset that you will regain your power if you set a boundary? What boundary you want to set?

Which Proactive or Reactive strategies will help you preserve your well-being while maintaining the relationship?

Take a first pass at scripting your boundary here:

_____

_____

_____.

***

Protection beyond Boundaries: Putting Up Barriers

Some of the people we have difficulties with in our lives act so squarely in our *no* zone that we are instantly kicked out of our power. Some are hypercritical, others brute bullies, and especially "crazy making" are people who have narcissistic qualities. And some environments still tolerate sexual harassers. With all of these types, even if you can't change their behavior, there's still a whole range of strategies you can try to protect yourself from absorbing the effects of their negative behavior.

The Special Problem of Narcissists

How do you know if you're dealing with a narcissist or someone with narcissistic tendencies? You will likely be on the receiving end of:

- *Criticism and blame:* You are repeatedly criticized whether your behavior merits it or not; you are held responsible for things that go wrong in the other person's world whether you had anything to do with it or not.

- *Lying and gaslighting:* The person will make assertions that are true only in their mind and not based on facts. They will create false narratives about how you are at fault and they are not, and they will outright deny their bad behavior or errors, even if they are obvious.

Narcissists must be dealt with strategically because they will stop at nothing to put themselves one up and you one down. If you don't recognize that you're dealing with a narcissist, you will repeatedly be confused by their lies and deflections. Their false assertions are likely to make you question your own view of the situation and your own judgment. This weakens you in relation to the narcissist with the effect you might even think you deserve their mistreatment. They might even convince you that you need their support because you don't trust yourself.

Mita Mallick is a knowledgeable and influential Chief Diversity Officer at Carta and co-host with Dee C. Marshall of *Brown Table Talk* podcast (which shares stories and solutions to the common microaggressions toward women of color). She described her experience of being gaslighted by a narcissistic colleague in an article in the *Harvard Business Review* and also on my *Power Shift* podcast. She recalled: "I would be putting together proposals recommendations, and my boss would say, "Of course you should come present it to the executive team, that would be wonderful." And then I'd be waiting for the invite. But it wouldn't come. The day of one meeting he'd suggested I attend, I texted him to check if I should attend and got no response. Then I got a note from another senior leader saying that my boss had said I was out on vacation and had presented my proposal to the team himself. He would also tell me that I was on the path for promotion but then turn right around and say that I was incompetent and that no one else in the organization would want me on their team."

Want to know why people act in such a destructive way toward others? Settle comfortably in your seat and let me walk you through what's going on backstage with a narcissist. A person who is narcissistic can often be charming and create a spiderweb of loyalists around them who will protect them. Early in your relationship they will indoctrinate you to become loyal to them (in a romantic relationship this is known as love bombing)— showering you with support to lure you into trust, and constantly reminding you what they do for you.

A high percentage of people who are difficult to deal with in this way have had repeated early childhood experiences in which they were helpless to control their physical and/or emotional safety. When children are in circumstances that are so emotionally (or physically) dangerous and harmful, it can be too unbearable to experience the terror and rage of it. Children also feel a sense of intense shame—even though they are not the doer of these acts—because they have been led to have a lead story that they deserved this treatment. Those who suffer such extreme experiences often find ways to not feel these intense emotions as a way of preserving themselves and preventing sheer emotional overwhelm. They systematically develop coping strategies to *not feel* their strong emotions in response to these experiences.

It seems hard to imagine someone so manipulative as previously so vulnerable, but that's the reason in their current life they deny these feelings of helplessness in themselves. Instead, they "split off this part of them" and project it outside of them so the vulnerable feelings are no longer "in" them or "about" them. They put their helplessness into you, psychologically speaking. Or else they make themselves psychologically powerful by acting toward you in a way that makes *you* feel the powerlessness *they* cannot feel inside themselves—known as "turning passive into active."

In other words, their controlling behavior toward you *is not actually about you*. And therein lies *your power* to deal with them. Your power is, first, to not internalize what is being projected onto you by them. You also have the power to limit as much as possible your interaction with the person.

Here are 7 strategies to protect yourself from people who are narcissistic or bullies:

1. <u>Accept that their behavior is not about you and it's never going to change. Don't waste your energy trying to change them.</u> This acceptance might even enable you to have some compassion for them. You only have to interact with them for a certain number of minutes or hours a day, but they have to live with themselves 24/7.

2. <u>Radically minimize engagement</u>. Stay away from interacting with them as much as possible. If you must interact, do so in a way that radically minimizes their ability to get their hooks into you. Show as little engagement as is humanly possible when interacting with them. The metaphor you want to aspire to is to be a "gray rock"—flat, drab, and monotone. Be robotic, straightforward, and concise in your communications. This is your opportunity to do your best "apathetic teenager" imitation, responding to all obnoxious communications with the equivalent of *whatever* (shoulder shrug and eyeroll are optional).

   Hint: Dealing with a narcissist is a great time to use cooling breath (from the Physiology portal) to keep yourself in a state of calm and connected to your own Horizon Point.

3. <u>Avoid futile attempts at accountability.</u> Keep in mind that a narcissistic person generally lives only in the moment, and all they care about is how the situation is making them feel *right now*. They often won't remember what they said earlier, even if it was contradictory. Calling them on past bad behavior will be futile.

   If you have to engage, you can make the relationship as good as possible by approaching them with empathy. You don't have to approve of their behavior, but it helps to avoid inflaming them. If you can be genuine and not have an obvious tone of shining them on, you can say something like "I know you have a lot of hopes for this project and are trying to steer it in a good direction."

4. <u>Narcissists respond to power.</u> They respect people who have and display power, that is, when responding directly to them. (I'm less encouraging of trying to pull a power play on them because they will stop at nothing to tear you down in retaliation.) Choose your battles, but sometimes it's important that the record stands corrected because it has implications for your review or reputation.

   If the criticism is systematic, you can put together irrefutable evidence that they are incorrect in their perception. Be firm when you bring it to their attention. In one of my programs, Beth, was constantly admonished by her narcissistic boss for having the worst record of missing deadlines for the projects she was managing, but she knew her counterparts were missing deadlines, too. The underlying problem was the manager's unrealistic deadlines. She accessed the group database that kept the schedules for projects, and was able to put together a memo that showed the reality, which was she actually had the second best record of meeting deadlines. She presented this information to her manager in a performance review meeting, and from then on her manager never again got on her case about missing deadlines.

   Bullies respect when you leverage your power, *but to prevent retaliation you must approach them in a calm but firm tone, in a one-on-one, not public, setting.* Be concise and neutral in your statement of the facts, and then move on to the next subject. Allow their silence to let them save face. Don't expect acknowledgment, just know you're justified.

   If their behavior will have an adverse implication for you with other people, it's more important to consider repairing your reputation with other decision makers who will have a say in your future than it is to do so in the impenetrable mind of the narcissist.

5. <u>Get Visibility:</u> It's always helpful to document disempowering treatment so that you have tangible evidence of it. If others you work with are also subject to this behavior, a collective report

of these incidents carries even more weight. Some people are unsure whether their HR professionals are able to protect them. If you have a close relationship with someone in the function, you can report the situation generically without naming names and ask for their advice on how to handle such a situation. If they have a response that makes you trust them, you could ask for an investigation to determine the facts of the matter.

6. <u>Join with them.</u> While the tone of criticism may be utterly inappropriate, and much of the substance of it may be off-base, some of what they are saying may have a kernel of truth to it. In these cases, you may be able to tone down their abuse by "agreeing" with them on the kernel with a light touch. *This takes the wind out of their sails,* leaving them nothing else to say about it.

    For example, my client had a hypercritical C-suite boss who intrusively berated her for missing a big meeting due to a flare-up of her health issues. This was truly a low blow. Her health issues developed after a prolonged traumatic divorce, and a great irony was that her boss was contributing to the flare-ups by causing her more stress with bullying. My client's strategy was to say to her boss, "Yeah, it's true that it's important for me to manage my health, and I'm actively working on it. Thank you for your interest." Done.

7. <u>Leave</u> As Mita Mallick shared, she followed the advice that "you can't heal in the place that hurt you." In her power, she took action to not stay in the organization where she was being gaslighted. And she learned to become much more attuned to and protect herself from organizations, relationships, or situations where someone might downplay her contributions or dim her light because of factors that have to do with the other person, not her.

    It's understandable if you've stayed, you may have been manipulated and gotten out of your power. But now, if the situation is beyond your desire to expend your energy on, you can leave. Find a new position/opportunity, whether inside the company or elsewhere—just to get away from them. Leaving a role can be your power move as long as it's a role you choose and are excited about.

[If you skipped all the way from Chapter 2 to read about dealing with a narcissist, I hope you got some useful strategies! Now it's time to start with the first portal and work your way through the rest of the book, because these strategies build on others.]

The Special Case of Harassment

If you are in a situation where you are being harassed, you must set firm barriers. *You are not to blame if someone else acts inappropriately toward you.* It is the responsibility of workplaces and our culture at large to provide a safe place to bring your talents and be compensated for them. You want to enforce minimal or no contact and get out from under the harasser.[5]

If you want to stay in your organization or community where the harassment or assault happened, you may be able to structure terms of protection that will allow you to stay in your position. A client of mine was groped by her company's CEO while they were on a business trip together. She asked HR for the requirement that she not ever have to travel together with him or be in a room alone with him, and this was granted and enforced. She was moved into a role in which she did not have daily contact with him. Within six months she found that unsatisfying, so she left to start her side hustle. She can control the narrative and was able to see this not as a cop-out or "him winning" but rather as a power move where she took a stand for her life.

If a lead story gets reactivated by the harasser's actions and makes you feel that you don't matter or are worthless, you can reclaim power. Use your energies to make every one of their insults an opportunity to make a stronger connection to your own self. Reinforce your new life story, and remind yourself to keep showing up at your Horizon Point.

Do you have someone in your life who is a narcissistic, harassing, or a boundary buster? It's *not* easy to deal with the force of someone like this. Which of the 7 barrier strategies will work to best protect yourself?

_____

_____

_____

***

Now that you are protecting yourself with strategies to preserve your well-being, you might notice that you wanted to tell the offending person what you really think and feel, and get them to show you the respect you deserve. You'll learn that in the next portal.

In Your Power Practices: Protection

1. Identify your internal signals of Yes and No so you will know when you need to protect yourself with boundaries or barriers.

2. Deepen your commitment to believing you are worthy of being treated with respect. This mindset will help you hold your boundaries once set.

3. What's a proactive boundary you can set today to prevent yourself from having to play whack-a-mole going forward?

4. Where is a situation in your life you can use the boundary-setting formula "If you do x, I will do y" or use active questions to deal with people who overreach and intrude?

5. You now have 7 strategies that set a barrier to minimize contact and protect yourself from someone who's narcissistic or bullying. Which can you apply to maintain your well-being starting today?

CHAPTER 12

Powerful Truth: From Angry to Authentic

"From caring comes courage."

—Chinese philosopher Lao Tzu

Lisa was the head of human resources, and she knew she needed to do *something*. This was 2019, when DEI leaders were already fighting a lack of urgency in their organizations (which we still are despite greater awareness of injustices and ROI data.) Frustrated that she wasn't being heard, she internalized the blame. She was a perfectionist who wanted to prove her worth and felt bad about herself. She was also dedicated to inclusive values. She had inner churn whether to stay or go.

Lisa was planning on approaching the next leadership team meeting with the usual—an elaborate PowerPoint with graphs of where the company stood on their metrics, accompanied by her strategic vision of their goals. She felt a sense of resignation, they'd just glaze over and go on with business as usual. Yet she wanted to take the company beyond scoreboards to embedding DEI in their DNA.

I told her she was ready to share with them her powerful truth: her observations about the lack of change and her passion about creating a culture of true inclusion and respect. We crafted a script for her to kick off the meeting, along the lines of "We're 30% of the way toward our diversity, equity, and inclusion goals, and it's the end of the year. *This is not okay with me.* Where else are we okay with accepting 30% of our business objectives? I'm holding us accountable for doing better, myself included. I want to hear from each of us: What do we *really* want in our culture? What is the real issue we are uncomfortable with that's getting in the way? I'll start by sharing where I haven't been doing enough. And then I want us to each personally commit to equity in our teams."

Lisa's firm statement and openness about her own need to do more rallied the leadership team to have a set of candid and vulnerable conversations that brought them closer and in alignment about making real progress. Culture initiatives became a priority, integrated into the fabric of daily business, led with personal ownership by each member of the executive team.

You speak a powerful truth because you need to express it and know it needs to be said. It aligns what you think and feel with what you say and do. It puts you back in your power because it helps you break through your reservations about speaking up, and allowing the status quo to get the better of you.

It's powerful because you have dared to speak it when others haven't. It's using your voice to own *your truth.* Then it is something that can—and must—be dealt with by others.

Using language or intonation outside of the norm of everyday conversation shakes us out of complacency. Your presence and delivery without waver or attempt to please sets a new standard. You are showing them more of who you really are, a new degree of your authenticity and humanity. It compels the listener to interact with you on new terms and requires them to pay attention to you with a new level of engagement. Whereas protection is about articulating what you won't stand for, your powerful truth is about giving voice to what you *do* stand for. With both, you stop the power leaks that came from feeling like you were spinning and couldn't use your voice.

Though not intended to get validation, you do want to engage people. In the portal of Powerful Truth you will learn to express your Powerful Truth so it moves others to action.

A Powerful Truth doesn't have to be a fancy polished speech. It can simply reflect what is true for you. Fun fact: You wouldn't be reading this book right now if I hadn't shared a Powerful Truth. I was approached by the publisher to write a follow-up to my first book, *Success under Stress*, because readers were hungry for advice on stress and resilience due to overwhelm and changes in our world. I said that I didn't think the world needed another book on how to deal with generic stress, because plenty of blogs and videos had been posted on the topic in the prior two years, and I had already covered that topic. I said I would only write a book that would add value.

We hopped on a call to discuss. I shared my perspective that while yes, burnout comes from the stress of too much to do, the real issue underlying mental well-being is a lack of a sense of power which grinds us down. I shared that people who are highly busy but in their power thrive (they just need more rest!), but the unifying theme causing stress in many people today is being in situations where they don't feel in control, don't feel seen/heard/impactful—and don't have skills to be in their power. If they were open to me writing a book on that, I was in!

I had no idea how my editor would respond. I didn't have a fully fleshed out idea yet. I just thought about all the people who might be going through their day reactively or made to feel diminished, and I shared my vision of how solutions would help them. I wasn't worried about what he would think about me, I had *non-attachment* to the outcome. In my meeting with him, I just "sang my song." My editor said nothing for some time while I described my vision for the book, but then he responded . . . that he loved the concept. Boom!

Speaking your Powerful Truth will make you feel vulnerable, but it unlocks new possibilities.

You can share your powerful truth with one person to compel them to see you or convey what you truly need in your relationship with them. Or you can share it with a team of people or an audience. You can share a powerful truth to hold others accountable because they've said something or acted in a way that violates your values or devalues you (or others).

You want to listen to the voice inside you saying this is *not okay* and things have to change. We often hold back on expressing these truths because we worry about how people will respond. We have also all been conditioned, especially in a professional setting, to minimize our expression of emotion and avoid raising hot button issues, especially ones that could make people in power uncomfortable or look bad.

For example, Catalyst research shows that 86% of men want to intervene to stop microaggressive acts toward women, but less than 20% do so directly because of fear of saying the wrong thing or risking impeding their career.[1] This is indicative that we *all* feel pressure not to speak up about uncomfortable or potential volatile truths. Which is why when you contemplate addressing them, you might freeze up, even though you feel rage coursing through your veins. You might even feel your throat constrict, making you feel literally voiceless. This is a vital message you are onto something that is deeply important to you.

If you don't share your truth, you leak your power and get the double whammy of being angry not only with the offending person or people but also with yourself—you'll probably kick yourself for the rest of the day if you don't speak up.

Vulnerable as speaking your truth may make you feel, when you share with such openness and authenticity, you are able to create space for conversations that haven't seemed possible.

When truth is spoken and acknowledged, tension is released from the room. The human body resonates with honesty.

When you are authentic, you allow others to be authentic as well, creating a virtuous cycle of deeper connection and alignment.

Nabeela Ixtabalan, who is Chief Operating Officer of Walmart Canada, expressed this beautifully when she told me about an experience of sharing her powerful truth.[2]

She recalls, "I was on a plane from Copenhagen to Toronto, where I was relocating to start my journey at Walmart Canada. As I was thinking through my first 100-day plan, I just kept writing two words over and over: "Stop pretending. Stop pretending." I hadn't spoken at work about my recent struggles with anxiety or postpartum depression, and my inner voice told me to be more authentic and vulnerable."

When she did speak about her reality, she said, "The response was overwhelming. So many people reached out and said, 'Thank you, I've had the same experience.'"

By sharing her powerful truth, she was a catalyst for her organization to focus more on the mental health and well-being of its employees, leading to substantial improvements. They launched a Compassionate Leadership training throughout the organization, and she recounts, "We destigmatized things that we wouldn't have talked about at work before, whether mental health or racial inequity, or any trauma that people are experiencing." Six months after the launch of the training, Walmart Canada, reported a 28% improvement in psychological safety. The company also reported many other positive effects for employees, such as healthier eating habits.

I asked Nabeela what enabled her to have the courage to share so authentically. She replied, "I asked myself, 'Do I believe in people's judgment? Or do I believe in their compassion?' Because anytime I take that leap of being vulnerable or authentic, I go through a door. I see one door which is the judgment of people I know and don't know. And the other door is the compassion of people I know and don't know. I choose to believe in people's compassion. That's what gets me over the hump, to be confident in sharing, taking the risk of judgment, or being disregarded, or being stigmatized."

When you share your powerful truth, it can have a snowball effect in creating the change you know needs to happen.

Call to mind all of the people you are championing, and they will give you courage. You won't be alone in that meeting room or that one-on-one or on that stage alone.

In addition to keeping in mind the good you may be able to do for others, here are five guidelines that will help you be intentional and firm about sharing your powerful truth.

Transcend Your Personal Hurt and Frame the Collective Hurt

You can transform the personal hurt of any situation into a memorable lesson from which others can learn.

This is what Representative Alexandria Ocasio-Cortez (D-NY) did when she gave a powerful speech in 2020 on the floor of the US House of Representatives[3] in response to being publicly called "f___ing b____" by a Representative from Florida. Ocasio-Cortez didn't make it about her. She took it out of the "me versus you" context and spoke to the underlying, systemic issues that would allow a Congressman to act with such disrespect. She stated that she represented not only her Congressional district, but "every congresswoman and every woman in this country. Because all of us have had to deal with this in some form, some way, some shape, at some point in our lives. . . . This is not new, and that is the problem. . . . It is cultural. It is a culture of impunity, of accepting violence and violent language against women, and an entire structure of power that supports that." She also busted myths and common justifications, saying "Just because he has a wife or a daughter doesn't mean he respects women."

Ocasio-Cortez processed the hurt privately and used her public statements to frame the collective hurt and raise visibility about the problem. If you're feeling hurt and angry about the behavior you want to address by speaking your truth, use the strategies in the Physiology portal to move those emotions through. Then take ownership of the narrative about the situation you're addressing, following the guidance in the Psyche portal. Once you are clear on your truth, ask yourself what's the collective issue that your personal hurt reflects.

Speaking a powerful truth is using your strength for the good of all.

In his article "What It's Like to Be a Black Man in Tech,"[4] technology professional LeRon Barton wrote about speaking his powerful truth concerning the pervasive discrimination he experienced along with other Black colleagues. Writing in *Harvard Business Review*, he shared "When I started to be more outspoken, I realized that I am not an individual, but part of a collective. My efforts to make tech more equitable are not just about me, but the networking engineer, the programmer, the project manager, and all of the other professionals that will come after."[3] By addressing the collective hurt, he made his powerful truth a catalyst for cultural reckoning.

Use a Strategic Display of Emotion

You can use to your advantage the discomfort people have been conditioned to feel about expression of emotion in the workplace. When *you* genuinely connect to your feelings and you can express them but still stay composed, you will rivet the attention of your listener. Even a slight rise in the tone of your voice makes others alert and even slightly fearful that your emotion will escalate out of control. This will stir others to listen to you intently.

An inspiring example of this is Greta Thunberg's impassioned speech at the UN Climate Summit in 2019[5] expressing her indignance at the lack of action about the crisis.

> People are suffering. People are dying. Entire ecosystems are collapsing. We are in the beginning of a mass extinction, and all you can talk about is money and fairy tales of eternal economic growth. How dare you!

> For more than 30 years, the science has been crystal clear. How dare you continue to look away and come here saying that you're doing enough, when the politics and solutions needed are still nowhere in sight.

> You are failing us. But the young people are starting to understand your betrayal. The eyes of all future generations are upon you. And if you choose to fail us, I say: We will never forgive you.

You can do this in an interpersonal scenario, too. The IT team leader Elisa, whom we met in the Partnership portal, did this gracefully in talking with the senior IT leader who had criticized her and told her she should fire her team. Recall that she and I scripted a constructive conversation with him using the POWERS of communication approach. When she got to the S (say what you mean, and mean what you say), she also shared her powerful truth.

She said, "My team and I worked very hard to prepare your department's budget, and help you get the resources you need. In response, you said I should fire my team. For you to not recognize the effort we've put in and come back to me with a criticism of my team, that hurt and disrespected me. I ask you to show me respect in our conversations going forward." (Depending on the relationship you could also say "in order for me to support your team I need you to show me respect." She eventually filed a report on an egregious public act of disrespect he did and he was moved out of his position 3 months later.)

Allow yourself a notch more latitude to increase the vigor of your emotional expression, especially when you are responding to injustice. Remember that you are channeling your voice for the good of *all*. Even if it's only a private interaction between you and someone else, anytime you speak against mistreatment and make a stand for respect, you contribute to creating a *world that we all want to live in.*

For women, being able to express emotion in this strategic way is especially important because women have been stigmatized as "overly emotional," and if they call out others on their bad behavior and express any anger in doing so, they're characterized as "strident." This no-win scrutiny of women has been an impediment to them ascending to leadership positions, and the discriminatory stereotypes are even more intense for Black and Latina women.

If you are speaking in the heat of the moment and you express a higher pitch of emotion than you would intend, allow yourself not to have to be "perfect." You are justified at being upset by disrespectful and rude treatment, and you do not have to apologize for doing so.

A great way to neutralize any bias that you are being "overly emotional" is to show your self-awareness. This involves showing others that you are being intentional in expressing your emotion. You might say something like, "I am aware that I am speaking with a high level of passion about this, and *let me tell you why I think this is so important . . .* " or ". . . *why I think we need to bring this level of urgency and emphasis to this issue . . .*"

It's best to speak once you have processed your raw emotion through, so even if your voice conveys a quiver, you're not fully reliving it while speaking. Yet you won't always have time to process your emotions, so it's to be expected that sometimes your powerful truth will just come out spontaneously even if you try to hold the feelings back. It's okay, you no longer have to keep something inside of you that is putting you out of your power. Know that anyone capable of empathy, and even people who have been impervious to your pleas, will be moved by your genuine display of emotion. Human beings are built to have emotional resonance with others.

If you are sharing with someone who genuinely cares about you and with whom you feel safe, this kind of release of emotion can bring you closer. If the person dismisses or attacks you, then this person is no longer safe for you, or at least you cannot be fully open with them. There is nothing wrong with you for having the feelings you are having. What that response to your display of feelings does mean is that this person is not capable of seeing or interacting with the authentic you. It would be better to accept that and protect yourself from that person. Talk to someone else who genuinely does care and would want to help you get your needs met.

When you open up with those you feel you can trust in this way, showing the intensity of the emotion you feel about your truth allows the other person to see you with a deeper level of humanity. Suddenly, things you may have tried to hint at or have asked for less forcefully can be seen as urgent for you, and the other person is required to reckon with the new truth. Adjusting to this new truth with another often brings forth a new level of honesty that goes both ways and raises your level of connection. The other person must now see you closer to the way you see yourself. Your openness about how strongly you feel requires them to challenge themselves to really hear you and be caring and thoughtful in response.

My friend Ann was able to understand her child more deeply and provide more empathetic parenting after her child shared a powerful truth. Ann's child shared about a difficult experience with a college professor who had made an intrusive and uninformed comment about gender identity in class. Her child opened up about feeling unsafe around the professor and showed anger and disappointment when talking about the incident. Her child shared that they experienced themselves as fluid in their gender identity, outside the prevailing understanding of gender and not identifying with either one. They said at different times and in different contexts they enjoy being seen as a boy and as a girl and expressing themselves across a range of what is considered masculine and feminine. They then asked Ann to refer from then on to them as "my child" rather than "my daughter." This was an eye-opening experience for Ann, and she has since been intentional about seeing the world through her child's eyes and supporting their experience.

This is a good example of how a powerful truth, whether scripted or not, becomes a game-changer.

How could you strategically display emotion as you share your powerful truth? What's the tone you want to set when sharing your powerful truth? Is there a powerful truth bubbling inside you that you might blurt out? How can you bring it forth in an intentional way? Write a first draft script here:

_____

_____

_____

Connect the Dots and Bust Myths That Perpetuate the Problem

Many people perpetuate status quo and make uninformed statements because they are not informed of (or choose to not take account of) the underlying factors that you are aware of and that make you uncomfortable, unsafe, or outraged. Just because they don't see it or abide by it doesn't mean it's not true. Sharing a powerful truth helps you connect the dots of events, circumstances, and personal experiences so others can come to see your perspective, too.

Connecting the dots to illuminate the larger injustice helps to turn dismissal into awareness. Deepa Purushothaman, the author of *The First, the Few, the Only: How Women of Color Can Redefine Power in Corporate America*, connected the dots about women of color's experiences in an article about what she calls "the inclusion delusion" in *Fortune* magazine.[6]

> Companies have stepped up to the plate to hire us, flaunt us in team photos and charity dinners, and offer us up as evidence that they have a diverse workforce. However, they don't pay attention to how challenging it is for us to feel a part of their cultures . . .
>
> When we arrive, we think our title and position of power will give us the opportunity to create change. Then the truth sets in: What's being asked of us is to fit into an existing culture, not to evolve it . . .
>
> As women of color, you need us more than we need your jobs. You need us because as the workplace becomes more diverse, you need diverse leaders with authentic power.

You can also share your powerful truth in a family or intimate relationship. A friend of mine was finally able to tell her father that his demeaning comments and behavior toward women had been hurtful to her. She connected the dots between his behavior and its effects on her, of which he was previously unaware. She wrote him a letter, when he was 89 years old, which shows that a powerful truth has no expiration date, and you can always benefit from sharing it. Here's an excerpt from the letter, which she agreed to share with you:

> Dad . . . You are NOT appropriate as much as You may think you are. And I have suffered the consequences of that. You've said whatever you want wherever you want without thinking for a moment about the message you are sending. I learned from you that women are meat to be used by men. That's thoughtless and self-centered parenting and it hurt your kids, especially your daughters. Not trusting men has impacted my life, my marriage, my well-being.

As a kid I dreamed of having a father who was gentle, caring, interested in me, and respectful of girls/women. For years, I justified your behavior by saying to myself, "Yeah, but Dad was an amazing provider." But, being a provider for your family is the baseline. It does not give you the right to mis-treat your family members. It's true, you've become more loving as you've aged but I am not here for your demeaning words anymore.

Her father passed away just four months later, but because she had shared her powerful truth with him, she was in a state of resolution and for the first time in her life could be at peace with him.

Stating her truth with her father also gave her more of a voice with everyone else in her life. In particular, she also shared her truth with her husband, saying that that she felt taken for granted by him at times and that she needed more quality and respectful attention from him, and less of his moodiness and irritability. He could hear the genuine interest in connection and the firmness in her tone. He responded by going to therapy and becoming much more engaged and aware of his behavior with her, regaining their previously positive connection and enjoying a summerlong trip together— again exemplifying the ripple effects of sharing your truth.

Sharing a powerful truth helps to educate offending actors about the issue they may have been perpetuating without the awareness. Once they are aware, you can hold them accountable for their actions.

What are the circumstances, injustices, or inefficiencies that harm you? How might you be able to concisely connect dots and bust some myths so others can understand the scenario like you do?

_____

_____

_____

Create an Opportunity to Educate and Encourage Partnership

In the wake of a disrespectful comment, you take your power back by shifting your focus away from your inner swirl and put the onus back onto the person who issued the insulting comment. This counter-response turns the attention and responsibility back on them, so they must be more precise about justifying the charged word or offending action. It spotlights the discomforts of their own experience instead of their vague or distorted perception about you.

As in the sport of Aikido, you can alchemize the negative energy of the attacking person and redirect it back to them more positively. You want to try not to shame the other person, or group of people, because that tends to shut them down, and they won't want to participate in growthful conversation. Engage them *with you* in surfacing the truth.

You don't have to get the words exactly right. In fact, the best response is simply to reply with a spirit of clarification and ask a neutral question. You can simply ask with genuine curiosity "What did you mean by that?" Or just stand firm in your power, look the person in the eye and ask "Did you mean that??"

Here are a few examples from a training I gave this year for women in health care of how you can be the steward even when others make uninformed or biased comments. One physician spoke her truth to a doctor who had slung the stereotyping accusation at her that she was "being emotional." She stopped him mid-sentence and stated clearly *"When I speak with clarity, it does not mean that I'm emotional.* I want you to recognize that you're likely saying that because I'm Black and I'm a woman. I ask you to reflect on that." He apologized immediately and later emailed her a formal apology. He stopped making any such devaluing comments in the future.

Another physician was in a meeting with colleagues reviewing candidates for their team, and one of the male participants commented about a candidate, who was a woman, that she was "a direct communicator," a not-so-subtle way of saying he saw her as too outspoken. Instead of calling him out for the comment, I suggested she ask him, "I think this is one of those words with different meanings for different people. What did *you* mean by that? How do you see her directness affecting her effectiveness as a physician and leader?" Now the onus was on him to explain himself.

Often when we highlight an inappropriate comment, the speaker says they were unaware of or deny the negative effect of their behavior. To educate them, you can use the language of "intent versus impact." You can help them see that even if their words were not intended to cause harm, they had a harmful impact. You could also say: "Sometimes people say things, and they are not aware of how it is received. Let me tell you how I received what you just said. . . ." Share your powerful truth about how you felt upon hearing their comment.

You're acting as the steward of the situation, helping achieve some greater good that can be served by making them aware of what is wrong about their language or actions. This again takes courage, so start with a nourishing deep breath! Spoiler alert— you are going to feel *so* proud of yourself after doing it!

Next you can suggest a better way. This shows that you want to engage in problem-solving with them, and you are giving them an opportunity to take you up on that possibility. In the case of the "direct communicator" comment, for example, you could share, "What would have felt different to me is if you had raised a concern about her behavior with an objective link to its implications for her as a doctor. Or if you made sure to compare your perception of her to other physicians we have interviewed with similar behavior." With this approach, you potentially invite those who have offended into a constructive conversation, and you may catalyze an important change in their perspective and behavior.

You can also share your powerful truth to inform other people of what you want and need and to create clarity about how to move forward. In these cases, it's best if you share your truth in a way that is neutral—it gives other people information about what you want to see if they want that, too. Then you'll know if you are a good fit. This is better than sharing your truth in a way that makes other people wrong for being who they are or wanting what they want.

This was a liberating approach for an architect, Leah, when asking the senior leaders of her firm for resources and a next-level role. The structure of her conversation was: "Here's the outcome I'm trying to get. . . . Here's what I need in terms of title, support, and resources in order to be successful." She went into that meeting with the idea that if they said *no*, as she expected they would, then it's clear they don't have the same vision she does, and it's time to leave. As she said, "It gave me so much freedom and confidence to have that conversation because I felt so much less that a no would be a judgment on me. My attitude was. "I'm presenting you an opportunity. And if you decide that it's not for you, then it's not about me and it just made the conversation so much easier to have." P.S. Because she presented it in terms of their WIIFT, of course they gave her all she wanted.

Reclaim the Definition of Words so They Don't Hurt You

Others can't hurt you with their words if you don't take their words or actions negatively. *You* get to choose how you define words. Then you win either way. Representative Ocasio-Cortez embraced the pejorative slung at her and used it with pride and whimsy. She tweeted later that week, "But hey, 'b*tches' get stuff done." I suggested to the female physician she say, "I've been a 'direct communicator' all my life, and I think that's helped me be successful here!" Or "I've been a direct communicator, and I think it's helping me point out this gender bias about being a direct communicator!" (Case closed!)

Humor can be an effective means of communicating about serious issues, bringing them out in the open in a way that shows you are very much in your power, despite attempts to disempower you. A friend who's a senior partner at a law firm told me she was in the middle of an important hallway discussion with two male colleagues when they broke off to head into the men's room. She knew they were going to continue talking without her, and she said to them, "Do you want to reach a final decision about this out here, or do you want me to come in there with you to finish up the conversation?"

You can inject a dose of snark if it fits your personality. As an example, if someone told me I am too "emotional" in a decision making meeting, I might counter, "OMG, you are SO right! I get more and more emotional each time I bring this up and we don't make a decision. Thank you for recognizing how exasperated I am that it took five conversations to get to this point." (Accompanied by a little wink to lighten the mood.) Have endless fun with this!

What is a common occurrence in your workplace or family life where you could prepare in advance with these response templates? Which of these powerful truth statements resonates for you, and whom do you want to say them to in order to create a more psychologically safe environment?

In sum, when you react, you leak your power and get derailed from the impact you are here to make. **When you share your powerful truth, you "raise the vibration" of everyone involved.**

In Your Power Practices: Powerful Truth

1. Your truth is *your truth. Own the value of your voice.* Check in with yourself—what is a powerful truth that needs to be said but you have not yet spoken?

2. When you are ready to share publicly and trying to create change, transcend your personal hurt to frame the collective hurt.

3. You can display emotion strategically to capture others' attention and move them to action. Move your raw emotion through before sharing your truth so that it's clear you are impassioned but not reliving it while speaking. Allow yourself to show your true emotion if it bubbles up; humans resonate with honesty.

4. Connect the dots to help people who may not share your perspective or have walked in your shoes to see the underlying reasons for your truth.

5. Use the opportunity to educate and create partnership so others learn how their words and actions impact you and others. Ask a neutral question, distinguish between the intent and impact of their words/actions, or flip the script on their words. If authentic to you, use humor to stay in your power! You got this!

CHAPTER 13

People: From Alone to Amplified

"I love, but I am not entirely sure how to be loved: how to be seen and known for the utterly flawed woman I am. It demands acknowledging that I am not perfect, but perhaps I deserve affection anyway."

—Roxane Gay, New York Times Best-selling Author of *Bad Feminist*

"I'm not the only one. That is such a relief." I hear this from numerous clients in our first conversation. Knowing others have been up against the same treatment and were confused or near the end of their rope helps us see it's not just about us.

You want reliable strategies you can use on your own to get back in your power to make the idea of home within yourself. But other people can play an important supplemental role in bringing you back there and helping you stay there. Some moments we are so disconnected from our inner resources that we *need* scaffolding from outside of us to bring us back to ourselves. Once you have a foundation of connection to yourself, then others' support, wisdom, and love is the delicious cherry on top of your self-empowerment sundae.

In the portal of People you will learn ways that people can help you reconnect to yourself by reminding you of aspects of yourself you haven't given yourself credit for and by creating an upward spiral taking one another higher.

Humans are deeply social animals, wired to seek a sense of belonging and to live in communities with common goals. Therefore, people can be both the source and solution to our power problems. You want to be mindful about those you trust to open up to and look to for perspective and support.

Here are some watch-outs to keep in mind.

Surround yourself with people who reflect the current empowered version of you, not an outdated perception of you. This disconnect is common in families or among old friends where *you* have come into your power, but they may have not—you need to become Teflon to their limited views of you or else set boundaries and minimize contact with them. Similarly, some friends from work may only see a narrow slice of who you are, so you want to be intentional about what you absorb from your interactions with them. And take active steps to avoid prolonged interaction with people who are not in their power.

When out of our power, we have a strong impulse to pull away from others or put on a show that everything is fine. It's such an instinct we may not even be aware how much we're isolating or hiding. Then we push people away. We deprive ourselves of emotional oxygen our trusted friends and family can provide, as well as perspective from colleagues who've experienced similar challenges.

People who are in their power can role-model for you and make it easier for you to act in your power. This is due to mirror neurons in our brains that cause us to experience what we witness others going through as a sort of simulation.[1] If I see you acting in your power, my mirror neurons will fire up and inspire me to feel that lift in the same way.

Be wary if your first instinct is always to go to others and unload on them, without realizing you are looking primarily for them to validate how wrong the other actors in the situation are. Hearing others' empathy or helpful insights might be the jump start you need to get back in your power. However, if seeking sympathy and talking about it but not doing anything about it has been your go-to strategy, then you now know it's keeping you out of your power. And its keeping your supply lines to your own power dependent on someone else. Time to ditch this pattern!

We Are Wired to Co-Regulate

Connecting with others can help us **regulate** our emotional state. Find people who will help you activate that safe and social state. People who are trusted and who are able to find calm within themselves can be a safe harbor for you, helping shelter you from your emotional storm. Built into humans is the ability to find resonance on an energetic level with others; that person can lend you their calm.

Some of us can find this especially beneficial because our life experiences have made regulating our internal storms on our own more difficult. This might be the case if you didn't receive reliable emotional regulation from caregivers when you were young. In our earliest years as children, our nervous system is chaotic and is regulated primarily by interactions with others. When we signal distress, such as by crying, we will be calmed if a caregiver speaks in a calming voice, picks us up and rocks us, or maybe rubs our hands and feet. From this outside regulation, we learn gradually to soothe ourselves, developing "muscle memory" about how to calm ourselves. But if you didn't consistently receive that emotional regulation from a caregiver, your body may have been more frequently in or stayed longer in emotional turmoil, and you didn't develop as reliable a muscle memory for self-soothing.

When you are really upset about something, you might need other people to help you bear feelings that are too much for you (or any one person) to hold. Especially when you are triggered, someone who's not in a triggered state can literally (or digitally) hold you in their arms, witness you, and be a presence that helps you to know there is an "other side" to the feeling. If you are really upset, regular check-ins with people who know what's going on can carry you through the aloneness of intense emotion. And when traumatic events happen that put us collectively out of our power, joining together gives us solidarity and strength to move through our emotions and regroup with strategic efforts to use our power.

We can even benefit from the emotional regulation we receive from trusting relationships when we're not actually with these people. We create mental representations of the people we care about, so we can conjure in our minds the calming sound of their voice and the soothing warmth of their embrace. If your inner critic is putting you out of your power, you can channel that person's tender voice in your mind. What would they say to you, what wise words would they provide about this situation? You can also use the voice you talk to your loved ones with (your children, spouse, pet) toward yourself.

We also experience emotional contagion—this is why you want to protect yourself from people who are negative and gossipy. The positive version of this can be leveraged, too. Indeed, as psychologist Adam Grant writes in the *New York Times*, "We find our greatest bliss in moments of collective effervescence . . . the sense of energy and harmony people feel when they come together in a group around a shared purpose."[2]

Our bodies have also been designed so that physical touch with someone who is safe for us can have a powerful calming effect and give us a release of the love hormone oxytocin. A six-second kiss, a 20-second hug, or holding hands have been proven to calm our nervous system and boost our sense of well-being.[3] Loving attention and touch communicates that you belong, you are safe, and that you matter.

People help us heal beyond what we can do ourselves. This opportunity is especially acute when we're feeling shame. Shame pulls us away from connecting with others, because it suggests to us that we are not worthy of connection or being loved. We speculate that if others knew what we know about ourselves, they wouldn't accept us.

Even a single interaction opening up to trustworthy others with shame we're feeling can be deeply restorative. As Brené Brown teaches, shame cannot survive being spoken and being empathized with.[4] As soon as you learn that someone else has felt what you are feeling—and you don't think *they* are an incorrigibly flawed human—your self-judgment can evaporate.

Make it part of your purpose to find people you can trust and share openly with so you can take in the effects of their empathy. (And be that person for others.)

If you can come to a clear idea of what would actually be helpful for you in those vulnerable moments, offering guidance to the other person will increase the likelihood you'll get it (rather than reach out to someone in a raw moment and then be angry at them for their disappointing response). For example, you can ask your spouse: "I'd really appreciate it if you would just listen" or "I'm feeling really tender right now so I appreciate your gentle response."

People Hold Up a Mirror for Us

Another way that your trusted confidants can help you stay in your power is by showing you a reflection of yourself. If you have not been nourishing yourself regularly, others may see a beauty, goodness, and capability that you might have forgotten exists in you. Loved ones, partners, trusted colleagues, and mentors open our eyes to aspects of ourselves and our contributions that we've lost sight of or maybe never appreciated or need to learn about. People can stand for your vision in moments when you are near giving up or are taking other people's behavior so personally you forget your purpose. Also, when others see you as more capable than you see yourself, their expectations can inspire you to push yourself to go higher than you thought you could.

So many of us have been taught to fear not having our stuff together. Those who know you see you not through your self-critical lens but as the rockstar you are. Being witnessed in this way and accepted helps you own those disliked parts of yourself rather than trying to hide them. When you experience this de-shaming, you no longer kick yourself out of your power with your self-criticisms, rather you walk in the world with a new boldness where no-one can have their hooks in you.

To get more technical, it's not "people," it's what you take in from people. It's about what your "parts" can take in from "their parts." I bet there are people in your family and work life right now who see your talents and your goodness. I bet they've told you that you're doing a great job(!) But you may shrug it off. You have to be in your power for their reflection of you to stick. You may have been so busy blaming others and berating yourself you that *you have yet to build that place where their sticky note of love can have somewhere to stick onto in you.*

You don't want to squander the love you deserve and the respect you've earned—that's pulling the plug on an oxygen tank that's right in front of you. Consider this as well: When you isolate from those who care for you or hide your pain and confusion from them, you're denying *them* the opportunity to show their love and share their perspective to assist you.

You want to receive others' acknowledgments and let it nourish your power. Sit with their reflections about your accomplishments and your good qualities and notice where do their words of affirmation land in your body? Once you have this experience of yourself in your own body you can recall it anytime and over and over again. Try adding this feeling into the times you upload your Horizon Point. You can also ask them what it is about you that makes them say that so you add texture to their words, and know what it is that you can appreciate about yourself.

Remember that those parts you dislike are parts that you internalized from other people or stories you had to tell yourself in order to keep their emotional and material support. Now you can wear your own mind and decide who *you* want to be and live from your own new life story. Take inspiration from the words of Mary Oliver, in this excerpt of the poem *Wild Geese*:[5]

> *You do not have to be good.*
> *You do not have to walk on your knees*
> *for a hundred miles through the desert repenting.*
> *You only have to let the soft animal of your body*
> *love what it loves.*

Similarly, remember that another person can only reflect back to you what they can know in themselves. If someone is uncomfortable with anger, they will distance from it in themselves and suppress it in you. If a close friend or romantic partner is not comfortable feeling vulnerable, they will avoid or attack you for ways you have healthy vulnerability—and if you didn't have the in-your-power toolkit you've been building, you might have otherwise taken their actions personally. Keep this alternative story at the ready: "They are only able to see me/love me/support me as much as they do themselves," so you won't get stuck in a lead story.

No matter what aspect(s) of yourself they accept or reflect, you want to be able to know the truth of who you are. You want to be able to accept all of you—all "88 keys of your emotional piano." Who you've been and who you are becoming. Then it takes the pressure off others to need to see us where we can't see ourselves.

The Power of the Posse

Participating in a community of others who have a shared experiences with you can be the ultimate in giving and receiving acceptance—like the reflective power of many mirrors combined. This might be a community of people who share your profession or social identity or personal life experiences, such as employee resource groups, women entrepreneurship forums, or survivor groups who have lacked support by systems. These community members have a foundation of common understanding—they get your common worries, take comfort in similar cultural experiences, and share intentions to make the world as it should be.

For people who have had a common experience of social denigration and disrespect due to race, gender, nationality, sexual orientation and identity, religion, physical impairment—any of the ways in which society "others" people—coming together in a community offers a protected place to share wounds and provides the opportunity to express the rage and grief of being subjugated. Others' distinctive words help you to understand your own experience more fully. These groups are safe forums for sharing your powerful truth.

Solidarity emboldens you with the strength in numbers for engaging in a common fight for justice. We are especially seeing a proliferation of community building by women locking arms in industry associations and women's leadership networks, such as the trailblazing organization Chief, coming together to break the legacy of sexism and collaborate in offering the ladder up to other women.

I have experienced the healing and inspiration such groups offer, whether with my friends, in mixed-gender groups of fellow coaches and entrepreneurs, and especially in the community of sisterhood fostered by Regena Thomashauer. This kind of intentional community provides a safe space to remove our masks and let others see us for who we are.[6]

This safety and connection is crucial. However, we also want to be intentional to raise each other, not keep one another out of our power. For example, as women, we've traditionally bonded with one another over stories of how we've been left out or mistreated because we were reacting to a culture that created scarcity and false competition among women. When we encountered a successful woman who loves herself, we might become threatened and judge her or question, "Who does she think she is?" In doing so we unwittingly constrained ourselves and perpetuated division. It's time to be in our power.

Instead we want to learn to bond around being in our power and celebrating one another. We want to praise, amplify, and reflect one another as a matter of course. If someone is upset, be empathic and hold space for emotion until she has "completed the cycle," and as she is ready, remind her to review approaches to get back in her power. Share your list of what you see is good in her until she can start to see it through her own eyes. Let's stand for one another's full expression so we can move beyond gritting through current conditions and instead create new realities.

Because I have witnessed the upward spiral created in a posse, I leverage this power in all my leadership development groups. I start each session with a round of brags, asking each participant to share a win of some kind, whether in their work or personal life. Recounting them in front of others allows them to own their accomplishment, which for so many of those I coach goes against their instincts. This practice offers you a mirror for seeing your true worth and gives you the practice to start appreciating all of who you are. And it inspires others in the group to emulate their win. (Invariably in the next coaching session someone will say they were so inspired by someone's "brag" that they immediately got off the call and did the same thing!)

I've been stretched by my posse(s). For example, speaking before an audience is for me an honor, so I don't consider a well-done presentation a reason to celebrate myself. Even after a speech when I had a stream of people enthusiastically sharing their powerful takeaways, I might only have a fleeting inner pat on the back to 'own it'.

That's because I've been conditioned by our culture, as most of us have, to maintain and share a constricted version of myself, so as not to make others uncomfortable or appear boastful. But then I'm not fully experiencing my power. I'm sure you similarly bleed yourself working hard on a successful project and then shrug off the compliments or feel them fleetingly. Where's our inner "Yes!"? Where's the replenishment of our exerted effort so we prevent burnout? How can we learn to authentically enjoy our own power while not having to worry about making others feel small?

In a posse! In the safety of my sisterhood posse we reflect the truth of one another. There I can share with my sisters about my speech: "I unleashed them!" Like confetti, the text chat blows up with emoji's celebrating me *100x more than I would ever celebrate myself*. This amplification expands what I think I'm capable of and reminds me to enjoy: "Oh, yeah, that's who I am!" Now *that* stretches the skin of my power suit! When I'm in that state, or you are, our presence reverberates. I can hold space for you to grow in a way I can't when I'm out of my power.

The truth is that the world needs me to be in this state and needs you to be there, too! We need to give this life force reflection to one another and receive it when given—it energizes both the giver and the receiver. We can neutralize the effects of a world that constricts us with a never-ending virtuous cycle keeping one another in our power.

Judging or being jealous of one another is based in scarcity, and being out of our power. As Sheila Robinson, founder of *Diversity Woman* magazine and events, and a huge connector, wisely put it, "Remember that you are a part of the community. If you are taking with one hand, give with the other." We need to celebrate one another's radiance and amplify one another every day.[7]

People Can Give You Feedback to See Your Blind Spots

Others' input can be a reality check, helping you overcome these distortions and see yourself and situations more accurately. Upon hearing your tale of an exhausting work or personal situation, a coach or friend might tell you that you need to set a boundary pronto! Their clarity can jolt you back to your senses and inspire you to take speedy action. Or their understanding of a scenario could be totally different from yours, reminding you that there are alternative stories with which to view the hologram of any situation. Their take on things might help you come up with new ideas about how to address the situation.

Feedback is a crucial mechanism to learn more about ourselves and even the part we might be playing in causing or perpetuating our out-of-power state. Research by Whitney Johnson, the author of *Smart Growth*, suggests that for people to operate at their best, they need to know what's working and what isn't. We want to aim for an optimized ratio of 4:1 positive to negative. "It's within that balance that people flourish," she writes. "Positive feedback balanced with constructive criticism from trusted others, especially when it is corroborated by more than one person, helps you get into that sweet spot."[8] When you are in your power you can vet whether the feedback giver has your best interests in mind, and take in constructive feedback objectively without getting stuck in your lead story. So seek out both.

Seek People Who Can Catalyze Your Power

Each person is limited to their own experience in a world that is unlimited. Other people's experience offers you a view of possibilities for yourself and for how you can raise others that you might not have even considered. Through other people you learn information, you get resources, you are exposed to new ideas and opportunities. People can refer opportunities to you and make introductions—all of these contributing to a sense of abundance that puts you in your power.

You can be inspired by people who have accomplished things that are so outside of your experience that they help you set a whole new bar for yourself. Through coaching and mentorship, you can get the blueprint from them for how they've done it so it's easier for you to do it, too.

Look for such role models. They will help you connect to a bigger vision of yourself to aspire to and bring about for others. One of my mentors, Marshall Goldsmith, a pioneer in executive coaching, inspired me with the way you can have an even bigger impact through generosity. At a "Design your Life" workshop by Ayse Birsel he was asked to think about what he learned from his role models. This prompt sparked in him the idea to teach a cohort of top coaches everything he knows—for free—as long as they would pass it forward. He put out an invitation on LinkedIn thinking he might start with 15 people, but he got over 18,000 applications from which to choose 100. Thus was born the "Marshall Goldsmith Top 100 Coaches," (MG100) a community of generosity and shared mission among top leaders, thinkers, and coaches throughout the world. It's been a genuine honor to be a part of this community, which has led to collaborations, mutual learning and amplification, and knowledge philanthropy around the world.

He grew power in others with no other agenda than generosity. Yet now he gets to meet people around the world with a shared mission, and has expanded the reach of his legacy. Now I'm inspired to form my own "SM100" of Change Agents in their power!

Seek Out Mentors, Sponsors, and Allies

Mentors can expand your view of the landscape at your organization or across the whole industry, such as helping you understand the politics of your organization and how to navigate potential pitfalls and alerting you to emerging opportunities in your industry, even providing you with a path for capitalizing on them.

As Charlene Li recounts on the *Power Shift* podcast:[9] "I remember in my very first job, brand-new college-minted person going out into the business world as a consultant, and having my manager pull me aside. He goes, 'You're way too quiet in meetings. You need to speak up with your ideas. I don't care if the other people are 50 or 60 years old. If you think that there's something there, it's your responsibility to speak up.' So he planted in me very early on in my career the sense of voice and agency. Growing up in Detroit, I was the only person of color in my neighborhood, so I grew up being a disruptive force in my classroom with my friends. I used his encouraging words to remind me to hold my own and be 'the only' in the room."

A sponsor is someone who will expend their social and political capital to advocate for your advancement. This is one of the most effective ways to get to a next-level opportunity, especially if you don't have the network or relationships with senior decision makers.

Jhaymee Tynan is an advisor in the Health Services, Public and Social Sector, and Diversity, Equity, and Inclusion practices of consultancy Egon Zehnder. She is a great example of how instrumental mentoring and sponsorship can be in helping us expand our power. In her prior role, she was being bullied by someone in her company who felt threatened by the success she was achieving and as she recounts, "wanted to squash the power that was growing within me." But a senior leader who saw her potential as a health care strategist gave her an opportunity to join her team and run a high-visibility program that put the organization on the path for future growth.

This mentor told Jhaymee, "I think you've got potential to be an executive in this organization, and I really want to see you in that role. I think you can take this project and run with it, and

I'll be there for you as bumper lane." Jhaymee says, "She gave me that courage to feel comfortable as a Black woman in a predominantly white organization."[10] Six months later, Jhaymee was promoted to an executive role. And she is paying it forward as the founder of the 100x2030™ initiative to sponsor women of color in leadership positions.

You can ask someone to be your sponsor. Start by being thoughtful to make sure it's someone who's at a high enough level that they have the relationships and visibility that will help you. Sometimes you already have an informal relationship with this person, such as if you have worked on projects with them, and if so, you can ask them if they would be open to formalizing your relationship with them to be a sponsor. When you talk with them, help them understand the context of your ask. Tell them the contribution you want to make so they can be inspired to help you. Share with them why you are choosing them—what is it about their approach or their role in the business that has convinced you they are the right person to stand for you.

When seeking a sponsor, it's best to choose someone you can have a bidirectional relationship with so you bring value to them as well their reflected glory of elevating a rockstar like you. Always give the person a graceful "out": "And if it's not a good time or a good fit, I'd love to hear your input on what I could do to strengthen my request for others." Sponsors could also be raving fans of your service or centers of influence who refer your business.

Also look for allies. Allies are colleagues who get the change you are trying to achieve and who champion your cause. They can help you fight the fight in a different way than you might be able to by yourself. They can bring their positional power to help marshal the resources of the organization. They can elevate the discussion and speak to other people who may listen to them out of commonality better than you will be listened to for now. You can pull people in to become allies by getting to know them on a personal level so they understand your experience more specifically, not only through their own preconceptions. Welcome their efforts, and give them grace to learn.

And there's a special place for a coach and/or a therapist who can know you deeply and support you to fulfill your purpose and goals for your life. You want someone in your life whom you feel totally safe and empathized with. Their encouragement is crucial, but also make sure what you are getting from someone in this role goes beyond encouragement to include empowerment, with specific approaches you can put into action.

Now that you've been reminded of the ways people can support you to be in your power and use it, you might want to make a map of people in your personal life, social life, and professional network. Think through how each person is currently helping you be in your power and where there is opportunity for even more of that. How can you deepen the relationships you already have? How can you expand the people in your life so you are stretched and reflected? How can you form a posse or uplevel the one(s) you're in?

Now that we've explored portals that expand your idea of "power" beyond its traditional definition, let's turn to the final portal, which will guide you to use the power of your Position.

In Your Power Practices: People

1. Make a map of people in your personal life, social life, and professional network. Think through how each person is currently helping you be in your power, and use your power. Where there is opportunity to deepen safe connections?

2. People can help you get into a place of calm and create a safe space that heals you when you feel shame. Who do you have in your life that is a calming force and you can share your vulnerabilities with?

3. People can reflect aspects of yourself you can't see yourself; a trusted posse will amplify your magnificence. Start to cultivate a posse (with girlfriends, family members, classmates, identity groups, professional communities, book club, gym buddies, etc.). If you don't have at least one yet, where could you build on a friendship with one or two people and start to make it into a posse?

4. Look for role models who expand your imagination, grow your network, and inspire you to make a bigger impact.

5. Identify a sponsor who can advocate for the expansion of your career. Use the scripts in this portal to reach out to ask the person you've identified if they would be your Sponsor. Be Impeccable for your 50%!

CHAPTER 14

Position: From Overlooking Your Power to Owning It

"If I am not for myself, who will be for me?
If I am only for myself, what am I?
And if not now, when?"
—Rabbi Hillel

You have power in your position no matter what position you're in. You want to enjoy the impact you can make by using it to its fullest.

We tend to think that the power we have in our position is defined by the responsibilities outlined in the job description and by the formal level of our position in the organization or community. But we generally have more power in any given position than we realize and are harnessing.

You want to go beyond a focus on performing the functions assigned to you and bring your own definition and creative use of power to any role. In the portal of Position, you will learn you have considerable latitude to support and uplift others, and that's true regardless of your spot within a company or community.

Bring Consciousness into the Use of Power in Your Position

If the term "position of power" is loaded for you, it's for good reason. Most of us have been subject to higher ups who lorded their power over us, so we think power is forceful or abusive. When we rise into positions of authority over others, we really don't want to be *that* person. (Yet a leader only acts in those ways if they are "in power," but not "in their power.")

And it's good to be mindful because research has found that when people get into positions of power, it can "go to our head" in a number of harmful ways. People in high-power mental states generally display less mirroring and empathy to others' distress. They tend to focus more on stereotypes rather than getting to know others as individuals. They are also prone to being less inclusive in their communication style, for example, more often interrupting others when they're speaking. In other words, they tend to pursue goals at others' expense.[1]

Bring consciousness into your position, and be a force for good. As a "power holder," you can establish norms for a team or a whole organization, and model in your power behavior and approaches. Remember, expert on executive power Ron Carucci, found in his research that the biggest abuse of power among those who assume a leadership position is not using it!

Carucci highlights that a common reason those who move into a more powerful position sometimes fail to make good use of their new power is that "it scares us. When you get to a broader level of influence, your life is now on the jumbotron. That sometimes leads to worry about disappointing people or making a decision that doesn't go well."[2]And the higher you go into leadership positions, the more lives you affect and the less opportunities you have for guidance. Now other people are looking to *you* for guidance. CEOs I coach benefit from a trusted sounding board because they can feel so alone in their power, without people to open up to about the questions they're wrestling with.

Focus on Your Why

Power is a sacred opportunity and responsibility. You *want* to sit with it and be intentional about how you use it. As talent executive Anne Gotte shared on my *Power Shift* podcast, "People on your team are likely talking about you over the dinner table with their families. What are they saying?"[3]

How do you get comfortable? You remember your why for wanting to be in the position. You've been wanting to call the shots so you wouldn't have to be put out of your power. What are the values you now have the chance to model in the culture? Enjoy the thrill of having resources to move the needle on that.

Take a little time now to think about all the ways you can leverage your position in pursuit of your vision and to empower and uplift others. Some of these will be types of power the job description of your position explicitly entails such as the power to hire team members, to direct resources as you believe they should be, to set the tone and strategy, to convene meetings, to promote people into roles they can flourish in, and to share information. But they also include other forms of power, of your choosing, that you can bring into your position by the style in which you lead, such as being an inclusive leader. The factors that will allow you to most successfully leverage your position are not necessarily those stressed in job descriptions.

Be Successful at Using Your Power

In a 10-year study of professionals who rose into executive positions, Ron Carucci discovered four behaviors that distinguished leaders who used their power most successfully. You can use them to maximize the power of your position no matter what level you are at.[4]

1. They Know the Whole Business

They see how the pieces of the organization fit together to create value and deliver results. They build bridges across silos and see things holistically, not as territorial.

2. They Are Great Decision Makers

They balance expressing their own views with seeking the input of others—asking questions, not imposing answers. Then they own the final call and communicate their decision clearly.

3. They Know the Industry

They have deep knowledge of their business context, they see trends and emerging possibilities, and they look to commonly held assumptions.

4. They Form Deep, Trusting Relationships

They develop strong bonds with those above and below them in position and in other parts of the company, as well as with outside stakeholders, and they become known for consistently delivering results while genuinely caring for those who deliver them.

Notice how these four success approaches parallel the qualities of being in your power—seeing the bigger-picture context, making mutually beneficial relationships, owning your decisions, and being the steward. I want you to get that *this* **is what power looks like**—approaches that likely already come naturally to you. (And for what it's worth, women in the study were better at these approaches, so if you're a woman, it's time to own it and use it!)

It's time for us to redefine power as a force for good. You can enjoy who you already are and the power you already have to create the world more as you think it should be.

Use the Leverage You Already Have but May Be Overlooking

One of my clients, Kathy, exemplified these success approaches when using her positional power to bring about a transformational change in her organization. She was a managing partner at a 150-person engineering firm. In this firm with all male-ownership, many of the highest revenue producers were women. In fact, from her earlier initiative to hire more women engineers, 50% of the top engineers were now women, well above industry average. But they held much less than 50% of the equity, which was majority owned by the two male owners of the firm. As she said: "Well, that's bullsh*t!"

She realized that this was not only unjust but a liability for the firm in terms of reputation and recruitment. She also noticed that the workplace culture was playing a role in attrition of their high performers and wanted to create a work environment in which their employees felt supported and thrived. And personally she needed to see some changes in order to feel good about her role at the firm and the impact the firm was having on the industry. Here's the story of how she evolved to use her power over the course of 90 days:

At first, she didn't think she had much. Though she had a vision of a more equitable workplace, she didn't know how to implement it. When she shared her ideas with the CEO, he dismissed them, which caused her to second-guess her vision and even take his remarks personally. "I brought things up, but nothing changed, so I brought it up louder (which didn't work either)."

When we thought through a strategic influencing campaign, she saw she had so much power she had been overlooking. She started with the power of her position: "I found that things kicked into gear when I actually just started doing the work." Along with her collaborator, the head of marketing, who was also the mother of young children, they brought in a consultant to run analyses comparing current firm ownership with the last several years of sales data for the female engineers, showing an imbalance of contribution to ownership. They pulled together DEI data to make a strong analytical case.

She started to leverage the relational power she had. She convened a meeting with the other partners to increase communication among them and initiate thoughtful workplace culture and workflow approaches—not waiting for permission but rather being the one to start leading change.

She reached out to deepen relationships with board members: "We were able to catalyze a number of conversations with key stakeholders including at the board level who were willing to engage. It started exploratory, like, 'What are you seeing?' We shared our fact-based understanding, and framed our business case in terms of the board's WIIFT such as growing the current reputation of the firm and increasing the company's future value. Then we got more specific about the outcome we sought: What's the succession plan?"

She shared her powerful truth by connecting the dots: "While keeping a premium for the founders who got the firm off the ground, how are we making sure that our agents for growth feel they have a real stake in the in the future of the company, which for me is the whole reason

I joined the firm? Otherwise I would have started my own firm. I want to own and be a part of it."

Then she used the ultimate leverage she had, namely her own value and that of her colleagues. She had spent years cultivating strong relationships with other partners and the members of the women's network she founded, and she was able to make clear that if the majority owners didn't see the opportunity they laid out, she and her collaborators would plan an exit. "We basically said, 'This is what we're going to build; let me know if it should be here or somewhere else!'"

Not only did the two major shareholders agree to wind down 30% of their equity to create a more equitable ownership, but Kathy had so impressed the board with her vision of an energizing and inclusive future that she was catapulted into the CEO position. And what was among her biggest thrills? "When the female employees were so inspired, saying: 'Thank you for creating one more crack in the glass ceiling!'"

She used the power she had been overlooking to create the world as she thought it should be. This is what it looks like when you use the power you already have to raise everyone around you!

Leverage Your Power

You want to think through the power you do have even when you don't think you have much. You can think first of relational power—Who is within your organization that can partner with you to accomplish a goal? Who can you text or call in order to advance a project or to get introduced to the person who can? Who's in your network who can help you understand the scoop on why a disempowering person is acting as such? Who can you pull in as a resource to reduce overwhelm? Who owes you a favor?

You also leverage your power when you show the value you can add to the goals of others or the consequences you can effect. This ability is available to you in any role, you don't need to be a senior executive to have the power of your position.

Marsha headed a team of nurses in a pharmaceutical company, and she believed her team was not being shown the respect they deserved or being given appropriate input into how the company was serving patients. Her requests repeatedly went unheard. We strategized to find her leverage, always starting with asking, "Where's my Power?" Look for all the ways you and/or your team has something that is valuable to other people. We considered that the nurses are the ones who have the most interaction with patients, helping to monitor their symptoms, and they have a lot of say in patients' decisions to renew medications for chronic diseases. We reframed the nurse team's power by tying it to the revenue they could influence.

This time she approached her manager quantifying how much revenue was at stake (his WIIFT) concerning medication renewals and advocating that the nursing team be included in sales discussions rather than only those about patient care. Her boss agreed, and her input became so valuable that she was then invited to a set of cross-functional meetings to explore other ways the company could elevate the nurses' contributions. She used her power to grow the respect of her team and grew her influence in the process.

You also have leverage when you can influence someone to act because there are enforcement mechanisms or consequences to their behavior. In addition to your position, power includes any contractual or legal leverage you have, whether that pertains to a client, a business partner, a job, or a roommate/tenant.[5] An important lever for Mary, the financial advisor, was revisiting their initial partnership agreement. Seeking advice from an attorney emboldened her because their contract had equal pay in its language but had not been enforced.

Business owners often get out of their power in sticky situations with clients, subcontractors, and team members. You have considerable power to negotiate terms of these contracts up-front, including how disputes will be resolved, and to be the steward who keeps everyone in their power for the greater good.

Create the Weather on Your Team

The best thing you can use your position for as a leader is creating *psychological safety* among your team, it's the factor with the biggest impact on team performance.[6] Harvard professor Amy Edmonson coined this term, which means "a sense of confidence that the team will not embarrass, reject or punish someone for speaking up . . . a team climate characterized by interpersonal trust and mutual respect in which people are comfortable being themselves."[7] This allows team members to speak up without fear (and perhaps even give you feedback you need to do better).

How can you foster psychological safety? Amy Edmonson offers three guidelines. First, convey that making mistakes is an opportunity to learn from them, all together. Second, role-model by acknowledging you are also fallible. Third, regularly and genuinely ask your team questions, not only about how their work is going but about their well-being and improvements they see for the team. Be aware of and constantly challenge personal and organizational biases, and be curious to understand and empathize with those who have other perspectives and experiences.[8] If you've been a person in a lower-power position at any time, you might have a heightened ability for empathy toward others; this is an asset you can leverage for psychological safety.

As the leader, you create the weather on the team. You can't do it alone, but you can set the tone. For example, you can decide the motto that people will rally around. For Jackie Frank, leader of a fast-growing mortgage originator team, it was "Excellence without the Drama," which everyone related to and wanted. As the leader, you get to share not only your vision for the team but also the metrics on which everyone would be evaluated. For her it wasn't just about getting the loan done but the customer satisfaction evaluations—her reputation was built on making clients happy. She shared with her team what she stands for, why it matters to her, and asks them why it matters to them. She made that metric concrete, for example, by sharing thank-you notes from clients. When you share your vision and what's in your heart, your team can care about it, too. You're not becoming exhausted by trying to get people to follow you, they *want* to.

And if you have been thoughtful and respectful in your approach, and Impeccable for your 50% using strategies in the portal of Partnership . . . and still someone on your team doesn't align with the culture you are creating, you can use the power of your position. Invite them to stay and be a part of the culture, or choose to not be a part of it. You stay in your power when you lay out choices you can stand behind and have non-attachment to the outcome.

How can you be the thermostat and set the tone for your team culture? What can you do starting today to ensure or increase the psychological safety on your team?

Growing Power in Others Grows Your Power

"One of the greatest human longings we have is to grow," says Whitney Johnson, best-selling author of *Smart Growth*. Growing power in others is good for them, and it's good for you. "When you help other people grow, you are saying to them, 'I see you.' If you create the conditions whereby they can respond to their own longings to grow, you're giving them the power they need. It's a predictor of whether or not people are going to stay with you."[9]

Growing power in others might sound good, but when it comes down to actually doing it, let's get real, isn't that giving up power you have? Charlene Li, expert on disruption and best-selling author of *The Disruption Mindset*[10] shared this on the *Power Shift* podcast: "Leaders say, 'Well I can't give up control,' believing they have to do all the thinking themselves, which is totally exhausting, and then lack of implementation makes things feel out of their control." She challenges leaders: "Tell me, What do you *actually* have control over?" Better she says to give people a container within which they are empowered to do whatever they need to do in order to accomplish the intent."[11]

She shared: "One of my favorite examples is from Comcast. They encouraged people on the front lines—in the call centers—to meet on a regular basis and talk about trends they were seeing. In typical organizational hierarchies, people on the front lines get everything dumped onto them and have no power. But they were encouraged to put together a brief telegram if they noticed something a department leader should know. The executive team looked at these escalations and responded. The power shifted to the front lines, where there is infinite untapped potential and energy."

You can think of this shift, as she says, *"not giving power away but growing it in others,"* which then leads to innovation and better implementation toward goals. Don't think about how much power *you want* but rather about what gives the people you're leading a sense of agency to accomplish your vision." As the Buddha is quoted as saying: "Thousands of candles can be lit from a single candle, and the life of the candle will not be short-ened. Happiness never decreases by being shared."

Become a Sponsor

As a mentor you are co-conspirator in someone else's career ambitions, both encouraging and championing them. As a spon-sor you use the power of your relationships and position and talk about the person you're sponsoring in rooms where they are not present. You will actively advocate for and introduce them to people in your network and use your professional capital on their behalf.

You can sponsor others. You have the power to spark a life course to unleash an important voice. Think of paying forward the sponsorship you've gotten. Who is already in your network that you could sponsor or mentor?

Engage in Allyship

"Allyship" is term used to describe efforts by members of a privileged in-group to advance the interests of marginalized groups. You can be an ally in interpersonal situations, by saying something, for example, when there has been a gender-, racial-, or identity-based discrimination or decision, and by showing your willingness to be open to understanding and supporting those whose life experience is different from yours and may lack the advantages you enjoy. You can also be an ally in ways that are more public and systemic—raising issues, questioning traditions, and endorsing new ideas and new talent. As an ally you play an important role because your voice is sometimes heard and accepted when the same message by a messenger who is "othered" may not.

Dave Smith and Brad Johnson, authors of *Good Guys*,[12] like to exemplify drawing from a slogan of pride from the gay community to be "loud and proud' as an ally. An example they give is if you are a working father, don't slink out the back door to go to your daughter's soccer game while the working mothers have the trepidation of announcing they have to leave at 5 p.m. to pick their kids up. Rather, normalize the challenges of working fathers as much as those of working mothers who have to fight career penalties.

Rather than shy away from being seen as an ally because you think people blame you for benefitting from the system in a way they don't, step into your power as an ally. Move beyond labels and be known for your actions.

Jennifer Brown, best-selling author of *How to Be an Inclusive Leader* and creator of the popular podcast *The Will to Change*, suggests an exercise to practice being an ally. "Put yourself in the position of ally (even if you feel that you are marginalized in the system). In certain situations you are an insider or in the majority, in others you are an outsider or in the minority. No matter who you are, in this way you have 'privilege.' This 'privilege' isn't a bad thing. It's something to accept and be utilized."[13]

Think about what power you have that you could share with others and what changes you could effect. Ask yourself, 'What power do I have in this system? What do I have access to that others don't? What rooms am I in that I can invite others into?' Going through the paces of this exercise can help you leverage your advantages to share power and empower others. It can also help you pinpoint where an ally has power you don't and then give you an idea of specific ways you can ask allies to support you."

Staying the course as an ally requires you to be in your power. Rather than have a scarcity mentality, consider the 3D perspective and how you can co-create a shared new vision of the workplace. Jennifer Brown advises: "Because of years of lip service, everyone's BS meter is high, so being authentic and talking 'real'—beyond public relations talking points—will be a welcome part of your power." Especially if it's the case that your team/organization/community is not at the point of equity, you want to "own your 50%." Say: "We are not where we need to be yet. Here's what I am personally doing, here's what our executive team has committed to do, here's how you can hold us accountable." This kind of candor and taking responsibility breeds others' trust in you, and it reduces the out-of-power reaction others have when lip service makes them feel unseen and unheard.

An Ally includes being an "upstander"—someone who is not the direct target of a microaggression or exclusion but recognizes that something is wrong and speaks or acts to make it right. If you witness bullying (or related disrespectful behavior) and don't do anything about it, it means you were out of your power feeling unsafe to speak up. Not speaking up can have a negative effect on you, parallel to how it can be traumatic for the target.

When I facilitated a panel on gender inclusion at one of the big tech companies, a panel member shared that when he was a junior manager one of the senior engineers on his team made some sexist comments in a team meeting, which made him uncomfortable. He was an upstander, speaking his powerful truth that the comments were inappropriate, suggesting that's "not how we do things here; we're trying to make a culture for all of us."

Where can you use your power to be an ally or upstander?

Leverage the Power of Platform

Even if you don't have a lot of leverage now, you can create the means to have power. There are abundant examples of this, a notable one being Reese Witherspoon, an American actress who a decade ago said she wasn't getting roles that portrayed strong women characters. So she started her own production company to showcase stories with powerful women.[14] Similarly with Shonda Rhimes, who didn't see women of color represented on TV in powerful roles, so she created shows and scripts that featured them in hit TV series.[15]

If you are a solo coach, consultant, business owner, entrepreneur, or an individual working in an organization, you might be thinking, What power do I have? Lots! It's the greatest time in history to get your story and your message out via existing platforms. We are living in a creator and influencer economy—your authentic documentation of how you alchemized your "mess into your message" is inspiration people are hungry for. A video of someone sharing a powerful truth can go viral, reaching 100,000 views within a few days or weeks. You can steadily build an audience from scratch by regularly posting authentic content. This could be you . . .

You can also use existing channels to become a leading voice. Minda Harts started by owning her story about the invisibility and microaggressions she faced as a Black woman in predominately white culture and corporate life. She used the power of existing channels by putting her story into a form that could go viral—a book, her first one titled *The Memo: What Women of Color Need to Know to Secure a Seat at the Table*. Standing for her end users, she and many other women of color have become important voices of conscience and healing in our media and organizations. You can use your own experience to create a movement that grows power in others as well as in yourself.

Or simply start like Greta Thunberg, stand outside with a sign. When you are in your power, you will find a way. You've had a vision of how things should be, use the leverage you have with your position and make it come to life. Look in every nook and cranny for the power you are overlooking, be creative in harnessing the power that is available to you. #Nowisyourtime.

Personally, I've loved the power of the position I have as author of this book—whispering in your ear to be in your power, feeding your brain with power potions, and cheering you on to use your power for the good of all.

Let's now bring together all the portals on using your power. On the next page you'll find a cheat sheet of reminders to help you remember which portal doors to open as you think through how to use your power. I'll also share two case studies of how one person used multiple strategies to resolve their scenario. Then we'll come up with a plan on how you can live your life in your power.

In Your Power Practices: Position

1. Review the description of your role whether in an organization or as a service provider (or write your own; you can get creative to do this for your role as a parent, family or community member, too). Are you maximizing the power already inherent in the role? Stay connected to your why to be comfortable using the power you have.

2. Regularly ask yourself, What are the unused levers of power you already have in your position? Where can you provide value to others that gives you leverage? How can you leverage your relational power? How can you "stitch the seams" of the organization to accomplish something bigger than the mandate of your role?

3. Create the weather on your team and in your family. Role-model and imbue all your team and family interactions with psychological safety.

4. Be intentional and maximize all the roles you can play: mentor, sponsor, upstander, ally. Grow power in others in order to grow theirs and your own.

5. Use (and expand) the power of your platforms in order to turn your out-of-power "pain" into an in-your-power "purpose" that you can share to mobilize many followers in the service of your vision

---

Use Your Power Checklist

Persuasion: Always identify the business and personal level WIIFT (What's In It For Them) of your decision maker before influencing them.

Partnership: Be the steward of the situation. Use each element of the POWERS framework to transfer the ownership of the issue and gain their partnership.

Protection: Do you feel your "No"? You can set proactive and reactive boundaries to protect yourself from others' behavior; set barriers with narcissists.

Powerful Truth: Do you have a Powerful Truth that needs to be spoken? Use your voice. State your needs. Connect the dots. Display strategic emotion. Or use humor.

People: Are you seeking out People to reflect you and help you get back in your power? Are you connecting with people who can sponsor and amplify you?

Position: Are you owning and using the full powers of your Position and Platform? What are you doing to grow power in others?

Case Study #1: Using Your Power to Overcome Overwhelm

Keisha is an executive director in a finance department. She is multi-talented and gets the job done with excellence, so a lot of work flowed to her. She handled all the fire drills from early morning til late evening. She had the opportunity for coaching to help her not have to do it all and elevate her role.

She said: "I lost control, was doing way too much, my job satisfaction withered. I was angry and frustrated. I had to take my power back."

Early in our work together she was exasperated and blurted out to her manager one day, "I CAN'T do this anymore!" She meant this as a boundary, but we turned it into a script for a powerful truth, connecting the dots that created the problem. She brought him the one-page "shock and awe" sheet of all she's doing, and a visual of the problem that showed how the work of three teams is funneled instead to her.

She became the steward of that situation. She convened a meeting with the heads of each of the functions and her manager, and proposed a go-forward solution of a new way of integrating the work, which was adopted by all the departments. She put together a master spreadsheet delegating and tracking of all the tasks for their functions and her own, freeing herself up to work on strategic initiatives to rework their accounting systems. Her manager and other participants raised their respect for her, and she was promoted and given a substantial bonus.

She had been asking for resources from the head of their department for months, but as she said, "It wasn't until I used her WIIFT that I got what I needed."

She had to deal with a narcissistic leader who was the head of IT and actively sabotaged her. "We were in a group meeting, and I wanted to go after him so many times. I did push back on him when he said something misleading about my function, but where I didn't need to intervene I just kept telling myself, 'gray rock, gray rock.' It totally worked!" I don't have any anger toward him anymore."

Keisha hadn't had a night off or cooked a meal in a year, but she spent the last two weekends renovating her house and cooking with her husband!

Case Study #2: Stay in Your Power When Sabotaged

Remember Mary from the introduction, who became the Partner in Charge of her group at her financial firm? Here's how she achieved her breakthrough. In our first discussion we deep-dived on the question "Where's your power?" She thought she was being pushed out but then realized it was in her partners' best interest to keep her and her clientele. That immediately shifted her: "I was not trapped by them, I was free to choose. I could either enjoy my time staying in the group or else *they would be paying me* to create my future somewhere else." She had the ultimate power because her client service approach led to such high satisfaction among her clients, they indicated they would hire her whether she stayed at her current firm or left. She had control over her income and reputation because of her proficiency in her craft.

She was so fear driven she made false assumptions. So she was able to tell an alternative story that her senior partner may have been threatened by the success she was building, not because she lacked competence or was a bully. Once she stopped taking his rumors personally, she could get out of her shame bath and focus on her values and purpose. She became less angry and more compassionate and lighthearted with them.

She started being intentional about showing up at her Horizon Point—joyful, poised, and abundant—so she immediately had a better mood and outlook. She shared her powerful truth of what she stands for, which led to getting what she wanted when she negotiated and initiated a vision to expand and diversify the group.

With a new approach to persuasion and partnership she forged neutral-toned conversations that shifted their undermining behavior toward collaboration. To reel in her biggest fish client ever she expanded the people in her network and once voted the Partner in Charge used the power of her position to establish equal pay and grow their partnership with diverse talent.

Mary was at her wit's end when we first talked. Within weeks she not only transformed her own situation, she had transformed her whole group. This is what it looks like to be in your power and use your power for the good of all!

PART IV

Create
a Ripple Effect

CHAPTER 15

Power Is a Lifestyle

"Every moment is an organizing opportunity, every person a potential activist, every minute a chance to change the world."

—Dolores Huerta, Co-Founder National Farmworkers Association

You now have an overstuffed stocking of strategies to be in your power in a world that can sometimes make you feel powerless. All are available to you, you just have to access them. You can transcend the automatic factory settings we have as humans, and instead be a creative force who steers any difficult situation to stay "good in you" and serve your good intentions.

Living in your power—it's a lifestyle. You walk through the world confidently, as if you have your own version of those Wonder Woman cuffs or a Batman utility belt.

When there's a situation that's pulling you out of your power, know that 360 degrees surrounding you are the 12 Power Portals. In any direction you look you can open the door and walk through the portal to see the new vista offered. Take your attention off the power problem, and instead look within yourself to know what you are making the situation mean. And lift your sights to the bigger-picture possibility where you lead yourself and others to the other side of the impasse.

These portals remind you to be **intentional**. You can always act with intention in the service of the outcome you want, and that's in the best interest of all. In the snap of a finger, you can shift your perspective and act toward your purpose. Instead of doing one of the five fight-or-flight spectrum behaviors, you can move your emotions through your body and reconnect to calm. You can use your know-how. No matter how obstructive other people are, you know how to persuade, partner, and proclaim your truth with them and bring more grace into the interaction. You can be a person who creates psychological safety within yourself and for others.

The portals guide you to stay **inviolable**. You are now the "home" you can come home to. You know how to protect yourself from your *no* and speak the truth of your *yes*. You can catch yourself stuck in a lead story and tell an alternative one. Moving forward from the storyline you developed as an adaptation to earlier experiences, you can live into the new life story you choose to tell about yourself. You can pursue "pleasure research," learning about what lights you up and fills you up, so you can show up with a radiant feeling from the inside-out and attract people who will help further brighten it. Other people can act from wherever they are in their journey—you're not reacting to them, you're about furthering your own. You're free.

Even when your heart breaks from the way the world is not as it should be, you can alchemize it and use it as fodder for your growth. When you have this ability to always come back home to a you that you love, you can pursue your biggest dreams. Because if you encounter difficult people along the way, they prompt you to reclaim even more acceptance of yourself and stand even more firm in your truth. Bring 'em on.

The portals exemplify the **infinite**. Always remember to look beyond the finite problem to the infinite possible solutions.

There is a current of divine love bigger than all of us that we can tap into when we connect with our purpose. The way your challenging situation is today is not all it could or will ever be—it will get better when you sprinkle your power dust on it. And if this situation isn't right for you, it's a big world, and there are people and opportunities waiting for someone just like you.

Are you committed to staying in your power from this day forward? I knew it! Here are practical ways you can stay in your power:

Have a go-to prompt to get back in your power: *Find a consistent prompt that sets in motion your series of in-your-power moves. What is a mantra that can remind you to be in your power? Maybe it's simply "Be in your power!" Or ask, "Where's my power?" Or have a phrase like the acronym Oops! (Out of power signal). Or remind yourself of your Horizon Point. Let this prompt put you in the mindset to sort through your abundant repertoire of in-your-power strategies.*

Put together a power inventory: *Review the strategies of this book by looking back through its pages and putting together your power inventory. Give a thorough answer for yourself to the question, Where's my power? (To feel proud of yourself, compare your full power inventory with the one you listed in Chapter 2 at the start of the book.)*

Surround yourself with reminders: *Many of my clients post the name or a symbol of their Horizon Point on their computer so they keep it in mind while having conversations they want to be intentional about.* I've put together a cheat sheet of the best strategies from each of the 12 portals so you can keep them as reminders in plain sight. You can download it at **www.inyourpowerbook.com**.

Have a daily ritual that keeps you in your power: *Have some ritual or exercise you do every day that reminds you of the truth of who you are. As part of* *this ritual, upload your Horizon Point. Make it an experience that gives you pleasure and keeps you in joy (I do a dance break, and energy exercises to clear out-of-power emotions). Find your own version of an electric car charging station, a power pump you can pull up to and refill yourself.*

Stay plugged into your posse: *Allow the reflection from your posse to reinforce and amplify this new version of yourself in your power. And, borrowing from popular anti-drunk driving phrase, think: "Friends don't let friends stay out of their power." Read this book with those in your posse so everybody can take a stand for one another to be in their power. Remind each other of the new standard you're each setting for yourselves and one another, you'll no longer settle for things happening to you. Notice if you are commiserating in complaint with someone who's reporting about being powerless, you know too much now to stay there. Better to ask, "Where's your power?"*

Grow power in others: *You can read this book with your team to identify opportunities where each team member becomes even more empowered (e.g., to set boundaries) and equipped to partner with others (e.g., to resolve breakdowns in systems). Make it your mantra to have an "In Your Power culture" on the team in which every person is Impeccable for their 50% in what they contribute to the overall culture. If you are the team leader, think how you can grow power in your team members to accelerate your goals. If you are a team member, think how you can use your power to accomplish goals and make workflow and collaboration better. To get the ideas deep in your bones, teach someone else on your team or in your family the new approaches you are using today.*

Be the steward: *Because you are in your power you bring a different level of consciousness than others may be operating with. You're not coming from reaction, you're not defensive or trying to survive or get one up on the others. Bring others along in a way they might not have* *experienced before—neutral, respectful, clear, fair, full of goodwill. Make this the new standard. Create the world as you think it should be.*

Be a role model: *Think of someone who's your role model. I bet they are in their power! You can be that role model for your children/mentees/clients/community/ team. Your corner of the world at large needs you to be in your power. Many of the pressing issues of our day have at their root an issue where participants are out of their power, but changes that have moved our world forward have been sparked by people like you who got back in their power and used it! If you've been treated with disrespect or unawareness by people in your workplace or family life, break the chain now. Don't let it perpetuate to your team members, your kids, your mentees.*

If you are ready to live in your power, I'd like to give you a challenge. Will you take the pledge to be in your power from this day forward? Do you commit to enter each scenario by asking, "Where's my Power?" If so, raise your right hand and repeat: "I, _____ (fill in your name), commit to being in my power and using my power for the good of all!"

Create a ripple effect, just by showing up as who you are. Because when you are in your power, you raise everyone around you.

Notes

Introduction

1. Except where identified by full name, my clients' names and companies have been disguised to preserve their anonymity.
2. Professor Sukhvinder Obhi interviewed by the author.
3. Carucci, Ron A., and Hansen, Eric C., *Rising to Power: The Journey of Exceptional Executives*, Austin, TX: GreenLeaf Book Press, 2014.
4. Johnson. W., *Smart Growth: How to Grow Your People to Grow Your Company*, Brighton, MA: Harvard Business Review Press, 2022.

Chapter 1

1. Fifteen years later I presented at the White House, so it turned out to not be once in a lifetime, but who knew? And this shows it's possible for a person to grow into her power!
2. Obhi, S. S., Swiderski, K. M., and Brubacher, S. P. "Induced Power Changes the Sense of Agency," *Consciousness and Cognition* 21, no. 3 (2012): 1547–1550, https://doi.org/10.1016/j.concog.2012.06.008.
3. Rock, D., *Your Brain at Work: Strategies for Overcoming Distraction, Regaining Focus and Working Smarter All Day Long*. New York, NY: Harper Collins, 2010.
4. Professor Sukhvinder Obhi interviewed by the author, April 7, 2022, via Zoom.
5. Bowlby, John, *A Secure Base*, New York, NY: Basic Books, 1988.
6. Kotler, S., and Wheal, J. *Stealing Fire: How Silicon Valley, the Navy Seals, and Maverick Scientists Are Revolutionizing the Way We Live and Work*. New York, NY: Dey Street Books, 2018.
7. "Priming," *Psychology Today*, https://www.psychologytoday.com/us/basics/priming.
8. Professor Sukhvinder Obhi interviewed by the author, April 7, 2022, via Zoom.

Chapter 2

1. Chabris, C., and Simons, D., *The Invisible Gorilla*, London, UK: Harper Collins, 2011.
2. Simons, Daniel, "Selective Attention Test," YouTube, March 2010, https://www.youtube.com/watch?v=vJG698U2Mvo.

Chapter 3

1. Parks, M., "Mandela Rejects S. African Terms for Prison Release," *Los Angeles Times*, February 11, 1985, https://www.latimes .com/archives/la-xpm-1985-02-11-mn-4278-story.html.
2. "1 in 60 Rule," Wikipedia, January 18, 2022, https://en.wikipedia. org/wiki/1_in_60_rule.
3. Clear, James, *Atomic Habits: Tiny Changes, Remarkable Results: An Easy & Proven Way to Build Good Habits & Break Bad Ones*. New York, NY: Avery, 2018.

Chapter 4

1. There are many things that grow a bottom line, but having more women in management and on boards has been consistently shown to "grow the pie" of a company's profitability.

Chapter 5

1. Nagoski, E., and Nagoski, A., *Burnout: The Secret to Unlocking the Stress Cycle*, New York, NY: Penguin Random House, 2019.
2. Brene Brown's 2022 book *Atlas of the Heart* suggests that empirically there are 87 types of emotion.
3. Andrew Huberman Stanford, accessed on April 7, 2021, "Reduce Anxiety & Stress with Physiological Sigh," YouTube accessed on April 7, 2021, https://www.youtube.com/watch?v=r BdhqBGqiMc.

4. Through the mouth bypasses the brain and goes right to work to cool down the heat in our lower-body organs, such as the liver, which is where negative emotions can be stored. This helps us stop impulsive reacting so you don't act in a way you will regret.

5. Dana, Deb, *The Polyvagal Theory in Therapy : Engaging the Rhythm of Regulation*. New York, NY: WW Norton & Co., 2018.

6. People who have experienced serious trauma are especially likely to develop this adaptive coping mechanism called dissociation, which helps them detach from their rageful or terrified emotions at the time.

7. Van der Kolk, B. A., *The Body Keeps the Score: Brain, Mind, and Body in the Healing of Trauma*, New York, NY: Penguin Books, 2015.

8. Ibid.

9. Nagoski, E., and Nagoski, A., *Burnout: The Secret to Unlocking the Stress Cycle*, New York, NY: Ballantine Books, 2019.

10. With a trauma response, the body's stress hormones do not in fact return to baseline after the threat has passed. If you notice you are having strong emotional responses to getting kicked out of your power, learn about additional approaches that are helpful to soothing yourself and finding safety in your own body. Some of these approaches can reduce intense emotions quickly, including those you can do on your own, such as Havening, or those you can do especially with a counselor such as Emotional Freedom Techniques (known as "tapping") and EMDR (Eye Movement Sensitization Reprocessing). For women, I also recommend the work of Sheila Kelley and Regena Thomashauer for moving emotions through your body and reconnecting with you pleasure and aliveness.

11. Dana, D., *The Polyvagal Theory in Therapy*, New York, NY: WW Norton & Co., 2018.

Chapter 6

1. There are four different patterns of indirect behaviors, such as seeking approval versus preventing disapproval versus focusing on never being good enough. Each has strategies that will help you overcome this approach or be counterproductive to it. Learn which pattern you use, and get strategies that are right for your type by taking my full Power Profile self-assessment at www.inyourpowerbook.com.

2. Tulshyan, R., and Burey, J.-A., "Stop Telling Women They Have Imposter Syndrome," *Harvard Business Review* (2021, February 11);

3. Tulshyan, R., and Burey, J.-A., "End Imposter Syndrome in Your Workplace," *Harvard Business Review* (2021, July 14).

4. McKinsey & Company and LeanIn.Org. "Women in the Workplace 2019," https://womenintheworkplace.com/2019.

5. Ibid.

6. Tulshyan, R., and Burey, J.-A., "Stop Telling Women They Have Imposter Syndrome."

7. "Understanding Diversity Journeys: Eli Lilly's World-Class D&I Research," Gallup, https://www.gallup.com/workplace/268769/understanding-diversity-journeys-eli-lilly-world-class-research.aspx.

8. Johnson, W. B., and Smith, D. G., "Mentoring Someone with Imposter Syndrome," *Harvard Business Review* (2019, February 22).

9. You want to develop objectivity to understand if you are facing bias that derails you from your purpose. Get feedback and 360-degree input from more than one manager so you can get a diversity of points of view and not overweight one. Drive performance conversations that detail the promotion or role expansion criteria and where your performance stands against them, and ask for the full array of possible career development pathways even if the information is not offered. Stay aware of known biases so you can recognize them when they are occurring in real time, and use the approaches you'll learn in the portal of Powerful Truth to require fairness. The power move is to develop relationships with allies, who can speak on your behalf to ensure equitable treatment and amplify your voice, and with sponsors, who can make introductions to help you get into ever-expanding positions where you can use your influence to create culture change.

10. "Five Whys," Wikipedia, accessed 15 April 2022, https://en.wikipedia.org/wiki/Five_whys.

11. Deborah Borg interviewed by the author.

12. Morrison, L. T., Hill, D., and Allen, J., *Be the Bridge: Pursuing God's Heart for Racial Reconciliation*, Colorado Springs, CO: WaterBrook, 2019.

13. Keyes, C., Fredrickson, B. L., and Park, N., "Positive Psychology and the Quality of Life," *Handbook of Social Indicators and Quality of Life Research*, Dordrecht, Netherlands: Springer, 2012, pp. 99–112.

Chapter 7

1. "This Author Was Mistaken for a Delivery Worker. Her Response Was Priceless." MSNBC, July 21, 2022, https://www-msnbc-com.cdn.ampproject.org/c/s/www.msnbc.com/msnbc/amp/ncna1297428.
2. Schwartz, R., *No Bad Parts: Healing Trauma and Restoring Wholeness with the Internal Family Systems Model*, Louisville, CO: Sounds True, 2021.

Chapter 8

1. If you are out of your power around growing your own business, learn how to offer your services effectively to corporate buyers; for this I recommend Bold Haus. To learn how to become a recognized expert I recommend Dorie Clark.

Chapter 9

1. "Women in the Workplace Report 2021," Lean In, https://leanin.org/women-in-the-workplace-report-2021/looking-ahead.
2. "The Real Reason Female Entrepreneurs Get Less Funding," Dana Kanze, TED Talk, https://www.ted.com/talks/dana_kanze_the_real_reason_female_entrepreneurs_get_less_funding?language=en.

Chapter 10

1. Women are often expected to do this emotional labor and are not compensated or recognized for it. However, it can be useful to intentionally play this role where it keeps you and others you care about in your power until you can find a root cause solution. Then you want to make sure it's reflected in your evaluations.

Chapter 11

1. Clarkson, K., "Kelly Clarkson Show | Brené Brown & Kelly Clarkson," YouTube, January 6, 2021. https://www.youtube.com/watch?v=RNCidRveJvU.
2. This language was inspired by the now infamous line by Arianna Huffington: "No is a complete sentence," sparking a well-being revolution.
3. Clarkson, K., "Kelly Clarkson Show | Brené Brown & Kelly Clarkson," YouTube, January 6, 2021, https://www.youtube.com/watch?v=RNCidRveJvU.
4. "One of the most important lessons Dr. Maya Angelou ever taught Oprah," The Oprah Winfrey Show, June 18, 1997, https://www.oprah.com/own-oprahshow/one-of-the-most-important-lessons-dr-maya-angelou-ever-taught-oprah.
5. Contact company security and local law enforcement if you are worried about violence toward you, and put together a safety plan.

Chapter 12

1. "Men Tell Why Other Men Don't Interrupt Sexism at Work," Catalyst Blog, July 2, 2020, https://www.catalyst.org/2020/07/02/why-men-dont-interrupt-sexism-work/; DiMuccio, S., Sattari, N., Shaffer, E., and Cline, J. "Masculine Anxiety and Interrupting Sexism at Work," Catalyst (2021), https://www.catalyst.org/reports/masculine-anxiety-workplace/.
2. Melnick, S. Power Shift podcast, episode #23: "The Power of Self-Authoring Your Life, with Nabeela Ixtabalan," February 2022, Apple Podcasts.
3. "Rep. Alexandria Ocasio-Cortez (D-NY) Responds to Rep. Ted Yoho," C-SPAN, YouTube, https://www.youtube.com/watch?v=LI4ueUtkRQ0.
4. Barton, L. L, "What It's like to Be a Black Man in Tech," Harvard Business Review (March 4, 2021), https://hbr.org/2021/03/what-its-like-to-be-a-black-man-in-tech.
5. "Watch: Greta Thunberg's Full Speech to World Leaders at UN Climate Action Summit," United Nations, YouTube, https://www.youtube.com/watch?v=KAJsdgTPJpU.

6. "Women of Color Can No Longer Buy into the 'Inclusion Delusion,'" *Fortune*, March 28, 2022, https://fortune.com/2022/03/28/women-careers-color-inclusion-delusion-kbj-supreme-court-gender-power-business-corporate-culture-deepa-purushothaman/.

Chapter 13

1. "The Mirror Neuron Revolution: Explaining What Makes Humans Social," *Scientific American*, July 1, 2008, https://www.scientificamerican.com/article/the-mirror-neuron-revolut/.
2. Grant, A., "There's a Specific Kind of Joy We've Been Missing. *New York Times*, July 10, 2021, https://www.nytimes.com/2021/07/10/opinion/sunday/covid-group-emotions-happiness.html.
3. Gottman, J., and Silver, N., *What Makes Love Last? Secrets from the Love Lab*, New York, NY: Simon and Schuster 2012; Grewen, K. M., Anderson, B. J., Girdler, S. S., and Light, K. C., "Warm Partner Contact Is Related to Lower Cardiovascular Reactivity," National Library of Medicine, National Center for Biotechnology Information, PubMed.gov; https://pubmed.ncbi.nlm.nih.gov/15206831/.
4. OWN, "Dr. Brené Brown: 'Shame Is Lethal, Oprah Winfrey Network, YouTube, https://www.youtube.com/watch?v=GEBjNv5M784.
5. Oliver, M., *Wild Geese*, Eastbourne, UK: Gardners Books, 2004.
6. It's important to establish safety and trust in the community. Anyone who puts others out of their power should not be invited into the posse. It can be helpful to start a posse as part of a formal group (a coaching mastermind, a professional community, an ERG, a learning program, and so on, so there is accountability at the beginning that becomes the standard over time). If people violate psychological safety, you can use approaches in the Partnership or Powerful Truth portals to help you navigate holding that person accountable to keep the posse safe.
7. Sheila Robinson interviewed by the author, April 21, 2022.
8. Whitney Johnson interviewed by the author, April 8, 2022.
9. Melnick, S., *Power Shift* podcast, episode #10: "Disruption and Power with Charlene Li," April 2021, Apple Podcasts.
10. Jhaymee Tynan interviewed by the author, April 29, 2022.

Chapter 14

1. Summarized from interview with Professor Sukhvinder Obhi, April 7, 2022. Specifics of Professor Obhi's work are that people in high-power mental states generally display less mirroring than people in lower-power states, consistent with research from other labs showing that high power is associated with less empathy when hearing about the distressing experiences others. Other work from a variety of social psychology labs has indicated that high-power individuals tend to focus more on stereotypes and devote less attention to getting to know specific characteristics of individuals. See also Obhi, S., "Beyond Unconscious Bias: Understanding Power Is Critical for Building Inclusive Organizations," McMaster University, January 2019; Guinote, A., *Annual Review of Psychology* 68, 2017.

2. Ron Carucci interviewed by the author, January 28, 2022.

3. Melnick, S., *Power Shift* podcast episode #14: "The Power of Noble Work with Anne Gotte," July 2021, Apple Podcasts.

4. Carucci, R., "A 10-Year Study Reveals What Great Executives Know and Do," *Harvard Business Review*, January 19. 2016, https://hbr.org/2016/01/a-10-year-study-reveals-what-great-executives-know-and-do.

5. If you ever face a documented pattern of egregious harm and other means have not been protective, you have access to and should use legal remedies up to and including a restraining order or lawsuit as a backstop.

6. Rozovsky, J., "The Five Keys to a Successful Google Team," re:Work, November 7, 2015, https://rework.withgoogle.com/blog/five-keys-to-a-successful-google-team/.

7. Edmondson, A. *The Fearless Organization: Creating Psychological Safety in the Workplace for Learning, Innovation and Growth*, New York: NY: Wiley.

8. Edmondson, A., "Building a Psychologically Safe Workplace," TEDxHGSE, 2014, https://www.youtube.com/watch?v=LhoLuui9gX8.

9. Whitney Johnson interviewed by the author, April 8, 2022.

10. Li, C., *The Disruption Mindset: Why Some Organizations Transform While Others Fail*, Washington, DC: Idea Press Publishing, 2019.
11. Melnick, S., *Power Shift* podcast, episode #10: "Disruption and Power with Charlene Li," April 2021, Apple Podcasts.
12. Smith, D., and Johnson, B., *Good Guys: How Men Can Be Better Allies for Women in the Workplace*, Brighton, MA: Harvard Business Review Press, 2020.
13. Jennifer Brown interviewed by with the author, May 2, 2022.
14. "Reese Witherspoon's Hello Sunshine Sold for $900 Million to Media Company Backed by Blackstone," *Variety,* August 2, 2021, https://variety.com/2021/film/news/reese-witherspoon-hello-sunshine-sold-1235032618/.
15. "Shonda Rhimes," Wikipedia, https://en.wikipedia.org/wiki/Shonda_Rhimes.

Acknowledgments

Reverence and huge thanks to the team at Wiley Publishers for their collaboration and enthusiastic support, starting with Mike Campbell, who believed in my vision; Jessica Filippo, whose passion elevated my flame of purpose and whose capable stewardship was key to the whole book project; and Richard Narramore and Deborah Schindlar, who brought their expert guiding hand. Thank you to my insightful literary agent Jessica Faust and to Amanda Plant for her gorgeous cover art.

"Couldn't have done it without you" thanks to Emily Loose, who brought a lifetime of experience, engagement, and strategic acumen to the writing process, as well as Karen Geier and Aldo Rosas for copyedits. Personal appreciation for crucial administrative support from Lauren Taylor and Michele Ericson-Stern, and Amy DeWolfe for beautiful work and fast turnarounds. A spirited thank you to Scott Osman and Jacquelyn Lane of 100Coaches for your caring leadership during the time of writing.

I'm honored to know giants of the MG100 who were consistently generous with their time, insights, and inspiring path as a fellow Change Agent. Warmest thanks to Ron Carucci, Anne Gotte, Charlene Li, Deborah Borg, Tricia Brouk, Beth Polish, Laine J. Cohen. A well-deserved nod to Karlen Lyons-Ruth, PhD, for her pioneering work to furthering our understanding of intergenerational attachment.

Deep bow to those who lent their energy, their story, and their blessing to the mission of this book: Marshall Goldsmith, Sheila Robinson, Jackie Frank, Neela Hummel, April Benetello, Tushar Nuwal, Brenda Salce-Garcia, Jackie Frank, Melanie Lewis, Latasha Stewart, Jhaymee Tynan, Cherie Bond, Jennifer Schwitzer, Seth Greene, Sally Helgesen, Kristen Clark, Sara Vetter, and Emily Pitts.

To those I interviewed to help me understand the power we each have within us and how it can create better careers, connections, and companies, I am grateful and fortunate to have your voice within this book: Tenzin Seldon, Milagros Phillips, Jen Davis, Lauren Camper, Mita Mallick, Sharon Hecker, MaryJo Gagliardi, Whitney Johnson, Deborah Braun, Mark Goulston, Annalisa Brown, Professor Sukhvinder Obhi, Nabeela Ixtabalan, Jennifer Mccollum, Ruchika Tulshyan, Efrie Escott, Chester Elton, Tonya Hempstead, Pamay Ekpedeme, Texanna Reeves, Danielle Matts, Lisa Mcleod, Sonia Sequiera PhD, and Steven Melnick.

To my parents Susan and Neil Melnick for a lifetime of love and setting an example of resilience, and my niece Maddie for always being my "focus group."

"Beyond words" gratitude to Dr. Joseph Michael Levry for opening the door to an endless repertoire of Naam Yoga tools so I could *know* the infinite creative force that is within me and available to each of us.

To my friends, I treasure you. Our connection filled me up and kept me in motion. Deep gratitude to my soul sister and disruptor Teri Cochrane; fellow explorer of all things related to power and inspiring visionary Jennifer Brown; pathbreaking innovator Dr. KellyAnn Petrucci; successful authors who were role models and personal cheerleaders Annmei Chang, Alisa Cohn, and Dorie Clark; and lifelong sharer of heart, hearth, and thoughtfulness Dr. Jennifer Hartwell. Special appreciation to Annette for our delicious love, and your generous unwavering support that set the foundation to bring this book to fruition.

Thank you to my sisterhood posse for giving me an opportunity to share myself fully with you and own my power. In the safety of our container, you inspired me, reflected me, held space for me, and gave me the gift of not feeling alone in the world. A flash to PLM sisters: Alyson Malloy, Andrea Aymer, Annika Ford, Anya Zurn, Ellen Storfer-Rainford, Jennifer Adams,

Jennifer Patterson, Julia Wells, Kimberly Agnew, Kristy Wood-ford, Lala Fletcher, Laurie Kowalevsky, Leslie Quigless, Liz Rafert, Mariska Nicholson, Renata Shelton, Sharon Kan, Sophie Luxton, Stacey Lewis, and Tamara Lukan; all this plus thank you to Caroline Ladzinski and Ayo Moore for dropping extra pearls. Extra shout out to my fellow Pleasure Guides Kristen Clark and Sara Vetter, for your fierce sisterhood and outrageous up-levelling—you are amazing humans who always lifted me; and to Stephanie Redlener for holding space for me to love all of myself and embodying the lioness so I could know it; eternal thanks to Regena Thomashauer, who is to me the most original visionary creating greater consciousness in our times. Thank you for the purity of your stance, for standing for my expansion, for your blazing unapologetic courage, and for birthing a whole un-imagined technology so I walk *juicy* in the world.

To my courageous clients who exemplified the shift from out of your power to in your power, and are creating ripple effects of good energy in your companies, families, and communities: Thank you for your trust, for allowing me to learn from and share your stories, and for the experience of total delight which I've gotten from seeing that you and every person in their power is a Change Agent.

Index